The Abolitionist Movement

DOCUMENTS DECODED

Titles in ABC-CLIO's Documents Decoded series

Presidential Campaigns: Documents Decoded
Daniel M. Shea and Brian M. Harward

The Death Penalty: Documents Decoded
Joseph A. Melusky and Keith Alan Pesto

Women's Rights: Documents Decoded
Aimee D. Shouse

The ABC-CLIO series *Documents Decoded* guides readers on a hunt for new secrets through an expertly curated selection of primary sources. Each book pairs key documents with in-depth analysis, all in an original and visually engaging side-by-side format. But *Documents Decoded* authors do more than just explain each source's context and significance—they give readers a front-row seat to their own investigation and interpretation of each essential document line-by-line.

The Abolitionist Movement

DOCUMENTS DECODED

Christopher Cameron

Documents Decoded

 ABC-CLIO

Santa Barbara, California • Denver, Colorado • Oxford, England

Library of Congress Cataloging-in-Publication Data

Cameron, Christopher, 1983–
    The Abolitionist Movement : documents decoded / Christopher Cameron.
        pages cm. — (Documents decoded)
    Includes bibliographical references.
    ISBN 978-1-61069-512-1 (alk. paper) — ISBN 978-1-61069-513-8 (ebook) 1. Antislavery movements—United States. 2. Antislavery movements—United States—Sources. 3. Abolitionists—United States—History. 4. Abolitionists—United States—History—Sources. I. Title.
    E441.C24 2014
    326'.80973—dc23   2014007502

ISBN: 978-1-61069-512-1
EISBN: 978-1-61069-513-8

18 17 16 15 14   1 2 3 4 5

This book is also available on the World Wide Web as an eBook.
Visit www.abc-clio.com for details.

ABC-CLIO, LLC
130 Cremona Drive, P.O. Box 1911
Santa Barbara, California 93116-1911

This book is printed on acid-free paper ∞
Manufactured in the United States of America

Contents

Introduction

The Rise of Slavery in British North America

African slavery began in the region that would become the United States in 1619, when 20 blacks were brought to the Virginia colony after their purchase from a Dutch warship. The status of all 20 of these individuals was uncertain—some were treated as slaves, while others were indentured servants who ended up gaining their freedom. Despite the presence of these African slaves and servants, Virginia actually relied primarily on white indentured servants before 1680. With land shortages and economic problems in England, many poor whites signed indentures whereby they agreed to work for a specified period of time, often between four and seven years, in return for passage to the colonies and room and board once they arrived. After completing their term of indenture, they might be given a small plot of land and tools and clothing with which to begin their free lives. Some became small farmers and even fewer became large planters, but many became part of a growing landless lower class.

High death rates and the high cost of slaves made indentured servitude more attractive to Virginia's planters for much of the 17th century, but things started to change in the 1650s. Around that time people started living longer in the colony, which increased the number of indentured servants who gained their freedom and competed economically with their former masters. The rights of commoners were reduced by leaders, and the courts started handing down harsher punishments for infractions such as running away, increasing the discontent of the indentured servant class. Wealthy speculators also bought up large tracts of land, making it difficult for those who did gain their freedom to achieve upward mobility, as land was the primary means of making money in an agricultural society.

These factors combined to produce widespread unrest among the lower classes, unrest that erupted into Bacon's Rebellion in 1676, which was an interracial movement of lower-class whites and blacks rebelling against Virginia's colonial government. The rebels were angry that the government did not protect citizens on the frontier, and they were likewise angry at the lack of economic opportunities and political rights. While the rebellion was put down fairly quickly, the interracial composition of the rebels and the rise of class warfare scared colonial elites and helped initiate the transition to racial slavery in Virginia. If there were fewer free and unfree lower-class white men in the colony, leaders reasoned, there would be less opportunity for future interracial rebellions to arise.

In 1680 the black population of Virginia stood at just 7 percent, some of whom were free blacks who had worked their way out of slavery. Twenty years later in 1700 that number had increased to 28 percent; however, the labor pool in the colony was still split roughly in half between African slaves and white indentured servants. By 1710, however, 40 percent of Virginia's population was enslaved, and the vast majority of the remaining 60 percent consisted of freedmen. A little more than 30 years after Bacon's Rebellion, the transition to racial slavery as the basis of the colonial economy was complete.

Slavery's rise in the neighboring Carolina colony developed very differently from the Virginia model. Carolina was settled in the late 1660s, as opposed to Virginia, which was first settled in 1607. But slavery was legal from the inception of the Carolina colony, while it had taken Virginia roughly 40 years to completely legalize the institution there. Carolina was first settled by smaller planters from Barbados, another British colony located in the Caribbean, and these planters brought their slaves with them, employing them primarily as cattle herders and artisans and in other trades until planters began rice cultivation in the mid-1690s. After this point slavery grew quickly in South Carolina, where blacks made up a majority of the population as early as 1708. Thirty years later there were two slaves for every one free white man or woman in the colony, and South Carolina would become a staunch advocate of slavery and slave trading until the American Civil War.

While slavery was strongest in the South, it was by no means strictly a southern institution, even in the colonial period. In fact, Massachusetts became the first colony in British North America to legalize slavery, which occurred in 1641 when the legislature declared that "there shall never be any bond slaverie, villinage or captivitie amongst us unless it be lawfull captives taken in just warres, and such strangers as willingly selle themselves or are sold to us. And these shall have all the liberties and Christian usages which the law of God established in Israell concerning such persons doth morally require." While the number of slaves throughout New England colonies such as Massachusetts always remained relatively small compared to the southern colonies, the numbers do not tell the entire story of how important slavery was to the region. Most enslaved Africans were clustered along the seacoast in major towns, which meant that slave populations were largest where those of the region's political and cultural leaders, the mercantile elite, were likewise heaviest. These were the figures among whom slaveholders were overwhelmingly represented, and gentlemen's households were often dependent upon slave labor as domestics. Even though slavery was not absolutely central to the New England economy, it did help to diversify it, partly by freeing masters to work outside the home, and was an important factor in the transition to capitalism during the 18th century.

In New England, slaveholders often regarded themselves as benevolent patriarchs and better masters than those elsewhere in the Atlantic world. They prided themselves on giving slaves what they felt was adequate clothing and proper medical attention. Yet the image of the good master in colonial New England is largely mythical. The long hours demanded of slaves could be very taxing. And unlike their southern counterparts, female slaves in New England who reproduced were actually more of a liability than a profit to their masters. In what would become an early harbinger for the tragedies associated with the internal slave trade, newspapers in colonial Massachusetts sometimes offered to give away the children of female slaves.

Early Antislavery Efforts, 1688–1765

The first protests against slavery in colonial America arose not in New England or the South but in the middle colony of Pennsylvania. The middle colonies consisted of New York, New Jersey, and Pennsylvania, and slavery had been present in all three nearly from their inception. While Pennsylvania, founded by the Quaker William Penn, was created as a haven for those escaping religious persecution in Europe, many early settlers accepted the institution of slavery, with Penn even noting that he preferred slaves to indentured servants because slaves would work for life. One exception was a group of four Quakers in Germantown who submitted the first known protest against slavery in 1688. Arguing that slavery was contrary to the Golden Rule of the Bible, which calls on Christians to do unto others as they would have done unto them, these Quakers called on the Society of Friends to ban their members from slaveholding. This would have been an important step because Quakers made up the bulk of Pennsylvania's population in this early period, and thus a ban by that religious body would likely have translated into a ban on slavery in the colony.

The Germantown petition eventually went to the Philadelphia Yearly Meeting of the Society of Friends, whose members responded by tabling the petition and taking no action. More individual Quakers began to speak out against slavery after the

Germantown Protest, however. One such person was Cadwalader Morgan, who had emigrated from Wales to Merion, Pennsylvania. In 1696 Morgan, a Quaker minister, argued against slavery on the grounds that owning slaves would be more trouble than good, especially if a slave ran away or committed some other infraction that had to be punished. Morgan also prayed extensively over the matter and concluded that buying slaves for profit was against the spirit of Christianity, which called for adherents to eschew worldly gain rather than to actively pursue it. Like the Germantown Protest, Morgan's opposition to slavery was of no avail in his lifetime, as the colony of Pennsylvania would go on to formally legalize the institution in 1700.

That same year Samuel Sewall penned the first antislavery tract in the American colonies. Sewall resided in Massachusetts, where he was a merchant and a member of the Superior Court of Judicature, the highest legal body in the colony. In his diary for June 19, 1700, he noted that "having been long and much dissatisfied with the Trade of fetching Negros from Guinea; at last I had a strong Inclination to Write something about it. . . . When I was thus thinking, in came Brother Belknap to shew me a Petition he intended to present to the General Court for the freeing of a Negro and his wife." It is unclear just what made Sewall unsatisfied with slavery in the years preceding, but it may very well have been the practice of giving away the children of slave mothers, which was somewhat common in New England. Sewall was also at that time deciding a freedom suit that had recently arisen in his court between a slave named Adam and his master John Saffin. These events pushed Sewall to write *The Selling of Joseph: A Memorial,* a pamphlet that outlined a number of arguments against slavery that became important to later abolitionist writers.

In this tract, Sewall argued that "it is most certain that all Men, as they are the Sons of Adam, are Co-heirs, and have equal Right unto Liberty." He also countered arguments for slavery that claimed that blacks were the children of the biblical figure Ham, pointing out that it was actually Ham's son Canaan who was cursed. Finally, Sewall refuted a common justification for slavery by arguing that conversion was not an excuse for enslaving Africans because men were not to do evil to bring about positive results. Sewall circulated his pamphlet among colonial leaders of Massachusetts, and just one year after he published his tract the Boston Selectmen passed the following resolution for the representatives of the General Court: "The Representatives ar farther desired To Promote the Encourrageing the bringing of white servts and to put a Period to negros being Slaves." While this resolution did not have the force of law, it did reflect a level of discomfort with slavery in these early years, a discomfort that Sewall's pamphlet likely played a role in creating.

While white Quakers and Puritans such as Sewall were active in calling for an end to slavery in the colonial era, blacks also took matters into their own hands when the opportunity arose to strike for their freedom. In 1739 the War of Jenkins' Ear arose between Spain and England, and Spain, which occupied the colony of

Florida, had recently declared that any slaves escaping to St. Augustine from an English colony would be given freedom and land. On September 9 that is just what slaves outside of Charles Towne, South Carolina, attempted to do. Led by an individual named Jemmy, about 20 slaves headed South, ransacking an ammunition store and killing the owner and other whites they encountered along the way in what has come to be known as the Stono Rebellion. Within hours their numbers had grown to about 50, but their luck ran out when they encountered the lieutenant governor of the colony, who escaped on horseback and quickly raised a posse to put down the rebellion. Most of the rebels were executed, and South Carolina passed strict new laws regulating the mobility of slaves and banning them from learning to read or write. The rebellion did make colonial leaders think twice about importing Africans, however, and the Atlantic slave trade to South Carolina slowed down considerably for the next decade before picking back up again in the 1750s.

The American Revolution and the Origins of the Abolitionist Movement

The greatest impetus for the start of the abolitionist movement came from the ideals and events of the American Revolution. After the Seven Years' War, in which Britain defeated France and established British supremacy on the North American continent, Parliament began to levy taxes on the colonists to help finance the war effort and their continued protection. These taxes included the Sugar Act of 1764 and the Stamp Act of 1765, both of which resulted in widespread opposition from the colonists, who were not represented in Parliament and believed that only their own colonial legislatures could tax them. The colonists began to argue that Parliament was treating them as second-class citizens and even had plans to enslave them. The colonists also drew from the ideas of political philosophers such as John Locke, who had argued in the 1680s that all people have the right to life, liberty, and property and that if governments do not support these "natural rights," then the people have the right to change their government as they see fit. These ideas helped justify widespread protest and opposition to British policies, opposition that sometimes took the form of mob activity such as tarring and feathering British officials. It was against this backdrop that the abolitionist movement arose in Revolutionary America.

One of the first white abolitionists to publicly voice his opposition to slavery after Samuel Sewall was James Otis Jr. Otis was a member of an old Massachusetts family. His father, James Otis Sr., had been the Speaker of the Massachusetts House of Representatives in the early 1760s, and Otis Jr. was himself a member of that body. Both father and son led the popular resistance in Boston to the Stamp Act and other parliamentary taxes in the mid-1760s. In his 1764 tract *The Rights of the British Colonies Asserted and Proved,* Otis deplored the practice of holding slaves because, he claimed, liberty is a gift from God that no man can take away. He further argued that slavery was a throwback to the days of barbarism and ignorance prevalent in the Dark Ages. While many of his contemporaries would have claimed that blacks were inferior to whites and deserved to be enslaved, Otis asked his readers "Does it follow that 'tis right to enslave a man because he is black? Will short curled hair like wool instead of Christian hair, as 'tis called by those whose hearts are as hard as the nether millstone, help the argument?" Otis believed that the colonists were being hypocritical in calling for their own natural rights while denying them to slaves and that slavery as an institution was harmful to white colonists on multiple fronts. These included stymieing the pace of Enlightenment and being able to value their own liberty.

Another white abolitionist to publicly voice his opposition to slavery during the 1760s was Nathaniel Appleton, son of a Congregational minister by the same name. Appleton's 1767 pamphlet *Considerations on Slavery* is significant both for the information it provides about the institution in Massachusetts and the arguments set forth, arguments that would serve as the crux for both white and black abolitionist thought for years to come. Among the first arguments that Appleton made against the slave trade was that it was "contrary to humanity, Christianity, the interest of the province, and of private families." He further claimed that Massachusetts would be stronger economically and militarily by importing white servants instead of slaves, who once freed would help settle the province and defend it from enemies in a way that blacks could not because whites barred them from military service.

Along with these considerations, Appleton's pamphlet stressed the moral question of slavery and its effects on both black and white people in Africa and Massachusetts. As far as blacks were concerned, the slave trade was destroying African life by promoting warfare and was harmful to African Americans in Massachusetts because it denied them the right to marry without fear of being sold while also promoting the sale of older slaves because of a lack of work for them to perform. Foreshadowing arguments that Thomas Jefferson would famously make in the 1780s, Appleton wrote that slavery was harmful to whites because it introduced haughtiness and cruelty into children in their treatment of slaves, character traits that then could carry over into other relationships. Speaking to the rising opposition of white colonists to the policies of Parliament during the era of the American Revolution, Appleton ended his appeal by noting that "it has always appeared very strange to me, how people can be so sensibly affected with what has but a remote tendency to deprive them of their smallest right or privilege, and yet remain so insensible of the deplorable state of so many of our species that live among us."

Like Otis's remarks three years earlier, Appleton's pamphlet drew strength from the increasing emphasis on natural rights being voiced by white colonists throughout British North America and helped build abolitionist sentiment in Massachusetts. On March 4, 1767, a bill for preventing the importation of slaves was read a first time in the House of Representatives. Nine days later the bill was amended to "A Bill to Prevent the Unwarrantable and Unusual Practice or Custom of Inslaving Mankind in This Province, and the Importation of Slaves into the Same." This amendment is significant because previous action by colonial leaders had targeted only the slave trade and not slavery itself. The move reflects a growing discontent with the institution of slavery among the Massachusetts colonists. The amended bill was read a third time but did not pass, perhaps because legislators felt that the governor would not approve of any restriction on slavery itself. Instead, the House brought a new bill that attacked only the slave trade, laying a large tax on all slave imports, but the Council passed a different version and the two houses could not agree, killing the legislation. These efforts, while initially unsuccessful, reveal the changing attitudes in the province toward slavery and would help spur continued efforts by individual blacks and groups to seek their freedom.

One such group was a committee representing slaves that began submitting abolitionist petitions to the Massachusetts legislature in January 1773. This committee, led by a slave named Felix Holbrook, argued against slavery on the grounds that it violated the natural rights of blacks and was unchristian and that it was hypocritical of colonists to argue for freedom from Great Britain while holding slaves at home. This group was the first antislavery committee in the American colonies, and its April 1773 petition to the Massachusetts legislature actually pushed that body to consider yet another abolition bill, although once the bill was reviewed by the Continental Congress it was killed. Blacks in Massachusetts continued their abolitionist campaign through petitioning and freedom suits throughout the 1770s and into the early 1780s, and they finally saw their efforts pay off in 1783, when William Cushing, chief justice of the Superior Court of Judicature, declared that slavery was incompatible with the new state constitution.

The Revolutionary era also saw slavery end in most northern states. When Vermont joined the Union in 1777, its new constitution specifically outlawed slavery, making it the first state in the young nation to take this step. In 1775, two years after the antislavery committee had formed in Massachusetts, the Pennsylvania Abolition Society was formed and worked to end slavery within that state, which was achieved with the passage of a gradual abolition bill in 1780. Gradual abolition laws would become common after the one in Pennsylvania. What they did was free the children of slaves born after a certain date when those children reached a certain age, generally 25 years old for males and 21 years old for females. The rationale behind these laws was that masters should be compensated somehow for the loss of their property and that black people needed time to prepare for freedom. If they were set free all at once, many contemporaries believed that they would become a burden on society.

Four years after Pennsylvania passed its gradual abolition law, Connecticut and Rhode Island followed suit with their own gradual emancipation acts. While neither

Connecticut nor Rhode Island had very large slave populations, Rhode Island was an important slave-trading center; thus, abolishing slavery was an important step for the nation's smallest state. New York gradually abolished slavery in 1799, and New Jersey followed suit just a couple of years later. Within 30 years of the start of the American Revolution, all northern states had either abolished slavery outright, as in Vermont and Massachusetts, or had passed laws for gradual abolition. There was no one route toward emancipation for blacks in the North, but the principles of the Revolution combined with the activity of antislavery groups, such as the committee of slaves in Massachusetts and the Pennsylvania Abolition Society, helped to usher in this widespread social movement.

While this movement was ongoing in the North, southerners also debated the morality of slavery. Indeed, Thomas Jefferson had included an attack on slavery and the slave trade in his original draft of the Declaration of Independence, where he wrote of King George III that "he has waged cruel war against human nature itself, violating it's [*sic*] most sacred rights of life & liberty in the persons of a distant people who never offended him, captivating & carrying them into slavery in another hemisphere, or to incur miserable death in their transportation thither." Jefferson's attack on slavery was struck out of the final draft of the Declaration of Independence, but it is indicative of the influence that Revolutionary principles had even on southern slaveholders. While an organized abolitionist movement never developed in the South during this era, southern states such as Virginia did relax their laws on manumission and made it easier for masters to free their slaves. From the 1770s to about 1815, thousands of slaves in Delaware, Maryland, and Virginia gained their freedom through the individual choices of their masters. Many of these slaves would then move North, contribute to the growth of northern black communities, and become actively involved in the antislavery movement.

Abolition of Slave Trade and Growth of Slavery in the 19th Century

While there was no concerted abolitionist movement in the South, many southerners did support the abolition of the slave trade for both moral and economic reasons. This was especially true of slaveholders in states of the Upper South such as Maryland and Virginia, where the continual importation of African slaves actually drove down the value of their bondmen. We have already seen Thomas Jefferson's critique of the slave trade in his draft of the Declaration of Independence. Luther Martin, a delegate to the 1787 Constitutional Convention from Maryland, proposed a ban on the slave trade that sparked one of the most heated discussions of the convention. Martin argued that "it was inconsistent with the principles of the revolution and dishonorable to the American character" to allow the importation of slaves in the U.S. Constitution. Roger Sherman of Connecticut was also opposed to the slave trade but did not think that the convention should take up the question, lest it hinder chances of ratifying the U.S. Constitution. This is exactly what delegates from South Carolina threatened would happen if abolition was a part of the U.S. Constitution. John Rutledge and Charles Cotesworth Pinckney both stated that their state would not join the Union if a ban on slave trading went into effect. The delegates ended up compromising and allowing the slaves to be imported into the country until 1807, so now the fight to end slave trading had to be waged at the state level, where they would be most successful.

During the summer of 1787, the New England Yearly Meeting petitioned the Rhode Island legislature to end slave trading among its residents, and within months lawmakers had passed a bill doing just that. The brevity of the debate actually surprised activists such as Congregational minister Samuel Hopkins, who had prepared for a protracted and bitter struggle. Rhode Island Quakers soon turned their attention to abolishing the slave trade in Connecticut, which they helped bring about in 1788. They felt that this was necessary because merchants and slavers could easily transfer their businesses outside of Rhode Island and conduct business as usual. With the slave trade abolished in most New England states, Rhode Island activists soon formed the Providence Society for Abolishing the Slave Trade to enforce the new abolition laws. Abolitionists formed the group in January 1789, and their goals were threefold. First, they wanted to suppress the African slave trade. Second, members felt that blacks should be able to exercise constitutional rights. And third, the group wanted to draw attention to the plight of those whites who, like Africans, "may be carried into slavery at Algiers or elsewhere."

By the time Congress banned the international slave trade for the entire nation, most states had already prohibited their citizens from engaging in slave trading. This ban, however, actually coincided with a rapid growth of slavery in the United States. In 1794 Eli Whitney patented the cotton gin, which allowed for the production of short-staple cotton at a rate hundreds times faster than possible before the machine. Less than a decade later Thomas Jefferson negotiated the Louisiana Purchase with France, which doubled the size of the United States and added states such as Alabama and Mississippi that would become leading cotton producers in the nation. In the first two decades of the 19th century cotton production in the United States would take off, going from 73,000 bales a year in 1800 to more than 730,000 bales by 1820, with nearly all of this being produced by slave labor. The slave population would likewise increase drastically, as it rose 30 percent between 1810 and 1820. So even as the Atlantic slave trade ended in the United States and as Latin American nations were likewise taking action to end both slavery and the slave trade, the institution of slavery itself become even more solidified in the early 19th century. This fact would lead to new strategies for achieving the abolition of slavery, as it was now clear that the principles of the American Revolution would not do the trick.

Black Emigration and Colonization

One such strategy to emerge during this era was a movement for black emigration from the United States to either Africa or Haiti. The black emigration movement during the early 19th century served a number of different functions. On the one hand, for activists such as Paul Cuffe and Prince Saunders, it became a way to attack the Atlantic slave trade and provide an asylum for those blacks freed from American slavery. African Americans would bring specialized commercial and agricultural knowledge to help develop African economies and would also bring Christianity to help convert the native inhabitants. Slaveholders would be more likely to free their slaves, activists believed, if there was a place outside of the United States to send them. On the other hand, black leaders such as James Forten pursued emigration schemes in part as a way to deal with the rising level of racism aimed at the free black population during the early republic. This racism manifested itself in the form of riots, efforts to disenfranchise blacks, and laws barring free black emigration to northern states such as Ohio and Pennsylvania.

Black emigration represented a continuation of tactics and strategies that early black activists employed as well as some significant departures that influenced the future course of the antislavery movement in America. Interracial cooperation, institution building, and fostering connections throughout the Atlantic world were central to the work of black emigrationists. In viewing Africa and Haiti as asylums for slaves who would eventually be freed, however, Cuffe, Saunders, and other leaders accepted the gradualist abolitionist sentiment that often dominated the antislavery ideology of white activists. In this sense, even as these leaders fostered important political connections among one another, black emigrationism represented something of a retreat from the radicalism of earlier generations of activists.

Schemes for immigrating to Africa in one form or another had been present in America since the American Revolutionary War. In their April 1773 petition to the Massachusetts General Court, black activists wrote that they desired "as soon as we can, from our joint labours procure money to transport ourselves to some part of the Coast of Africa, where we propose a settlement." That same year Congregational ministers Samuel Hopkins and Ezra Stiles raised a subscription to send two black men, John Quamine and Bristol Yamma, to Africa to evangelize the natives. For Hopkins and Stiles, this effort would have served a dual purpose. First, it would have spread the Christian religion to what they saw as a heathen people. Second, Hopkins and Stiles sought support for this plan because "it is humbly proposed to those who are convinced of the iniquity of the slave trade; and are sensible of the great inhumanity and cruelty of enslaving so many thousands of our fellow men every year . . . and are ready to bear testimony against it in all proper ways, and do their utmost to put a stop to it: Whether they have not a good opportunity of doing this, by chearfully [*sic*] contributing, according to their ability, to promote the mission proposed."

The foremost proponent of black emigration in the early 19th century would be the black businessman and Quaker Paul Cuffe. Cuffe's business and Quaker connections introduced him to a network of abolitionists throughout the United States and England, and this network helped to facilitate his plans for emigration starting around 1810. Cuffe embarked on his first voyage to the British colony of Sierra Leone in December 1810 and upon arrival immediately began to organize the Friendly Society of Sierra Leone, a trading group that would promote trade in legitimate goods such as rice and cotton versus the trade in slaves that was rife in other regions of Africa. Upon his return to the United States, Cuffe traveled along the Eastern Seaboard establishing groups to correspond and build connections with the Friendly Society in Baltimore, Philadelphia, and New York City. Cuffe's efforts had the practical effects of promoting emigration as a political strategy while also connecting black leaders throughout the nation and the larger Atlantic world.

After a second trip to Sierra Leone in 1816 when Cuffe brought more than 40 American blacks to the colony, he continued to correspond with black leaders throughout the Eastern Seaboard and whites interested in black emigration. Within a year, however, widespread black interest in African emigration waned due to blacks' distrust of white colonizers' motives. White leaders such as Samuel Mills and Robert Finley asked Cuffe for information about his voyage and his thoughts about the establishment of a permanent government-funded colony for blacks in Africa. Finley played a key role in creating the American Colonization Society (ACS) in 1817 and believed that if a colony was established on the coast of Africa, laws could then be passed "permitting the emancipation of slaves on condition that they shall be colonized." John T. Peters of the Hartford Auxiliary Colonization Society likewise noted that his organization wanted to "encourage, and ultimately to produce an entire emancipation of slaves in America; and last, though not least—to break up and destroy that inhuman and accursed traffic, the SLAVE TRADE."

Although Finley, Peters, and other colonizationists supported the abolition of slavery and the slave trade, other members who started the ACS were prominent slaveholders who were more interested in strengthening slavery by colonizing free blacks. John Randolph of Roanoke, one of the first members of the ACS, stated that "it was a notorious fact . . . that the existence of this mixed and intermediate population of free negroes was viewed by every slave holder as one of the greatest sources of insecurity, and also unprofitableness, of slave property." At this same meeting, Henry Clay wondered whether there could be "a nobler cause than that which, while it proposes to rid our country of a useless and pernicious, if not a dangerous portion of its population, contemplates the spreading of the arts of civilized life" to Africa. Years earlier, Thomas Jefferson had supported colonization because he believed that blacks and whites could never live peaceably in the same nation. Writing in his *Notes on the State of Virginia,* he stated that "Deep-rooted prejudices entertained by the whites; ten thousand recollections, by the blacks, of the injuries they have sustained; new provocations; the real distinctions which nature has made; and many other circumstances, will divide us into parties, and produce convulsions which will probably never end but in the extermination of the one or the other race." Jefferson suggested that blacks be educated for a trade until 18 years old for women and 21 years old for men, at which time "they should be colonized to such place as the circumstances of the time should render most proper."

These sentiments led black leaders such as James Forten and Richard Allen of Philadelphia to reconsider their support for African emigration. Forten came to believe that colonization would strengthen slavery in the United States because "diminished in numbers, the slave population of the southern states, which by its magnitude alarms its proprietors, will be easily secured." This was exactly the sentiment that John Randolph of Roanoke had expressed, and the *National Intelligencer* reported that at the first ACS meeting "it was not proposed to deliberate on, or consider at all, any question of emancipation, or that was connected with the abolition of slavery. It was upon this condition alone . . . that many gentlemen from the south and west" had attended the meeting. Forten noted also that African Americans in Philadelphia believed that colonization was a scam designed to rid the nation of free blacks. "We had a large meeting of males at the Rev. R. Allen's Church, the other evening," he wrote. "Three Thousand at least attended, and there was not one sole that was in favor of going to Africa."

Despite the growing hostility to emigration and colonization plans, the efforts of black leaders such as Paul Cuffe played a central role in connecting black abolitionists throughout the North and making them determined to fight for equal rights in America. Black emigration plans helped keep antislavery activism alive and well at a time when many white abolitionists felt that their work was finished, having secured the abolition of the slave trade in 1807. The institutions and abolitionist networks that Cuffe helped build would prove vital to the movement in the 1820s. Through trial and error, black abolitionists came to realize that immediatism, and not gradual abolition coupled with emigration or colonization, was their best option, and they set out with renewed vigor to try to convince Americans of this notion.

The Rise of Garrisonian Abolition

The emphasis on immediate emancipation would be the central point of what has come to be called Garrisonian abolition, a new phase of the struggle against slavery. The 1820s and 1830s saw a number of important changes in this struggle. First, the number of people involved in antislavery activity was a sharp increase over previous eras. While this number still constituted only a small percentage of the population in the North, there were thousands more activists committed to ending slavery. Second, while abolitionists such as Prince Hall had alluded to the specter of Saint Domingue as an implicit warning to whites of the consequences of slavery, activists in the 1820s such as David Walker explicitly called for southern slaves to rebel against their masters and free themselves.

In one of the seminal texts in the history of American abolitionism, *Appeal to the Coloured Citizens of the World,* Walker built his case for antislavery by first calling for black unity and self-help. He began with the premise that American blacks were "the most degraded, wretched, and abject set of beings that ever lived since the world began" and stated that his purpose was "to awaken in the breast of my afflicted, degraded, and slumbering brethren, a spirit of inquiry and investigation respecting our miseries and wretchedness in this Republican Land of Liberty." In the first article of the text, in an attempt to arouse blacks to greater exertions on behalf of the antislavery movement, Walker argued that slaves in America were worse off than those in any country the world had known. The plight of the ancient Israelites paled in comparison, according to Walker, because slaves such as Joseph had great authority in Egypt, while black men in America could not even serve as constables or on juries. Furthermore, Egyptian slavery was milder because masters at least recognized the humanity of their bondsmen, something that masters in the United States denied.

Walker also stated that blacks' degraded condition in America was due to ignorance, and he called for black leaders to help educate their brethren. Ignorance caused both violence and disunity in the slave community and also caused blacks to have an irrational fear of white people, so that 8 whites could effectively control 50 blacks. The solution to this problem was self-help and a stronger sense of community among blacks in America—slave and free. "Men of colour, who are also of sense," he wrote, "I call upon you . . . to cast your eyes upon the wretchedness of your brethren, and to do your utmost to enlighten them—go to work and enlighten your brethren!" He likewise implored black leaders to "let the aim of your labours among your brethren, and particularly the youths, be the dissemination of education." As black abolitionists in Massachusetts had thought since the 1780s, Walker believed that increased educational opportunity was one of the best means for fighting slavery.

Walker's fiery denunciation of American slaveholders helped contribute to unified southern opposition to abolition and had long-term implications for the politics of slavery. By pushing southerners toward censoring and confiscating mail, which northern whites would strongly object to as a violation of their constitutional liberties, Walker helped bring thousands of new activists into the movement. Perhaps even more significant was his influence on white abolitionists such as William Lloyd Garrison, who started his antislavery career as a colonizationist and an advocate of gradual abolition, yet by 1831 was a proponent of immediate emancipation, writing one year later that "I am constrained to declare, with the utmost sincerity, that I look upon the colonization scheme as inadequate in design, injurious in its operation, and contrary to sound principle." Garrison never did adopt the belief that violence was necessary to overthrow slavery, but he did say that if his strategy of moral suasion did not convince masters to free their slaves, then the physical strength of the slaves would do so. Walker and Garrison also shared very similar rhetorical styles. In his opening editorial to *The Liberator,* Garrison wrote: "I am aware that many object to the severity of my language, but is there not cause for severity? I will be as harsh as truth, and as uncompromising as justice." Garrison's language here is very similar to the rhetoric that Walker himself employed in his own writings. And Garrison's newfound insistence on immediate as opposed to gradual abolition strongly suggests the powerful influence that activists such as Walker had on Garrison's thinking in particular and the growth of abolitionism in general.

A key development in the growth of interracial activism among abolitionists in the early 1830s was cooperation in antislavery societies. Prior to this period, organizations such as the Pennsylvania Abolition Society and the Massachusetts General Colored Association consisted solely of either whites or blacks, but this changed in 1832. In December 1831, David Lee Child, Garrison, and other activists met at the African Baptist Church in Boston to organize the New England Anti-Slavery Society (NEASS). The constitution of this institution stated that "every person of full age, and sane mind, has a right to immediate freedom from personal bondage," demonstrating again the impact that black abolitionists' insistence on immediate emancipation had on their white coworkers. Along with pushing for the abolition of slavery, the NEASS endeavored "by all means sanctioned by law, humanity, and religion . . . to improve the character and condition of free people of color." Signers of the constitution included black activists John T. Hilton, James G. Barbadoes, Hosea Easton, and Thomas Paul, making this organization the first interracial antislavery society in the nation.

Antiabolitionist Violence and Proslavery Thought

The rise of this robust, interracial antislavery movement during the 1830s precipitated a backlash among northerners and southerners alike, a backlash that took the form of violent antiabolitionist mobs and a new body of proslavery thought based upon hardened racial ideologies. In the mid-1830s mob activity began to rise, with much of it directed toward free blacks and abolitionists. In 1835 Harrison Gray Otis gave an antiabolition speech in Boston, and soon thereafter a mob attacked William Lloyd Garrison and nearly killed him. That year there were 68 mobs in the northern states that killed 8 people, while 79 southern mobs killed 63 people. Most of these mobs were led by local leaders; elites, especially businessmen, were very hostile to the spread of abolitionist principles, as this spread could potentially harm businesses that depended on trading with the southern states. So while abolitionists in the North had their share of successes in this era, they also saw a rise in white racism and had to deal with violent reactions to their antislavery work.

In this context, South Carolina senator John C. Calhoun gave his 1837 speech to the U.S. Senate, where he argued that "abolition and the Union cannot coexist." His statement is indicative of the effect that abolitionists had in pushing southerners and defenders of slavery to more radical positions. Whereas many slaveholders in the Revolutionary and early national eras had expressed hope that slavery, an institution seen as a necessary evil, would eventually die away, by the late 1830s slaveholders such as Calhoun were defending slavery on the grounds that it was a positive good for society. Indeed, in a later speech to the Senate, Calhoun posited slavery as a superior economic and social system to the free labor of the North. "The difference between us," Calhoun noted, "is that our slaves are hired for life and well compensated; there is no starvation, no begging, no want of employment among our people, and not too much employment either. Yours are hired by the day, not cared for, and scantily compensated, which may be proved in the most painful manner, at any hour in any street in any of your large towns. Why, you meet more beggars in one day, in any single street of the city of New York, than you would meet in a lifetime in the whole South." For Calhoun and many proslavery thinkers of his era, slavery was now seen as a positive good rather than a necessary evil.

The notion of slavery as a positive good was intimately tied to shifting racial ideologies in the 1830s and 1840s. Influenced by the Enlightenment, early thinkers such as Thomas Jefferson had advanced theories of race based on the environment, meaning that racial differences between blacks and whites were often seen as environmental and cultural rather than biological. This line of thought began to shift in the 1830s, especially with the rising popularity of pseudosciences such as phrenology whereby the size of one's cranium was supposed to determine one's intelligence and capacity for civilized life. Now, racial theorists such as Thomas R. R. Cobb and Alexander Stephens, future vice president of the Confederacy, would argue that blacks were biologically inferior to whites and in essence were made to be slaves. The significance of this line of thought cannot be overstated, as it now meant that blacks and other racial minorities could do little if anything to overcome the stigma attached to their color. Thus, new developments in racial thought during the 1830s and beyond helped to provide a foundation for proslavery arguments.

The Slaveocracy, Black Republicans, and the Coming of the Civil War

For the next 30 years, abolitionist and proslavery forces would view each other with suspicion and distrust. Abolitionists argued that there was a slaveocracy in the country that was engaged in a calculated plot to undermine American civil liberties as long as the institution of slavery was protected. Their fears were seemingly confirmed by the presence of antiabolition mobs, many of which tried to prevent people from exercising the right of free speech, as well as by events such as the passage of the Gag Rule in 1836 whereby the House of Representatives refused to discuss any antislavery petitions that came to Congress. In 1836, members of Congress also tried to annex Texas, which had recently declared its independence from Mexico, in a move that was likewise seen as an attempt by the slaveocracy to expand their power in Congress and the nation at large. Texas was finally admitted to the Union in 1845 over the opposition of many northerners, and the war with Mexico that raged from 1846 to 1848 was seen as further evidence that slaveholders did not have the interests of the country in mind but instead were merely interested in preserving and protecting the institution of slavery.

From the point of view of slaveholders, it was abolitionist agitators who were the true enemies of American liberty and equality. With calls for the nonextension of slavery in the West after the formation of the Free Soil Party in 1848, slaveholders became increasingly fearful that their property rights would not be safe in the nation. By 1854, the Free Soilers and other parties had merged into the new Republican Party, and members were referred to derisively as "Black Republicans" by southerners because their free soil ideology seemingly favored the interests of blacks over whites. Slaveholders argued that the "Black Republicans" were in favor of race mixing and perhaps even wanted to start a race war in the South. Both southerners and northerners came to view each other with intense suspicion and believed that the other was committed to undermining American freedom and democracy.

Against this backdrop, some of the most significant events in the history of slavery and abolition would further galvanize the nation during the 1850s. The same year that the Republican Party was formed, 1854, also witnessed the passage of the Kansas-Nebraska Act, a law that repealed the Missouri Compromise of 1820 and allowed slavery to exist in a northern territory if the residents voted for it. Many northerners, while opposed to the extension of slavery, had at least taken solace from the fact that slavery could not exist in the North because of the Missouri Compromise, and its repeal caused many to fear that the slaveocracy would now be able to extend its reach and influence even farther. Settlers from throughout New England and the neighboring slave state of Missouri, as well as other areas of the South, flocked to Kansas to ensure that its new constitution would be either antislavery or proslavery. In what came to be known as Bleeding Kansas, skirmishes broke out around the state as dozens if not hundreds lost their lives fighting for slavery or free soil.

The violence in Kansas soon spilled over into the U.S. Congress in 1856. That year, Senator Charles Sumner of Massachusetts gave a speech titled "Crime against Kansas" in which he insulted the honor of proslavery advocates such as South Carolina senator Andrew Butler. Butler's nephew Preston Brooks was a U.S. representative from South Carolina and decided to take revenge on Sumner for the insult to his uncle. On May 22, 1856, after the Senate session had ended, Brooks slipped into the chamber and began beating Sumner with his cane while Sumner was working at his desk. The beating lasted just a minute but would have enormous repercussions for the sectional divisions characterizing the nation in the 1850s. Brooks was seen as a hero by southerners and was sent hundreds of new canes to replace the one he broke in the beating. Northerners, looking at the admiration shown Brooks, increasingly came to believe that they could no longer do business with southerners and that the democratic system was simply not working. Brooks passed away shortly after the attack, while Sumner, after taking a break from his duties to recover, would go on to serve 18 more years in the Senate.

The Civil War and the Abolition of Slavery

The final straw in the move toward the Civil War and the eventual abolition of slavery was the election of Abraham Lincoln in 1860. During this election, the Democratic Party split into northern and southern wings, thus almost ensuring the election of the Republican candidate. Lincoln won the election without being on a single southern ballot, and roughly one month after election day, South Carolina seceded from the Union. South Carolina was followed by six other states in the next two months, and together they formed the Confederate States of America in February 1861. Upper South states such as Virginia and Tennessee held out for a few months, but after the commencement of hostilities between the North and South in the April 1861 Battle of Fort Sumter, four other states would join the Confederacy, marking the official beginning of the Civil War.

At the start of the conflict, Lincoln proclaimed that the goal of the war was not to free the slaves. He noted that if he could save the Union by freeing some and leaving others enslaved, he would do that. If he could save the Union by freeing all the slaves, he would also do that, and if the task could be accomplished by freeing none of the slaves, he would do that as well. For Lincoln, the paramount goal was saving the Union. Things started to change when the war actually began, however. As Union troops moved into Southern territory, enslaved blacks would run to Union lines hoping to attain their freedom. Some generals sent the slaves back to their masters, but other generals realized that slaves could be a valuable resource to the Southern war effort and did not want to risk sending them back. Eventually, enough slaves ran to Union lines that Lincoln became convinced that declaring the abolition of slavery could be justified as a necessary wartime measure. This move came with Lincoln issuing the Emancipation Proclamation in 1863, which declared that all slaves in regions under control of the Confederacy were now free and that blacks could serve in the military. What had begun as a war to save the Union in 1861 had shifted into a war to end slavery in just two years. While the Emancipation Proclamation did not free all slaves in the nation, it was an important symbolic gesture that helped pave the way for the eventual abolition of slavery, which came with the passage of the Thirteenth Amendment in 1865.

The Abolitionist Movement
DOCUMENTS DECODED

Slavery and Racial Thought in Colonial and Revolutionary America

Quakers and Abolitionism
Petition of Germantown Quakers
1688

INTRODUCTION

On February 18, 1688, a small group of Quakers and Mennonites in Germantown, Pennsylvania, submitted a petition to their local meeting protesting the slave trade and the institution of slavery. At this time, Pennsylvania was a fledgling colony made up largely of Quakers and other religious dissenters seeking to practice their faiths openly and freely. The Quakers argued here that slavery was contrary to divine law and implied that its existence in Pennsylvania would reflect negatively on the colony, which the founder William Penn was actively trying to promote in Europe. This local petition made its way to the Yearly Meeting in Burlington, New Jersey, where it was eventually tabled. While it was unsuccessful, this petition represents the beginning of Quaker activism in the antislavery movement and would provide a model for future activists.

This is to ye monthly meeting held at Richard Worrell's.

By "traffik of men-body," the petitioners are referring to the transatlantic slave trade.

These are the reasons why we are against the **traffik of men-body,** as followeth.

Is there any that would be done or handled at this manner? viz., to be sold or made a slave for all the time of his life?

Just as Christians enslaved members of different religions, so too did Muslims (Turks) enslave Christians and others they considered infidels. This slave trade ran in the opposite direction, generally going east across the Sahara desert in Africa.

How fearful and faint-hearted are many on sea when they see a strange vessel—being afraid it should be a Turk, and they should be taken, and sold for slaves into Turkey. Now what is this better done, as Turks doe?

The Old Testament contains multiple strictures against "man-stealing," proscribing a penalty of death for any who do so. Protests against slave trading often relied upon this biblical injunction not to steal other people.

Yea, rather is it worse for them which say they are Christians, for we hear that ye most part of such negers are brought hitherto against their will and consent and that many of them are stolen.

3

Now tho they are black we cannot conceive there is more liberty to have them slaves, as it is to have other white ones. **There is a saying that we shall doe to all men like as we will be done ourselves; making no difference of what generation, descent or colour they are.**

> Here the petitioners draw from the Golden Rule in the New Testament, which urges believers to do unto others as they would have done to themselves. This would be a standard refrain in abolitionist arguments well into the 19th century.

And those who steal or rob men, and those who buy or purchase them, are they not alike? Here is liberty of conscience wch is right and reasonable; here ought to be likewise liberty of ye body, except of evil-doers, wch is an other case.

> The petitioners are speaking to one of the primary reasons their colony was founded, namely as an area of religious freedom for people of all faiths. If religious liberty exists in Pennsylvania, they argue, then so too should physical liberty for all people.

But to bring men hither, or to rob and sell them against their will, we stand against. In Europe there are many oppressed for conscience sake; and here there are those oppossd who are of a black colour. **And we who know that men must not commit adultery—some do commit adultery, in others, separating wives from their husbands and giving them to others; and some sell the children of these poor creatures to other men. Ah! doe consider well this thing, you who doe it, if you would be done at this manner? and if it is done according to Christianity?**

> The sin that resulted from slavery, whether it was adultery, separating families, or other offenses, constitutes another important strand of abolitionist arguments.

You surpass Holland and Germany in this thing. This makes an ill report in all those countries of Europe, where they hear off, that ye Quakers doe here handel men as they handle there ye cattle. And for that reason some have no mind or inclination to come hither.

> For the petitioners, having slavery in the colony could have a direct impact on its success because some people may not want to migrate to such an area. In 1688, the colony of Pennsylvania was in its infancy and was trying to attract more settlers from Europe to increase the population.

And who shall maintain this your cause, or pleid for it? Truly we can not do so, except you shall inform us better hereof, viz., that Christians have liberty to practise these things. Pray, what thing in the world can be done worse towards us, than if men should rob or steal us away, and sell us for slaves to strange countries; separating housbands from their wives and children. Being now this is not done in the manner we would be done at therefore we contradict and are against this traffic of men-body. And we who profess that it is not lawful to steal, must, likewise, avoid to purchase such things as are stolen, but rather help to stop this robbing and stealing if possible. And such men ought to be delivered out of ye hands of ye robbers, and set free as well as in Europe. Then is Pennsylvania to have a good report, instead it hath now a bad one for this sake in other countries. Especially whereas ye Europeans are desirous to know in what manner ye Quakers doe rule in their province—and most of them doe look upon us with an envious eye. But if this is done well, what shall we say is done evil?

Another way that slavery could weaken the colony would be introducing the possibility of slave rebellions. These had already occurred in British colonies such as Barbados and thus were a possibility for Pennsylvania. Slave rebellions represented even more of a threat in Pennsylvania than elsewhere, however, because the Quakers were pacifists and were opposed to war. Therefore, slavery was also a sin in that it might foster violence in their society.

If once these slaves (wch they say are so wicked and stubborn men) should joint themselves—fight for their freedom,—and handel their masters and mastrisses as they did handel them before; will these masters and mastrisses take the sword at hand and warr against these poor slaves, licke, we are able to believe, some will not refuse to doe; or have these negers not as much right to fight for their freedom, as you have to keep them slaves?

Now consider well this thing, if it is good or bad? And in case you find it to be good to handel these blacks at that manner, we desire and require you hereby lovingly that you may inform us herein, which at this time never was done, viz., that Christians have such a liberty to do so. To the end we shall be satisfied in this point, and satisfie likewise our good friends and acquaintances in our natif country, to whose it is a terror, or fairful thing that men should be handeld so in Pennsylvania.

This is from our meeting at Germantown, held ye 18 of the 2 month, 1688, to be delivered to the Monthly Meeting at Richard Worrell's.

Garret hendericks
derick up de graeff
Francis daniell Pastorius
Abraham up Den graef

Source: "Germantown Friends' Protest against Slavery, 1688," Library of Congress.

Puritan Protests

Samuel Sewall, *The Selling of Joseph*
1700

INTRODUCTION

Samuel Sewall was a businessman and a judge of the Supreme Judicial Court of Massachusetts. By the year 1700 slavery had begun to take off in the colony, with nearly 1,000 bondmen in the province that year. Some of these slaves attempted to use the less restrictive Massachusetts legal system to gain their freedom. One such individual was named Adam, the slave of John Saffin; Adam sued his master for his freedom in 1700. Sewall was one of the judges deciding the case, which Adam eventually won in 1703, gaining his freedom. While the case had just begun, Sewall decided to publish this pamphlet, which was circulated among the leading figures in the colony. Sewall attempts here to undermine the common proslavery arguments of the era, including the Curse of Ham and the biblical basis of slavery. The pamphlet was unsuccessful in getting slavery abolished in the colony but did push other leaders, including Cotton Mather, to publish tracts urging better treatment and Christianization of slaves. This short piece was the first antislavery publication in New England, the region that would eventually become the center of American abolitionism.

Sewall's title immediately brings to mind for his readers the story of the biblical Joseph being sold into slavery by his brothers. Joseph would go on to distinguish himself in the service of the Egyptian pharaoh and became a trusted adviser, bringing into even starker light the decision of his brothers to sell him in the first place.

Sewall here makes his case for political equality based on his belief that all people descended from one common ancestor, the biblical Adam, and thus deserve all the same considerations when it comes to freedom and slavery. He also anticipates here an important strain of 19th-century proslavery thought, which would posit that not all men were descended from Adam but that there had in fact been multiple creations.

The Selling of Joseph

For as much as Liberty is in real value next unto Life: None ought to part with it themselves, or deprive others of it, but upon most mature Consideration.

The Numerousness of Slaves at this day in the Province, and the Uneasiness of them under their Slavery, hath put many upon thinking whether the Foundation of it be firmly and well laid; so as to sustain the Vast Weight that is built upon it. **It is most certain that all Men, as they are the Sons of Adam, are Coheirs; and have equal Right unto Liberty, and all other outward Comforts of Life.**

7

GOD hath given the Earth [with all its Commodities] unto the Sons of Adam, Psalm 115.16. And hath made of One Blood, all Nations of Men, for to dwell on all the face of the Earth; and hath determined the Times before appointed, and the bounds of their habitation: That they should seek the Lord. Forasmuch then as we are the Offspring of GOD &c. Act 17.26, 27, 29. **Now although the Title given by the last ADAM, doth infinitely better Mens Estates, respecting GOD and themselves; and grants them a most beneficial and inviolable Lease under the Broad Seal of Heaven, who were before only Tenants at Will: Yet through the Indulgence of GOD to our First Parents after the Fall, the outward Estate of all and every of the Children, remains the same, as to one another. So that Originally, and Naturally, there is no such thing as Slavery.**

By saying "the last Adam," Sewall refers to Jesus, commonly known as the second or last Adam and not the man thought by Christians of his time to be the first human on Earth. So, according to Sewall, all men deserve liberty because they descended from the first Adam and have been made acceptable to God by the sacrifice of the second Adam.

Joseph was rightfully no more a Slave to his Brethren, then they were to him: and they had no more Authority to Sell him, than they had to Slay him. And if they had nothing to do to Sell him; the Ishmaelites bargaining with them, and paying down Twenty pieces of Silver, could not make a Title. Neither could Potiphar have any better Interest in him than the Ishmaelites had. Gen. 37. 20, 27, 28. For he that shall in this case plead Alteration of Property, seems to have forfeited a great part of his own claim to Humanity. There is no proportion between Twenty Pieces of Silver, and LIBERTY. The Commodity it self is the Claimer. If Arabian Gold be imported in any quantities, most are afraid to meddle with it, though they might have it at easy rates; lest if it should have been wrongfully taken from the Owners, it should kindle a fire to the Consumption of their whole Estate. 'Tis pity there should be more Caution used in buying a Horse, or a little lifeless dust; than there is in purchasing Men and Women: When as they are the Offspring of GOD, and their Liberty is,

"Auro pretiosior omni" means "More precious than gold." Sewall wrote at a time when Latin was a required language to even enter college and was still the favorite of many European intellectuals. That trend was beginning to change in this era but had not completely done so.

—Auro pretiosior Omni.

And seeing GOD hath said, He that Stealeth a Man and Selleth him, or if he be found in his hand, he shall surely be put to Death. Exod. 12.16. This Law being of Everlasting Equity, wherein Man Stealing is ranked amongst the most atrocious of Capital Crimes: What louder Cry can there be made of the Celebrated Warning,

"Let the buyer beware!"

Caveat Emptor!

And all things considered, it would conduce more to the Welfare of the Province, to have White Servants for a Term of Years, than to have Slaves for Life. Few can endure to hear of a Negro's being made free; and indeed they can seldom use their freedom well; yet their continual aspiring after their forbidden Liberty, renders them Unwilling Servants.

Even though he argued against slavery, Sewall was not immune to the prejudices of his day, claiming that blacks were inferior and could never be incorporated into Puritan society. Thus it would be better to have white servants.

And there is such a disparity in their Conditions, Color & Hair, that they can never embody with us, and grow up into orderly Families, to the Peopling of the Land: but still remain in our Body Politick as a kind of extravasat Blood.

Sewall argues that because blacks cannot be a part of the "Train Bands," or the colonial militia, having them in the colony tends to weaken it militarily. Notions of black inferiority and fear of what slaves could do if given weapons precluded them from serving in the military for most of the colonial era.

As many Negro men as there are among us, so many empty places there are in our Train Bands, and the places taken up of Men that might make Husbands for our Daughters.

And the Sons and Daughters of New England would become more like Jacob, and Rachel, if this Slavery were thrust quite out of doors. Moreover it is too well known what Temptations Masters are under, to connive at the Fornication of their Slaves; lest they should be obliged to find them Wives, or pay their Fines.

It seems to be practically pleaded that they might be Lawless; 'tis thought much of, that the Law should have Satisfaction for their Thefts, and other Immoralities; by which means, Holiness to the Lord, is more rarely engraven upon this sort of Servitude. It is likewise most lamentable to think, how in taking Negros out of Africa, and Selling of them here, That which GOD ha 's joyned together men do boldly rend asunder; Men from their Country, Husbands from their Wives, Parents from their Children. How horrible is the Uncleanness, Mortality, if not Murder, that the Ships are guilty of that bring great Crouds of these miserable Men, and Women. Methinks, when we are bemoaning the barbarous Usage of our Friends and Kinsfolk in Africa: it might not be unseasonable to enquire whether we are not culpable in forcing the Africans to become Slaves amongst our selves. And it may be a question whether all the Benefit received by Negro Slaves, will balance the Accompt of Cash laid out upon them; and for the Redemption of our own enslaved Friends out of Africa. Besides all the Persons and Estates that have perished there.

Obj. 1. These Blackamores are of the Posterity of Cham, and therefore are under the Curse of Slavery. Gen. 9.25, 26, 27.

Sewall is responding to notions that blacks were the offspring of the biblical Ham, also known as Cham. According to this story, Ham saw his father Noah drunk and naked one night. Noah cursed Ham's son Canaan and all his descendants to serve the sons of Ham's two brothers. Those who argued in favor of slavery in America argued that blacks were the descendants of Ham and that slavery was thus biblically sanctioned.

Answ. Of all Offices, one would not begg this; viz. Uncall'd for, to be an Executioner of the Vindictive Wrath of God; the extent and duration of which is to us uncertain. If this ever was a Commission; How do we know but that it is long since out of date? Many have found it to their Cost, that a Prophetical Denunciation of Judgment against a Person or People, would not warrant them to inflict that evil. If it would, Hazael might justify himself in all he did against his Master, and the Israelites, from 2 Kings 8: 10, 12.

But it is possible that by cursory reading, this Text may have been mistaken. For Canaan is the Person Cursed three times over, without the mentioning of Cham. Good Expositors suppose the Curse entailed on him, and that this Prophesie was accomplished in the Extirpation of the Canaanites, and in the Servitude of the Gibeonites, Vide Pareum. Whereas the Blackmores are not descended of Canaan, but of Cush. Psal. 68. 31. Princes shall come out of Egypt [Mizraim] Ethopia [Cush] shall soon stretch out her hands unto God. Under which Names, all Africa may be comprehended; and the Promised Conversion ought to be prayed for. Jer. 13, 23. Can the Ethiopian change his skin? This shews that Black Men are the Posterity of Cush: Who time out of mind have been distinguished by their Colour. And for want of the true, Ovid assigns a fabulous cause of it.

Sanguine tum credunt in corpora summa vocato Aethiopum populos nigrum traxisse colorem. Metamorph. lib.2.

Perhaps the most common justification for slavery was the Christianization of Africans that would follow. Spanish Catholics emphasized conversion to a far greater degree than the Protestant English, although in New England, where Sewall lived, more blacks were converted than in the southern colonies during the early 18th century.

Obj. 2. The Nigers are brought out of a Pagan Country, into places where the Gospel is Preached.

Answ. Evil must not be done, that good may come of it. The extraordinary and comprehensive Benefit accruing to the Church of God, and to Joseph personally, did not rectify his brethrens Sale of him.

Obj. 3. The Africans have Wars with one another: our Ships bring lawful Captives taken in those Wars.

Answ. For ought is known, their Wars are much such as were between Jacob's Sons and their Brother Joseph. If they be between Town and Town; Provincial, or National: Every War is upon one side Unjust. An Unlawful War can't make lawful Captives. And by Receiving, we are in danger to promote, and partake in their Barbarous Cruelties. I am sure, if some Gentlemen should go down to the Brewsters to take the Air, and Fish: And a stronger party from Hull should Surprise them, and Sell them for Slaves to a Ship outward bound: they would think themselves unjustly dealt with; both by Sellers and Buyers. And yet 'tis to be feared, we have no other kind of Title to our Nigers. Therefore all things whatsoever ye would that men should do to you, do ye even so to them: for this is the Law and the Prophets. Matt. 7. 12.

Obj. 4. Abraham had servants bought with his Money, and born in his House.

Answ. Until the Circumstances of Abraham's purchase be recorded, no Argument can be drawn from it. In the mean time, Charity obliges us to conclude, that He knew it was lawful and good.

It is Observable that the Israelites were strictly forbidden the buying, or selling one another for Slaves. Levit. 25. 39, 46. Jer. 34. 8–22. And GOD gaged His Blessing in lieu of any loss they might conceipt they suffered thereby. Deut. 15. 18. And since the partition Wall is broken down, inordinate Self love should likewise be demolished. GOD expects that Christians should be of a more Ingenuous and benign frame of spirit. Christians should carry it to all the World, as the Israelites were to carry it one towards another. And for men obstinately to persist in holding their Neighbours and Brethren under the Rigor of perpetual Bondage, seems to be no proper way of gaining Assurance that God ha's given them Spiritual Freedom. Our Blessed Saviour ha's altered the Measures of the Ancient Love-Song, and set it to a most Excellent New Tune, which all ought to be ambitious of Learning. Matt. 5. 43, 44. John 13. 34. These Ethiopians, as black as they are; seeing they are the Sons and Daughters of the First Adam, the Brethren and Sister of the Last ADAM, and the Offspring of GOD; They ought to be treated with a Respect agreeable. . . .

Source: Samuel Sewall, *The Selling of Joseph: A Memorial* (Boston: Bartholomew Green and John Allen, 1700), 1–3.

Race and the Enlightenment

David Hume, "Of National Characters"

1758

INTRODUCTION

David Hume was a Scottish philosopher and historian who was widely known as one of the principal figures of the British Enlightenment. Hume's most popular works include titles such as *A Treatise of Human Nature* and *Dialogues Concerning Natural Religion*. In this excerpt, taken from his book *Essays Moral and Political,* Hume expounds upon what he sees to be the deficiencies in the nature of blacks. For Hume, philosopher and "enlightened" citizen, any group of people who had not produced important accomplishments in the arts and sciences were inferior. This train of thought represents the viewpoint of many during the 18th and 19th centuries and would provide the foundation for the racial caste system in both Britain and the United States.

I am apt to suspect the negroes to be naturally inferior to the whites. There scarcely ever was a civilized nation of that complexion, nor even any individual eminent either in action or speculation. No ingenious manufactures amongst them, no arts, no sciences.

On the other hand, the most rude and barbarous of the whites, such as the ancient GERMANS, the present TARTARS, have still something eminent about them, in their valour, form of government, or some other particular. Such a uniform and constant difference could not happen, in so many countries and ages, if nature had not made an original distinction between these breeds of men. Not to mention our colonies, there are NEGROE slaves dispersed all over EUROPE, of whom none ever discovered any symptoms of ingenuity; though low people, without education, will start up amongst us, and distinguish themselves in every profession. In JAMAICA, indeed,

In this short excerpt, David Hume articulates perhaps the most important strain of racial thinking of this time period, namely that blacks were inferior to whites because blacks had not achieved as much intellectually. Hume was writing during the Age of Enlightenment, an era that saw reason, science, and literature as the chief markers of civilization. Since enslaved blacks had not produced great works of literature or achieved fame in the sciences, the argument went, then they were lower on the scale of humanity than whites and deserving of inferior treatment. While Hume was personally opposed to slavery, his ideas could easily be used by supporters of the system.

they talk of one negroe as a man of parts and learning; but it is likely he is admired for slender accomplishments, like a parrot, who speaks a few words plainly.

Source: David Hume, "Of National Characters." In *Essays, Moral and Political,* Vol. 1 (London: A. Millar, 1758), 125n.

The Colonial Crisis and Abolitionism

James Otis, *The Rights of the British Colonies Asserted and Proved*

1764

INTRODUCTION

James Otis was a Harvard-educated lawyer in Boston who became an early advocate of colonial rights and resistance to Great Britain. His work in the Writs of Assistance cases in 1761 put him on the map as a leader of popular resistance in Massachusetts, as he championed the rights of privacy and protection from illegal searches. His publication *The Rights of the British Colonies Asserted and Proved* in 1764 denied Parliament's right to enforce the Navigation Acts in the colonies, and it was here that he drew parallels between the position of the colonists and the position of slaves. Asserting the natural rights of blacks and their equality with whites, Otis went far beyond the comfort level of most abolitionists of his time, who worked against slavery but also harbored prejudice toward blacks. Otis recognized from an early period the intimate connection between the movement to end slavery and the movement for racial equality.

In order to form an idea of the natural rights of the colonists, I presume it will be granted that they are men, the common children of the same Creator with their brethren of Great Britain. Nature has placed all such in a state of equality and perfect freedom to act within the bounds of the laws of nature and reason without consulting the will or regarding the humor, the passions, or whims of any other man, unless they are formed into a society or body politic. . . .

Otis begins his tract with a discussion of John Locke, a British philosopher of the late 17th and early 18th centuries, and his ideas of natural rights. In response to the Glorious Revolution of 1688, which replaced James II with William and Mary, Locke wrote *Two Treatises on Government* in which he argued that all men are endowed with the rights to life, liberty, and property and that these rights are natural and inalienable. Natural rights theory would play a critical role in both the American Revolution and the origins of American abolitionism.

The colonists are by the law of nature freeborn, as indeed all men are, white or black. No better reasons can be given for enslaving those of any color than such as Baron Montesquieu has humorously given as the foundation of that cruel slavery exercised over the poor Ethiopians, which threatens one day

16

Otis does what few white intellectuals had
done before him, namely apply notions of
natural rights to blacks and argue that physical differences bear no weight when considering one's rights in society.

to reduce both Europe and America to the ignorance and barbarity of the darkest ages. **Does it follow that 'tis right to
enslave a man because he is black? Will short curled hair
like wool instead of Christian hair, as 'tis called by those
whose hearts are as hard as the nether millstone, help the
argument? Can any logical inference in favor of slavery
be drawn from a flat nose, a long or a short face?** Nothing
better can be said in favor of a trade that is the most shocking
violation of the law of nature, has a direct tendency to diminish the idea of the inestimable value of liberty, and makes
every dealer in it a tyrant, from the director of an African
company to the petty chapman in needles and pins on the
unhappy coast. It is a clear truth that those who every day
barter away other men 's liberty will soon care little for their
own. . . .

The colonists, being men, have a right to be considered
as equally entitled to all the rights of nature with the
Europeans, and they are not to be restrained in the exercise
of any of these rights but for the evident good of the whole
community.

The idea that Britain was engaged in a tyrannical plot to enslave the colonists was common
during the American Revolutionary era and
provided a useful rhetorical tool with which
black and white abolitionists could argue for
an end to slavery. If whites recognized that
they were not born to be slaves, then surely
they would come to the same conclusion for
blacks, the reasoning went.

**By being or becoming members of society they have not
renounced their natural liberty in any greater degree
than other good citizens, and if 'tis taken from them
without their consent they are so far enslaved.**

I also lay it down as one of the first principles from whence
I intend to deduce the civil rights of the British colonies, that
all of them are subject to and dependent on Great Britain,
and that therefore as over subordinate governments the Parliament of Great Britain has an undoubted power and lawful
authority to make acts for the general good that, by nam-
ing them, shall and ought to be equally binding as upon the
subjects of Great Britain within the realm. This principle,

I presume, will be readily granted on the other side the Atlantic. It has been practised upon for twenty years to my knowledge, in the province of the *Massachusetts Bay;* and I have ever received it that it has been so from the beginning in this and the sister provinces through the continent. . . .

> **That the colonists, black and white, born here are free-born British subjects, and entitled to all the essential civil rights of such is a truth not only manifest from the provincial charters, from the principles of the common law, and acts of Parliament, but from the British constitution, which was re-established at the Revolution with a professed design to secure the liberties of all the subjects to all generations. . . .**

Otis is referring to the aforementioned Glorious Revolution of 1688, where Parliament passed laws designed to recognize and promote the liberties of British subjects, including the Act of Toleration that went far toward promoting religious liberty, at least for Protestants. Otis argues that this legacy of liberty is the birthright of both black and white colonists.

The liberties of the subject are spoken of as their best birthrights. No one ever dreamed, surely, that these liberties were confined to the realm. At that rate no British subjects in the dominions could, without a manifest contradiction, be declared entitled to all the privileges of subjects born within the realm to all intents and purposes which are rightly given foreigners by Parliament after residing seven years. These expressions of Parliament as well as of the charters must be vain and empty sounds unless we are allowed the essential rights of our fellow subjects in Great Britain.

Now can there be any liberty where property is taken away without consent? Can it with any color of truth, justice, or equity be affirmed that the northern colonies are represented in Parliament? Has this whole continent of near three thousand miles in length, and in which and his other American dominions His Majesty has or very soon will have some millions of as good, loyal, and useful subjects, white and black, as any in the three kingdoms, the election of one member of the House of Commons?

Parliament? As it is agreed on all hands the crown alone cannot impose them, we should be justifiable in refusing to pay them, but must and ought to yield obedience to an act of Parliament, though erroneous, till repealed. I can see no reason to doubt but the imposition of taxes, whether on trade, or on land, or houses, or ships, on real or personal, fixed ort floating property, in the colonies is absolutely irreconcilable with the rights of the colonists as British subjects and as men. I say men, for in a state of nature no man can take my property from me without my consent: if he does, he deprives me of my liberty and makes me a slave. If such a proceeding is a breach of the law of nature, no law of society can make it just. The very act of taxing exercised over those who are not represented appears to me to be depriving them of one of their most essential rights as freemen, and if continued seems to be in effect an entire disfranchisement of every civil right.

Source: James Otis, *The Rights of the British Colonies Asserted and Proved* (Boston, 1764).

Organized Black Abolitionism

Petition of Massachusetts Blacks to the General Court

1773

INTRODUCTION

In the midst of the conflict with Great Britain, petitioning emerged as a key tactic of the American Revolutionaries and would become a key tactic of the early antislavery movement. Massachusetts law granted slaves rights that they were denied in other colonies, including the right to petition the legislature. They took advantage of this with a petition campaign begun in January 1773. Receiving no response to their first entreaty, a committee of slaves, led by Felix Holbrook, petitioned the legislature again in April 1773 and were more successful in getting their voices heard. The petition was published in multiple venues, and the Massachusetts House of Representatives acted on the petition, forming a committee to consider the abolition of slavery. The law passed the House and Council of Massachusetts but was killed when it was sent to the Continental Congress, which included many delegates from slaveholding states. This would be one of six petitions that Massachusetts blacks submitted during the 1770s to end slavery. Their efforts helped weaken the institution within the Bay State and inspired activists throughout New England to use petitions as a means to end slavery.

Sir,

The efforts made by the legislative of this province in their last sessions to free themselves from slavery, gave us, who are in that deplorable state, a high degree of satisfaction.

Here the petitioners reference the political context of the American Revolution to bolster their case against slavery. At this time Committees of Correspondence had been set up throughout Massachusetts so that people could communicate and coordinate resistance activities against Britain.

We expect great things from men who have made such a noble stand against the designs of their fellow-men to enslave them. We cannot but wish and hope Sir, that you will have the same grand object, we mean civil and religious liberty, in view in your next session. The divine spirit of freedom, seems to fire every humane breast on

Pointing out the hypocrisy of Americans contending for liberty while holding slaves was a common tool employed by both abolitionists who wanted to undermine slavery and Loyalists who wanted to undermine the American Revolution.

The petitioners reference the Spanish practice of coartación whereby enslaved men and women were sometimes allowed to purchase their own freedom. Since the English liked to think of themselves as more humane and benevolent than the Catholic Spaniards, the petitioners felt that this comparison would assist their cause.

In 1767 the Massachusetts legislature had debated a bill to outlaw slave trading in the state, and thus the petitioners may have been referring to that. In mentioning their "natural right" they employed the ideas of John Locke—which were widespread throughout Revolutionary America—that all human beings possess natural rights to life, liberty, and property.

While they clearly desire their freedom, the petitioners also make it clear that they are peaceful and will not revolt to get it. Instead, they will continue to use lawful means such as petitions and freedom suits to achieve their goals.

this continent, except such as are bribed to assist in executing the execrable plan.

We are very sensible that it would be highly detrimental to our present masters, if we were allowed to demand all that of right belongs to us for past services; this we disclaim. **Even the Spaniards, who have not those sublime ideas of freedom that English men have, are conscious that they have no right to all the service of their fellow-men, we mean the Africans, whom they have purchased with their money; therefore they allow them one day in a week to work for them-selve[s], to enable them to earn money to purchase the residue of their time, which they have a right to demand in such portions as they are able to pay for (a due appraizment of their services being first made, which always stands at the purchase money).**

We do not pretend to dictate to you Sir, or to the honorable Assembly, of which you are a member: We acknowledge our obligations to you for what you have already done, but as the people of this province seem to be actuated by the principles of equity and justice, we cannot but expect your house will again take our deplorable case into serious consideration, and give us that ample relief which, as men, we have a natural right to.

But since the wise and righteous governor of the universe, has permitted our fellow men to make us slaves, we bow in submission to him, and determine to behave in such a manner, as that we may have reason to expect the divine approbation of, and assistance in, our peaceable and lawful attempts to gain our freedom.

We are willing to submit to such regulations and laws, as may be made relative to us, until we leave the province, which we determine to do as soon as we can from our joynt labours procure money to transport ourselves to some part of the coast of Africa, where we propose a settlement. We are very desirous that you should have instructions relative to us, from your town, therefore we pray you to communicate this letter to them, and ask this favor for us.

In behalf of our fellow slaves in this province, And by order of their Committee.

PETER BESTES,
SAMBO FREEMAN,
FELIX HOLBROOK,
CHESTER JOIE.

For the REPRESENTATIVE of the town of Thompson

Source: "Peter Bestes and Other Slaves Petition for Freedom (April 20, 1773)," Leaflet in the collection of the New York Historical Society Library.

African and Indian Alliances

Phillis Wheatley, "Letter to Samson Occom"

1774

INTRODUCTION

Phillis Wheatley was brought to Boston aboard the slave ship *Phillis* in 1761 at the age of seven or eight years old and was purchased by John Wheatley, a local businessman. Phillis Wheatley proved to be a precocious child and was able to acquire an education, something that was unavailable to most slaves in the British North American colonies.

A number of Wheatley's letters survive, and these provide scholars with excellent insights into the lives and thoughts of black evangelicals during the era of the American Revolution. Here Wheatley writes to Samson Occom, a Native American minister. The letter indicates an ongoing correspondence between the two figures, both of whom were likely the most well known of their respective races during this period. Wheatley uses biblical examples and arguments to make her case against slavery, noting that God will not look kindly on a nation that continues the practice of slaveholding.

The Connecticut Gazette
March 11, 1774

Rev'd and honor'd Sir,

I have this Day received your obliging kind Epistle, and am greatly satisfied with your Reasons respecting the Negroes, and think highly reasonable what you offer in Vindication of their natural Rights: **Those that invade them cannot be insensible that the divine Light is chasing away the thick Darkness which broods over the Land of Africa; and the Chaos which has reign'd so long, is converting into beautiful Order,** and [r]eveals more and more clearly, the glorious Dispensation of civil and religious Liberty, which are so inseparably Limited, that there is little or no

Wheatley references ongoing missionary attempts to bring Africans into the fold of Christianity. This is a theme that she would highlight in numerous poems, including her well-known work, "On Being Brought from Africa to America."

Enjoyment of one Without the other: **Otherwise, perhaps, the Israelites had been less solicitous for their Freedom from Egyptian slavery; I do not say they would have been contented without it, by no means, for in every human Breast, God has implanted a Principle, which we call Love of Freedom; it is impatient of Oppression, and pants for Deliverance; and by the Leave of our modern Egyptians I will assert, that the same Principle lives in us.**

Comparing contemporary slaveholders to Egyptians was a powerful symbol for abolitionists, especially during the American Revolutionary era. During this time many still believed that the New England colonies represented the New Israel, a promised land that could help bring the world to the one true religion—Protestant Christianity.

God grant Deliverance in his own Way and Time, and get him honour upon all those whose Avarice impels them to countenance and help forward tile Calamities of their fellow Creatures.

The phrase "get him honour" referred to God having revenge upon all who insisted on slave trading and holding slaves in bondage. Wheatley notes that punishment from God, perhaps in the form of a military loss or slave rebellion, might be necessary for those who continue this sinful practice.

This I desire not for their Hurt, but to convince them of the strange Absurdity of their Conduct whose Words and Actions are so diametrically, opposite. How well the Cry for Liberty, and the reverse Disposition for the exercise of oppressive Power over others agree,—**I humbly think it does not require the Penetration of a Philosopher to determine.**

In this barb at Enlightenment philosophers who have written extensively on the subject of liberty, Wheatley claims the intellectual authority, even as an African slave, to enter and contribute to this important discussion.

Source: Phillis Wheatley, "Letter to the Reverend Samson Occom," *Connecticut Gazette*, March 11, 1774.

Black Masons Protest Slavery

Petition of Prince Hall to the General Court

1777

INTRODUCTION

After 4 years of submitting unsuccessful petitions, slaves and free blacks in Massachusetts were growing increasingly restless. They had begun their campaign in 1773 while the colonists were still part of the British Empire. By 1777 the colonies were in the midst of war, and this petition was submitted just weeks after George Washington's stunning victories at Trenton and Princeton. The tone of the petitioners grew increasingly radical over the course of the decade. Beginning with humble entreaties for their rights, by this point the petitioners are impatient, and their rhetoric shows this. Instead of deferentially asking for their freedom as they did earlier, the petitioners now boldly assert it based upon their understanding of natural rights. This petition campaign is the first recorded political activity of Prince Hall, who founded the African Masonic Lodge of Boston and would go on to be the recognized leader of the black community for the next 30 years.

To the Honorable Counsel & House of Representatives for the State of Massachusetts Bay in General Court assembled, January 13, 1777:

The petitioners articulate a number of the key themes in American abolitionism. Especially prevalent during the Revolutionary period, as the document from James Otis highlights, was the notion that blacks had not forfeited their natural rights. According to Locke, all people possessed these rights in a state of nature but gave some of them up when forming a society. Since blacks never voluntarily gave up their rights, they are calling for whites to recognize them. The petitioners likewise note that they were stolen from a populous and pleasant country, not the barren, heathen wasteland that many likely pictured when they thought of African nations. And finally, like many abolitionists would do, they point out that their enslavers are supposedly Christian and thus should follow their own religious principles.

The petition of A Great Number of Blackes detained in a State of slavery in the bowels of a free & Christian County Humbly sheweth that your Petitioners apprehend that they have in Common with all other men a Natural and Unalienable Right to that freedom which the Grat Parent of the Universe that Bestowed equally on all menkind and which they have Never forfeited by any Compact or agreement whatever but that wher Unjustly Dragged by the hand of cruel Power and their Derest friends and sum of them Even torn from

the Embraces of their tender Parents from A populous Pleasant and Plentiful country and in violation of
Laws of Nature and of Nations and in Defiance of all
the tender feelings of humanity Brough here Either to
Be sold like Beast of burthen & Like them Condemned
to Slavery for Life Among A People Professing the mild
Religion of Jesus A people Not Insensible of the Secrets
of Rational Being Nor without spirit to Resent the
unjust endeavors of others to Reduce them to a state
of Bondage and Subjugation your hononuer Need not
to be informed that A Live of Slavery Like that of your
petitioners Deprived of Every social privilege of Every
thing Requisite and render Life Tolable is far worse
than Nonexistance.

(In imitat)ion of the Lawdable Example of the Good
People of these States your petitioners have Long and
Patiently waited the Event of petition after petition By
them presented tot the Legislative Body of this state
and cannot but with Grief Reflect that their Success
hath been but too similar they Cannot but express their
Astonishment that It have Never Bin Considered that
Every Principle from which America has Acted in the
Course of their unhappy Difficulties with Great Briton
Pleads Stronger than A thousand arguments in favors
of your petitioners they therfor humble Beseech your
honours to give this petition its due weight and consideration & cause an act of the legislature to be past Wherby
they may be Restored to the Enjoyments of that which is
the Natural right of all men and their Children who wher
Born in this Land of Liberty may not be held as Slaves
after they arrive at the age of twenty one years so may
the Inhabitance of this States No longer chargeable with
the inconstancy of acting themselves that part which they

Their first petition to the legislature was the one above in 1773, and while the Massachusetts General Court did debate an abolition bill after an April 1773 petition, nothing came out of it. The General Court would likewise debate an abolition measure after this 1777 petition but deferred to the Continental Congress on the matter, and the presence of slaveholders in that body doomed any antislavery legislation.

condemn and oppose in others Be prospered in their present Glorious struggle for Liberty and have those Blessings to them, &c.

Source: "Petition of a Great Number of Negroes," Presented to the Massachusetts House of Representatives on January 13, 1777, Massachusetts Historical Society, 5th Series, Vol. 3 (Boston, 1877), 432–433.

Antislavery Poetry

Phillis Wheatley, "On the Death of General Wooster"

1778

INTRODUCTION

Phillis Wheatley published her first poem in 1767 and just six years later, in 1773, became the first African American and the first woman to publish a book of poems, titled *Poems on Various Subjects, Religious and Moral*. In this piece, published in 1778, she honors General David Wooster, who died after the Battle of Ridgefield in Connecticut in May 1777. Wheatley reflects on the ideals for which Wooster died and pushes the colonists to live up to those ideals by addressing the problem of slavery in a land fighting for freedom.

A poem by Phillis Wheatley (July 1778)

From this the Muse rich consolation draws
He nobly perish'd in his Country's cause
His Country's Cause that ever fir'd his mind
Where martial flames, and Christian virtues join'd.
How shall my pen his warlike deeds proclaim
Or paint them fairer on the list of Fame—
Enough, great Chief-now wrapt in shades around,
Thy grateful Country shall thy praise resound—
Tho not with mortals' empty praise elate
That vainest vapour to the immortal State
Inly serene the expiring hero lies.
And thus (while heav'nward roll his swimming eyes):
"Permit, great power, while yet my fleeting breath
And Spirits wander to the verge of Death—

It was a common idea that freedom was a necessary foundation for a life of virtue and morality. Revolutionaries made this claim in their resistance to the policies of Great Britain, and abolitionists would likewise argue that it was essential to black virtue.

Permit me yet to point fair freedom's charms

For her the Continent shines bright in arms,

By thy high will, celestial prize she came—

For her we combat on the field of fame

Without her presence vice maintains full sway

And social love and virtue wing their way

O still propitious be thy guardian care

And lead Columbia thro' the toils of war.

With thine own hand conduct them and defend

And bring the dreadful contest to an end—

For ever grateful let them live to thee

And keep them ever Virtuous, brave, and free—

Wheatley argues that God will not favor the Revolutionaries in their struggle unless they free their slaves, putting into practice their own rhetoric of freedom. Wheatley here draws from the long-standing Puritan tradition of the jeremiad, which tied together social and political change with religious rhetoric.

But how, presumptuous shall we hope to find

Divine acceptance with th' Almighty mind—

While yet (O deed Ungenerous!) they disgrace

And hold in bondage Afric's blameless race?

Let Virtue reign—And thou accord our prayers

Be victory our's, and generous freedom theirs."

The hero pray'd—the wond'ring spirits fled

And sought the unknown regions of the dead—

Tis thine, fair partner of his life, to find

His virtuous path and follow close behind—

A little moment steals him from thy sight

He waits thy coming to the realms of light

Freed from his labours in the ethereal Skies

Where in succession endless pleasures rise!

Source: "Phillis Wheatley to Mary Wooster, 15 July 1778," Hugh Upham Clark Collection, 1778, Massachusetts Historical Society.

"No Taxation without Representation"

Petition of John and Paul Cuffe to the General Court

1780

INTRODUCTION

Paul and John Cuffe were the freeborn children of Ruth and Cuffe Slocum. When Paul was 16 years old he went to sea and traveled aboard whaling ships to the Gulf of Mexico and the West Indies. While Paul was on his third voyage in 1776 his ship was captured by the British, and he was briefly imprisoned in New York before returning to Westport. He sailed to the Caribbean again in 1778 and the following year decided to go into business with his brother, building a small boat to carry on trade with the islands just off the Massachusetts and Rhode Island borders. These many experiences proved formative to Paul's growing political consciousness, allowing him to witness the treatment of blacks throughout the Western Hemisphere and to become conversant with the discourses of natural rights and the duty of resisting tyranny. His familiarity with these discourses is evident in the petition that he and six others submitted in February 1780.

To the Honorable Council and House of Representatives, in General Court assembled, for the State of the Massachusetts Bay, in New England:

The petition of several poor negroes and mulattoes, who are inhabitants of the town of Dartmouth, humbly showeth,—

That we being chiefly of the African extract, and by reason of long bondage and hard slavery, we have been deprived of enjoying the profits of our labor or the advantage of inheriting estates from our parents, as our neighbors the white people do, having some of us not long enjoyed our own freedom; yet of late, contrary to the invariable custom and practice of the country, we have been, and now are, taxed both in our polls and that small pittance of estate

The petitioners note that their economic situation prevents them from being able to pay recently imposed taxes. Hard circumstances such as theirs were often considered by governmental authorities as exceptions to tax laws, but these exceptions came on an individual basis. Without relief from taxation, they argue, blacks will be forced onto the poor rolls, which will be paid for from tax dollars anyway.

30

which, through much hard labor and industry, we have got together to sustain ourselves and families withall. We apprehend it, therefore, to be hard usage, and will doubtless (if continued) reduce us to a state of beggary, whereby we shall become a burthen to others, if not timely prevented by the interposition of your justice and your power.

The context of the American Revolution is critical to the petitioners' argument, as it allows them to claim that they are being taxed without the benefit of representation, the same argument that white Revolutionaries used to justify war with Great Britain. If American colonists want to be intellectually consistent, the petitioners suggest, they need to either not tax blacks or extend to them voting privileges.

Your petitioners further show, that we apprehend ourselves to be aggrieved, in that, while we are not allowed the privilege of freemen of the State, having no vote or influence in the election of those that tax us, yet many of our colour (as is well known) have cheerfully entered the field of battle in the defence of the common cause, and that (as we conceive) against a similar exertion of power (in regard to taxation), too well known to need a recital in this place.

We most humbly request, therefore, that you would take our unhappy case into your serious consideration, and, in your wisdom and power, grant us relief from taxation, while under our present depressed circumstances; and your poor petitioners, as in duty bound, shall ever pray, &c.

John Cuffe,

Adventur Child,

Paul Cuffe,

Samuel Gray, X his mark.

Pero Howland, X his mark.

Pero Russell, X his mark.

Pero Coggeshall.

Dated at Dartmouth, the 10th of February, 1780.

Source: George W. Williams, *History of the Negro Race in America,* Vol. 2 (New York: Putnam, 1883), 126.

"A Suspicion Only"

Thomas Jefferson, Excerpt from *Notes on the State of Virginia*

1785

INTRODUCTION

Thomas Jefferson wrote his *Notes on the State of Virginia* as a response to queries about his home state. The book contained information about the natural resources of the state and Jefferson's reflections on the ideal society, which he believed Virginia represented. In this selection Jefferson reports on efforts to gradually abolish slavery in the state, and he also discusses his views on blacks and whites living together in the same society. The first part reflects the influence of the American Revolution in pushing many states to consider abolishing slavery, while the second part represents one answer to the question that arose once the question of abolition was brought up, namely what would be done with the black population once they were freed. Jefferson would argue that blacks and whites could not live together in the same society, and thus blacks should be repatriated to Africa.

To emancipate all slaves born after passing the act. The bill reported by the revisors does not itself contain this proposition; but an amendment containing it was prepared, to be offered to the legislature whenever the bill should be taken up, and further directing, that they should continue with their parents to a certain age, then be brought up, at the public expence, to tillage, arts or sciences, according to their geniusses, till the females should be eighteen, and the males twenty-one years of age, when they should be colonized to such place as the circumstances of the time should render most proper, sending them out with arms, implements of houshold and of the handicraft arts, seeds, pairs of the useful domestic animals, &c. to declare them a free and indepandant people, and extend to them our alliance and

Jefferson is referring to a bill discussed in the Virginia House of Burgesses during the American Revolution. The bill was a gradual emancipation plan, meaning that no slaves would be immediately freed by the act. Instead, the children of current slaves would gain their freedom at a specific age. In the case of Virginia, it appears that emancipation was to be tied to colonization, or deportation of blacks to Africa. This bill never passed the Virginia legislature.

protection, till they shall have acquired strength; and to send vessels at the same time to other parts of the world for an equal number of white inhabitants; to induce whom to migrate hither, proper encouragements were to be proposed.

Jefferson and many others of his time argued that racial prejudice and the possibilities of a race war would prevent the incorporation of blacks into the larger society. While they wrote 80 years apart, Jefferson in essence makes a similar argument that Samuel Sewall did in *The Selling of Joseph*.

It will probably be asked, Why not retain and incorporate the blacks into the state, and thus save the expence of supplying, by importation of white settlers, the vacancies they will leave? Deep rooted prejudices entertained by the whites; ten thousand recollections, by the blacks, of the injuries they have sustained; new provocations; the real distinctions which nature has made; and many other circumstances, will divide us into parties, and produce convulsions which will probably never end but in the extermination of the one or the other race.

Jefferson notes that the differences between whites and blacks are "fixed in nature." This was one common way of viewing racial difference, basing it on biology and nature. Many abolitionists, on the other hand, viewed race in environmental and cultural terms, arguing that any differences between whites and blacks were a result of different environments.

To these objections, which are political, may be added others, which are physical and moral. The first difference which strikes us is that of colour. Whether the black of the negro resides in the reticular membrane between the skin and scarf-skin, or in the scarf-skin itself; whether it proceeds from the colour of the blood, the colour of the bile, or from that of some other secretion, the difference is fixed in nature, and is as real as if its seat and cause were better known to us.

And is this difference of no importance? Is it not the foundation of a greater or less share of beauty in the two races? Are not the fine mixtures of red and white, the expressions of every passion by greater or less suffusions of colour in the one, preferable to that eternal monotony, which reigns in the countenances, that immoveable veil of black which covers all the emotions of the other race? Add to these, flowing hair, a more elegant symmetry of form, their own judgment in favour of the whites, declared by their preference of them, as uniformly as is the preference of the Oran-ootan for the black women over those of his own species. **The circumstance of superior beauty, is thought worthy attention in the propagation of our horses, dogs, and other domestic animals; why not in that of man? Besides those of colour, figure, and hair, there are other physical distinctions proving a difference of race. They have less hair on the face and body. They secrete less by the kidnies, and more by the glands of the skin, which gives them a very strong and disagreeable odour. This greater degree of transpiration renders them more tolerant of heat, and less so of cold, than the whites.**

In this list Jefferson articulates what would come to be some of the most lasting stereotypes of African Americans, namely that they were ugly and smelled bad and were lustful.

Perhaps too a difference of structure in the pulmonary apparatus, which a late ingenious experimentalist has discovered to be the principal regulator of animal heat, may have disabled them from extricating, in the act of inspiration, so much of that fluid from the outer air, or obliged them in expiration, to part with more of it. They seem to require less sleep. A black, after hard labour through the day, will be induced by the slightest amusements to sit up till midnight, or later, though knowing he must be out with the first dawn of the morning. They are at least as brave, and more adventuresome. But this may perhaps proceed from a want of forethought, which prevents their seeing a danger till it be present. When present, they do not go through it with more coolness or steadiness than the whites. They are more ardent after their female: but love seems with them to be more an eager desire, than a tender delicate mixture of sentiment and sensation. Their griefs are transient. Those numberless afflictions, which render it doubtful whether heaven has given life to us in mercy or in wrath, are less felt, and sooner forgotten with them. In general, their existence appears to participate more of sensation than reflection. To this must be ascribed their disposition to sleep when abstracted from their diversions, and unemployed in labour. **An animal whose body is at rest, and who does not reflect, must be disposed to sleep of course. Comparing them by their faculties of memory, reason, and imagination, it appears to me, that in memory they are equal to the whites; in reason much inferior, as I think one could scarcely be found capable of tracing and comprehending the investigations of Euclid; and that in imagination they are dull, tasteless, and anomalous.**

It would be unfair to follow them to Africa for this investigation. We will consider them here, on the same stage with the whites, and where the facts are not apocryphal on which a judgment is to be formed. It will be right to make great allowances for the difference of condition, of education, of conversation, of the sphere in which they move.

Many millions of them have been brought to, and born in America. Most of them indeed have been confined to tillage, to their own homes, and their own society: yet many have been so situated, that they might have availed themselves of the conversation of their masters; many have been brought up to the handicraft arts, and from that circumstance have always been associated with the whites. Some have been liberally educated, and all have lived in countries where the arts and sciences are cultivated to a considerable degree, and have had before their eyes samples of the best works from abroad. The Indians, with no advantages of this kind, will often carve figures

These were perhaps Jefferson's most damning critiques of blacks, namely that they were unintelligent beings incapable of rational thought and artistic production. In the Age of Enlightenment, one's humanity was based on one's capacity to reason. By arguing that blacks could not reason, Jefferson diminished that humanity.

Here Jefferson alludes to the environmental theories of racial difference, but he would soon discount this line of thought.

on their pipes not destitute of design and merit. They will crayon out an animal, a plant, or a country, so as to prove the existence of a germ in their minds which only wants cultivation. They astonish you with strokes of the most sublime oratory; such as prove their reason and sentiment strong, their imagination glowing and elevated. But never yet could I find that a black had uttered a thought above the level of plain narration; never see even an elementary trait of painting or sculpture. In music they are more generally gifted than the whites with accurate ears for tune and time, and they have been found capable of imagining a small catch. Whether they will be equal to the composition of a more extensive run of melody, or of complicated harmony, is yet to be proved. Misery is often the parent of the most affecting touches in poetry.—Among the blacks is misery enough, God knows, but no poetry. Love is the peculiar oestrum of the poet. Their love is ardent, but it kindles the senses only, not the imagination. **Religion indeed has produced a Phyllis Whately; but it could not produce a poet. The compositions published under her name are below the dignity of criticism.**

Here Jefferson refers to Phillis Wheatley. In the 18th century her name would have been pronounced "Whately." While Wheatley was the first African American poet to publish a book of her works, Jefferson argues that she does not deserve the title.

The heroes of the Dunciad are to her, as Hercules to the author of that poem. **Ignatius Sancho has approached nearer to merit in composition; yet his letters do more honour to the heart than the head. They breathe the purest effusions of friendship and general philanthropy, and shew how great a degree of the latter may be compounded with strong religious zeal. He is often happy in the turn of his compliments, and his stile is easy and familiar, except when he affects a Shandean fabrication of words. But his imagination is wild and extravagant, escapes incessantly from every restraint of reason and taste, and, in the course of its vagaries, leaves a tract of thought as incoherent and eccentric, as**

Ignatius Sancho was one of the most well-known blacks in London at the time who gained notoriety for a series of letters that he published. By noting that "his letters do more honour to the heart than the head," Jefferson repeats his argument that blacks can feel but not think.

is the course of a meteor through the sky. His subjects should often have led him to a process of sober reasoning: yet we find him always substituting sentiment for demonstration.

Upon the whole, though we admit him to the first place among those of his own colour who have presented themselves to the public judgment, yet when we compare him with the writers of the race among whom he lived, and particularly with the epistolary class, in which he has taken his own stand, we are compelled to enroll him at the bottom of the column. This criticism supposes the letters published under his name to be genuine, and to have received amendment from no other hand; points which would not be of easy investigation. The improvement of the blacks in body and mind, in the first instance of their mixture with the whites, has been observed by every one, and proves that their inferiority is not the effect merely of their condition of life. **We know that among the Romans, about the Augustan age especially, the condition of their slaves was much more deplorable than that of the blacks on the continent of America. The two sexes were confined in separate apartments, because to raise a child cost the master more than to buy one. Cato, for a very restricted indulgence to his slaves in this particular, took from them a certain price. But in this country the slaves multiply as fast as the free inhabitants.**

Their situation and manners place the commerce between the two sexes almost without restraint.—The same Cato, on a principle of oeconomy, always sold his sick and superannuated slaves. He gives it as a standing precept to a master visiting his farm, to sell his old oxen, old waggons, old tools, old and diseased servants, and every thing else become useless. "Vendat boves vetulos, plaustrum vetus,

This would be Jefferson's primary critique of environmentalist racial theory. Using a historical comparison, he argues that Roman slaves had it far worse than African slaves in America, yet the Romans produced great works of art and were active in political affairs.

ferramenta, vetera, servum senem, servum morbosum, &
si quid aliud supersit vendat." The American slaves cannot enumerate this among the injuries and insults they
receive. It was the common practice to expose in the island
of Aesculapius, in the Tyber, diseased slaves, whose cure
was like to become tedious. The Emperor Claudius, by an
edict, gave freedom to such of them as should recover, and
first declared, that if any person chose to kill rather than to
expose them, it should be deemed homicide. The exposing
them is a crime of which no instance has existed with us;
and were it to be followed by death, it would be punished
capitally. We are told of a certain Vedius Pollio, who, in
the presence of Augustus, would have given a slave as food
to his fish, for having broken a glass. With the Romans,
the regular method of taking the evidence of their slaves
was under torture. Here it has been thought better never to
resort to their evidence. When a master was murdered, all
his slaves, in the same house, or within hearing, were condemned to death. Here punishment falls on the guilty only,
and as precise proof is required against him as against a
freeman. Yet notwithstanding these and other discouraging
circumstances among the Romans, their slaves were often
their rarest artists. They excelled too in science, insomuch
as to be usually employed as tutors to their master's children. **Epictetus, Diogenes, Phaedon, Terence, and Pha-
edrus, were slaves. But they were of the race of whites.
It is not their condition then, but nature, which has
produced the distinction.**

The reason that Roman slaves achieved their artistic success, in Jefferson's view, was not because their environments were different but because they were white.

Whether further observation will or will not verify the
conjecture, that nature has been less bountiful to them in
the endowments of the head, I believe that in those of the
heart she will be found to have done them justice. That

"That a change in the relations in which a man is placed should change his ideas of moral right and wrong, is neither new, nor peculiar to the colour of the blacks."

disposition to theft with which they have been branded, must be ascribed to their situation, and not to any depravity of the moral sense. The man, in whose favour no laws of property exist, probably feels himself less bound to respect those made in favour of others. When arguing for ourselves, we lay it down as a fundamental, that laws, to be just, must give a reciprocation of right: that, without this, they are mere arbitrary rules of conduct, founded in force, and not in conscience: and it is a problem which I give to the master to solve, whether the religious precepts against the violation of property were not framed for him as well as his slave? And whether the slave may not as justifiably take a little from one, who has taken all from him, as he may slay one who would slay him? That a change in the relations in which a man is placed should change his ideas of moral right and wrong, is neither new, nor peculiar to the colour of the blacks. Homer tells us it was so 2600 years ago.

hemisu gar t' aretes apoainutai euruopa Zeus
aneros eut' an min kata doulion emar helesin
(Od. 17. 323.)

Jove fix'd it certain, that whatever day
Makes man a slave, takes half his worth away.

But the slaves of which Homer speaks were whites. Notwithstanding these considerations which must weaken their respect for the laws of property, we find among them numerous instances of the most rigid integrity, and as many as among their better instructed masters, of benevolence, gratitude, and unshaken fidelity.—The opinion, that they are inferior in the faculties of reason and imagination, must be hazarded with great diffidence. To justify a general conclusion, requires many observations, even where the subject may be submitted to the Anatomical knife, to Optical glasses, to analysis by fire, or by solvents. How much more then where it is a faculty, not a substance, we are examining; where it eludes the research of all the senses; where the conditions of its existence are various and variously combined; where the effects of those which are present or absent bid defiance to calculation; let me add too, as a circumstance of great tenderness, where our conclusion would degrade a whole race of men from the rank in the scale of beings which their Creator may perhaps have given them. **To our reproach it must be said, that though for a century and a half we have had under our eyes the races of black and of red men, they have never yet been viewed by us as subjects of natural history. I advance it therefore as a suspicion only, that the blacks, whether originally a distinct race, or made distinct by time and circumstances, are inferior to the whites in the endowments both of body and mind.**

Jefferson backtracks from the strong statements made regarding black inferiority, noting here that his ideas on this matter are "a suspicion only."

It is not against experience to suppose, that different species of the same genus, or varieties of the same species, may possess different qualifications. Will not a lover of natural history then, one who views the gradations in all the races of animals with the eye of philosophy, excuse an effort to keep those in the department of man as distinct as nature has formed them? This unfortunate difference of colour, and perhaps of faculty, is a powerful obstacle to the emancipation of these people. Many of their advocates, while they wish to vindicate the liberty of human nature, are anxious also to preserve its dignity and beauty. Some of these, embarrassed by the question "What further is to be done with them?" join themselves in opposition with those who are actuated by sordid avarice only. Among the Romans emancipation required

Thomas Jefferson, Excerpt from *Notes on the State of Virginia*

but one effect. The slave, when made free, might mix with, without staining the blood of his master. But with us a second is necessary, unknown to history. When freed, he is to be removed beyond the reach of mixture. . . .

In this query Jefferson switches gears to discuss the negative effects of slavery on the white population. We see the ambivalence that Jefferson held on the subject of slavery in general. In some instances he seemingly supports slavery by arguing for black inferiority to whites, while elsewhere he argues against slavery.

It is difficult to determine on the standard by which the manners of a nation may be tried, whether catholic, or particular. It is more difficult for a native to bring to that standard the manners of his own nation, familiarized to him by habit. There must doubtless be an unhappy influence on the manners of our people produced by the existence of slavery among us. The whole commerce between master and slave is a perpetual exercise of the most boisterous passions, the most unremitting despotism on the one part, and degrading submissions on the other.

Our children see this, and learn to imitate it; for man is an imitative animal. This quality is the germ of all education in him. From his cradle to his grave he is learning to do what he sees others do. If a parent could find no motive either in his philanthropy or his self-love, for restraining the intemperance of passion towards his slave, it should always be a sufficient one that his child is present. But gen-

Jefferson argues that slavery naturally produces a tyrannical disposition because of the violence necessary to maintain the institution. As such, slavery is not only an injustice to blacks but is also harmful to the morals of whites.

erally it is not sufficient. **The parent storms, the child looks on, catches the lineaments of wrath, puts on the same airs in the circle of smaller slaves, gives a loose to his worst of passions, and thus nursed, educated, and daily exercised in tyranny, cannot but be stamped by it with odious peculiarities. The man must be a prodigy who can retain his manners and morals undepraved by such circumstances.**

"Amor patriae" refers to love of country. Jefferson notes that slaves would have little reason to be patriotic. By keeping slaves, masters are thus harboring enemies to the state.

And with what execration should the statesman be loaded, who permitting one half the citizens thus to trample on

the rights of the other, transforms those into despots, and these into enemies, destroys the morals of the one part, and the amor patriae of the other.

For if a slave can have a country in this world, it must be any other in preference to that in which he is born to live and labour for another: in which he must lock up the faculties of his nature, contribute as far as depends on his individual endeavours to the evanishment of the human race, or entail his own miserable condition on the endless generations proceeding from him. With the morals of the people, their industry also is destroyed. For in a warm climate, no man will labour for himself who can make another labour for him. This is so true, that of the proprietors of slaves a very small proportion indeed are ever seen to labour. **And can the liberties of a nation be thought secure when we have removed their only firm basis, a conviction in the minds of the people that these liberties are of the gift of God? That they are not to be violated but with his wrath? Indeed I tremble for my country when I reflect that God is just: that his justice cannot sleep for ever: that considering numbers, nature and natural means only, a revolution of the wheel of fortune, an exchange of situation, is among possible events: that it may become probable by supernatural interference! The Almighty has no attribute which can take side with us in such a contest.**

Just as Phillis Wheatley and other writers noted, a just God would always be on the side of slaves if a rebellion were to erupt. This statement is even more significant considering the fact that Jefferson was a Deist who very rarely invoked notions of a providential God, or a God who was intimately involved in Earthly affairs.

But it is impossible to be temperate and to pursue this subject through the various considerations of policy, of morals, of history natural and civil. We must be contented to hope they will force their way into every one's mind. I think a change already perceptible, since the origin of the present revolution. The spirit of the master is abating, that of the slave rising from the dust, his condition mollifying, the way I hope preparing, under the auspices of heaven, for a total emancipation, and that this is disposed, in the order of events, to be with the consent of the masters, rather than by their extirpation.

Source: Thomas Jefferson, *Notes on the State of Virginia* (Philadelphia: Prichard and Hall, 1788), 146–154.

Slavery and the Constitution

Gouverneur Morris, "Constitutional Convention Speech"

1787

INTRODUCTION

Gouverneur Morris was a Founding Father who signed both the Articles of Confederation and the U.S. Constitution, the latter of which he also had a hand in writing. Morris was an opponent of slavery at least from 1776, when he and John Jay attempted to amend the New York Constitution to include a clause abolishing slavery. In 1787 Morris was representing the state of Pennsylvania at the Constitutional Convention and once again registered his protest against slavery. While his earlier argument against slavery was based on the rhetoric of equality, here Morris argued that the prosperity of the southern states depended on their imitating the example of the North in using free labor. Morris and other opponents of slavery at the convention were unsuccessful in their attempts to abolish the institution at the national level. With southern members threatening to leave should slavery be interfered with, the delegates took no action on slavery itself and allowed the transatlantic slave trade to continue uninterrupted for at least another 20 years.

He never would concur in upholding domestic slavery. It was a nefarious institution. It was the curse of heaven in the States where it prevailed.

> This record of Morris's speech is written in the third person, taken from the notes of James Madison during the Constitutional Convention.

Compare the free regions of the Middle States, where a rich & noble cultivation marks the prosperity & happiness of the people, with the misery & poverty which overspread the barren wastes of Va. Maryd & the other States having slaves.

> By 1787, the sectional divide that would eventually lead to the Civil War was starting to form. Whereas most northern states had either abolished or gradually abolished slavery by 1787, the institution seemed stronger than ever in the southern states. Morris argues here that a society run by free labor is much more prosperous than one run by slave labor.

Travel thro' the whole Continent & you behold the prospect continually varying with the appearance and disappearance of slavery. The moment you leave the E. Sts. & enter N. York, the effects of the institution become visible,

> Here Morris refers to the disparity in urbanization and industrialization prevalent in the North and South. The biggest cities in the country are in the North, and the South is a backwater because of slavery.

44

passing thro' the Jerseys & entering Pa. every criterion of superior improvement witnesses the change. Proceed southwdly & every step you take thro' the great region of slaves presents a desert increasing, with the increasing proportion of these wretched beings.

Morris is speaking to a critical issue at the Constitutional Convention, namely whether slaves should be counted for purposes of representation. Southerners argued yes, while northerners such as Morris argued no, claiming that if slave property could be counted then other forms of property should be as well. This was such a critical question because on it rested the balance of power in the U.S. House of Representatives, which was to be determined by population.

Upon what principle is it that the slaves shall be computed in the representation? Are they men? Then make them citizens, and let them vote. Are they property? Why, then, is no other property included? The houses in this city (Philadelphia) are worth more than all the wretched slaves who cover the rice swamps of South Carolina.

The admission of slaves into the Representation when fairly explained comes to this: that the inhabitant of Georgia and S.C. who goes to the Coast of Africa, and in defiance of the most sacred laws of humanity tears away his fellow creatures from their dearest connections & damns them to the most cruel bondages, shall have more votes in a Govt. instituted for the protection of the rights of mankind, than the Citizen of Pa. and N. Jersey who views with a laudable horror, so nefarious a practice.

The type of government that the Founders were trying to build was a republic, and their political philosophy was republicanism, which emphasized the equality of all men and opposed aristocracy. For Morris, keeping slavery was antirepublican.

He would add that Domestic slavery is the most prominent feature in the aristocratic countenance of the proposed Constitution. The vassalage of the poor has ever been the favorite offspring of Aristocracy.

And What is the proposed compensation to the Northern states for a sacrifice of every principle of right, of every impulse of humanity. They are to bind themselves to march their militia for the defence of the S. states; for their defence agst those very slaves of whom they complain. They must supply vessels & seaman, in case of foreign Attack. The

Legislature will have indefinite power to tax them by excises, and duties on imports: both of which will fall heavier on them than on the Southern inhabitants; for the bohea tea used by a Northern freeman, will pay more tax than the whole consumption of the miserable slave, which consists of nothing more than his physical subsistence and the rag that covers his nakedness.

On the other side the Southern States are not to be restrained from importing fresh supplies of wretched Africans, at once to increase the danger of attack, and the difficulty of defence; nay they are to be encouraged to it by an assurance of having their votes in the Natl Govt increased in proportion. And are at the same time to have their exports & their slaves exempt from all contributions for the public service. Let it not be said that direct taxation is to be proportioned to representation. It is idle to suppose that the Genl Govt. can stretch its hand directly into the pockets of the people scattered over so vast a Country. They can only do it through the medium of exports imports & excises. For what then are all these sacrifices to be made? He would sooner submit himself to a tax for paying for all such negroes in the U. States, than saddle posterity with such a Constitution.

Source: Max Farrand, ed., *The Records of the Federal Convention of 1787,* Vol. 2 (New Haven, CT: Yale University Press, 1911), 221–223.

Atlantic Crossings

Josiah Wedgwood, "Am I Not a Man and a Brother?"

1787

INTRODUCTION

It is sometimes said that a picture is worth a thousand words. The same year that the U.S. Constitution was drawn up, Josiah Wedgwood, an English abolitionist, created the most famous antislavery image of the 18th century. Wedgwood produced this medallion for the English Society for Effecting the Abolition of the Slave Trade, which was also formed in 1787. The Society distributed thousands of these medallions, which were reproduced in antislavery publications and were even worn as bracelets and hairpins. The image quickly became well known as a symbol for the abolitionist movement in both England and the United States.

This image depicts a typical slave on an English plantation, a man in his mid-20s, in a posture of prayer. While nudity in art was usually a sign of freedom, Wedgwood provides a stark contrast to that symbol with the chains. The figure is on his knees but looks as if he will rise shortly, displaying confidence that his prayer will be answered. This confidence speaks to notions of moral progress that were prevalent during the Age of Enlightenment, when many thinkers believed that reason was undermining the barbarism in Western civilization that was a remnant of the medieval period. The image likewise evokes notions of Christian brotherhood and was intended to convince viewers that Africans were also the children of God and deserved their freedom. Despite this argument, the Society for Effecting the Abolition of the Slave Trade maintained that its goal was not to eradicate slavery but merely to end slave trading.

Source: Josiah Wedgwood, "Am I Not a Man and a Brother?," 1787, Library of Congress.

47

Abolitionism and Proslavery Thought in Antebellum America

Slavery and Power

Thomas Ruffin Opinion in *State v. Mann*, North Carolina Supreme Court

1829

INTRODUCTION

Thomas Ruffin was a lawyer and a justice of the North Carolina Supreme Court from 1829 to 1852, serving as chief justice for the last 20 years of that period. He is best known for his legal decisions that promoted economic development in North Carolina, but the case *State v. Mann* revolved around the institution of slavery and the rights that slaves should enjoy. Different colonies and states answered this question in various ways. When Massachusetts had legal slavery, slaves were treated as both persons and property before the law, meaning they could be sold like property but could sue others like people. This situation was common throughout New England but much less so in the South. In this decision, Mann attempted a definitive response to this question, arguing that slaves had no rights and that the power of the master must be absolute if any slave system was to survive. This decision predated the U.S. Supreme Court's decision in the Dred Scott case, which expanded this ruling in 1857 to argue that blacks in general had no rights in the United States.

PRIOR HISTORY: The Defendant was indicted for an assault and battery upon Lydia, the slave of one Elizabeth Jones.

Hiring slaves out was a common practice in the Old South. Some masters bought slaves specifically for this purpose, using them in the same manner that companies today use rental cars. Other masters hired slaves out when they just did not have enough work for them to perform. Whatever the reason, the practice was widespread but created particular problems of authority, as there were now two masters over the slaves but only one legal owner.

On the trial it appeared that the Defendant had hired the slave for a year—that during the term, the slave had committed some small offence, for which the Defendant undertook to chastise her—that while in the act of so doing, the slave ran off, whereupon the Defendant called upon her to stop, which being refused, he shot at and wounded her.

His honor Judge DANIEL charged the Jury, that if they believed the punishment inflicted by the Defendant was cruel and unwarrantable, and disproportionate to the offence

51

committed by the slave, that in law the Defendant was guilty, as he had only a special property in the slave.

A verdict was returned for the State, and the Defendant appealed.

DISPOSITION: **Judgment reversed, and judgment entered for the Defendant.**

In a decision of a lower court the defendant was found guilty of assault, but that decision was reversed by the Supreme Court of North Carolina.

OPINION: RUFFIN, Judge.—A Judge cannot but lament, when such cases as the present are brought into judgment. It is impossible that the reasons on which they go can be appreciated, but where institutions similar to our own, exist and are thoroughly understood. The struggle, too, in the Judge's own breast between the feelings of the man, and the duty of the magistrate is a severe one, presenting strong temptation to put aside such questions, if it be possible. It is useless however, to complain of things inherent in our political state. And it is criminal in a Court to avoid any responsibility which the laws impose. **With whatever reluctance therefore it is done, the Court is compelled to express an opinion upon the extent of the dominion of the master over the slave in North-Carolina.**

The relationship between masters and slaves was both a personal one and a political one. It involved labor and plantation economics but also the safety of the state. Ruffin acknowledges here what has been long understood, namely that to the extent possible, southern governments tried to steer clear of these types of questions. In cases of rebellion, running away, or other types of resistance, however, governments had to insert their voice.

. . . Our laws uniformly treat the master or other person having the possession and command of the slave, as entitled to the same extent of authority. The object is the same—the services of the slave; and the same powers must be confided.

For all intents and purposes, it does not matter if the owner of a slave or the person renting a slave out chastises the slave. Both instances must be treated, Ruffin argues, as a master-slave relation, with all the rights and obligations inherent in those titles on both sides.

In a criminal proceeding, and indeed in reference to all other persons but the general owner, the hirer and possessor of a slave, in relation to both rights and duties, is, for the time being, the owner. This opinion would, perhaps dispose of this particular case; because the indictment,

Ruffin notes that masters cannot be charged in criminal court for assaulting their slaves. Dating back to 17th-century Virginia, it was an established fact that even if a slave died from a beating the master would not be held criminally liable because no master would willingly destroy his own property. If a death occurred, in the eyes of the law it must have been a mistake.

which charges a battery upon the slave of *Elizabeth Jones,* is not supported by proof of a battery upon Defendant's own slave; since different justifications may be applicable to the two cases. But upon the general question, whether the owner is answerable *criminaliter,* for a battery upon his own slave, or other exercise of authority or force, not forbidden by statute, the Court entertains but little doubt.—That he is so liable, has never yet been decided; nor, as far as is known, been hitherto contended. There have been no prosecutions of the sort.

The established habits and uniform practice of the country in this respect, is the best evidence of the portion of power, deemed by the whole community, requisite to the preservation of the master's dominion. If we thought differently, we could not set our notions in array against the judgment of every body else, and say that this, or that authority, may be safely lopped off. This has indeed been assimilated at the bar to the other domestic relations; and arguments drawn from the well established principles, which confer and restrain the authority of the parent over the child, the tutor over the pupil, the master over the apprentice, have been pressed on us. The Court does not recognize their application. There is no likeness between the cases. They are in opposition to each other, and there is an impassable gulf between them.—The difference is that which exists between freedom and slavery—and a greater cannot be imagined. In the one, the end in view is the happiness of the youth, born to equal rights with that governor, on whom the duty devolves of training the young to usefulness, in a station which he is afterwards to assume among freemen. To such an end, and with such a subject, moral and intellectual instruction seem the natural means; and for the most part, they are found to suffice. Moderate force is superadded, only to make the others effectual. If that fail, it is better to leave the party to his own headstrong passions, and the ultimate correction of the law, than to allow it to be immoderately inflicted by a private person.

With slavery it is far otherwise. The end is the profit of the master, his security and the public safety; the subject, one doomed in his own person, and his posterity, to live without knowledge, and without the capacity to make any thing his own, and to toil that another may reap the fruits. What moral considerations shall be addressed to such a being, to convince him what, it is impossible but that the most stupid must feel and know can never be true—that he is thus to labour upon a principle of natural duty, or for the sake of his own personal happiness, such services can only be expected from one who has no will of his own; who surrenders his will in implicit obedience to that of another.

In this legal decision Ruffin articulates a definition of slavery itself, namely a condition in which the slave completely surrenders his or her will to that of the master. While this was the ideal slave for the southern planter class, in reality, of course, slaves were individual moral beings who constantly asserted their own wills, as the record of abolitionism and resistance to slavery attests.

Such obedience is the consequence only of uncontrolled authority over the body. There is nothing else which can operate to produce the effect. The power of the master must be absolute, to render the submission of the slave perfect. I most freely confess my sense of the harshness of this proposition, I feel it as deeply as any man can. And as a principle of moral right, every person in his retirement must repudiate it. But in the actual condition of things, it must be so.

Ruffin recognizes the moral problems with his views on slavery, noting that the idea of complete domination of one man by another is morally repugnant but must be upheld in a slave society.

There is no remedy. This discipline belongs to the state of slavery. They cannot be disunited, without abrogating at once the rights of the master, and absolving the slave from his subjection. It constitutes the curse of slavery to both the bond and free portions of our population. But it is inherent in the relation of master and slave.

That there may be particular instances of cruelty and deliberate barbarity, where, in conscience the law might properly interfere, is most probable. The difficulty is to determine, where _a Court_ may properly begin. Merely in the abstract it may well be asked, which power of the master accords with right. The answer will probably sweep away all of them. But we cannot look at the matter in that light. The truth is, that we are for-bidden to enter upon a train of general reasoning on the subject. We cannot allow the right of the master to be brought into discussion in the Courts of Justice. **The slave, to remain a slave, must be made sensible, that there is no appeal from his master; that his power is in no instance, usurped; but is conferred by the laws of man at least, if not by the law of God.**

The danger would be great indeed, if the tribunals of justice should be called on to graduate the punishment appropriate to every temper, and every dereliction of menial duty. No man can anticipate the many and aggravated provocations of the master, which the slave would be constantly stimulated by his own passions, or the instigation of others to give; or the consequent wrath of the master, prompting him to bloody vengeance, upon the turbulent traitor—a vengeance generally practised with impunity, by reason of its privacy. The Court therefore disclaims the power of changing the relation, in which these parts of our people stand to each other.

We are happy to see, that there is daily less and less occasion for the interposition of the Courts. The protection already afforded by several statutes, that all-powerful motive, the private interest of the owner, the benevolences towards each other, seated in the hearts of those who have been born and bred together, the frowns and deep execrations of the community upon the barbarian, who is guilty of excessive and brutal cruelty to his unprotected slave, all combined, have produced a mildness of treatment, and attention to the

Ruffin may have been aware of the workings of slavery in British colonies such as Berbice, where slaves were actually allowed to appeal excessive punishments to a legal authority known as the Fiscal. As he penned this opinion there was a widespread antislavery movement in the British Empire, perhaps causing him to fear the effect that concessions such as appeal of punishment would have on the entire system of slavery.

comforts of the unfortunate class of slaves, greatly mitigating the rigors of servitude, and ameliorating the condition of the slaves. The same causes are operating, and will continue to operate with increased action, until the disparity in numbers between the whites and blacks, shall have rendered the latter in no degree dangerous to the former, when the police now existing may be further relaxed. This result, greatly to be desired, may be much more rationally expected from the events above alluded to, and now in progress, than from any rash expositions of abstract truths, by a Judiciary tainted with a false and fanatical philanthropy, seeking to redress an acknowledged evil, by means still more wicked and appalling than even that evil.

I repeat, that I would gladly have avoided this ungrateful question. But being brought to it, the Court is compelled to declare, that while slavery exists amongst us in its present state, or until it shall seem fit to the Legislature to interpose express enactments to the contrary, it will be the imperative duty of the Judges to recognize the full dominion of the owner over the slave, except where the exercise of it is forbidden by statute. And this we do upon the ground, that this dominion is essential to the value of slaves as property, to the security of the master, and the public tranquillity, greatly dependent upon their subordination; and in fine, as most effectually securing the general protection and comfort of the slaves themselves.

PER CURIAM.—Let the judgment below be reversed, and judgment entered for the Defendant.

Source: *State v. Mann,* 13 North Carolina Reports 263 (1829).

Early Black Nationalism

David Walker, *Appeal to the Coloured Citizens of the World*

1829

INTRODUCTION

David Walker was a free black man who was born in Wilmington, North Carolina, in the late 18th century. By the early 1820s Walker had made his way to Charleston, where he may have been involved in Denmark Vesey's planned uprising of 1822. A couple of years later Walker was living in Boston, Massachusetts, where he ran a used clothing store and became involved in the political life of the black community. He was a member of the Massachusetts General Colored Association, an organization aimed at securing racial equality and abolishing slavery, and he was also an agent for the *Freedom's Journal,* the first black newspaper published in the United States. Walker, a self-educated man, wrote the *Appeal to the Coloured Citizens of the World* in 1829 in order to promote black unity, self-respect, racial uplift, and the abolition of slavery. Walker's book was one of the most radical antislavery works ever published and precipitated death threats from southern slaveholders.

IT will be recollected, that I, in the first edition of my "Appeal," promised to demonstrate in the course of which, viz. in the course of my Appeal, to the satisfaction of the most incredulous mind, that we Coloured People of these United States, are, the most wretched, degraded and abject set of beings that ever lived since the world began, down to the present day, and, that, the white Christians of America, who hold us in slavery, (or, more properly speaking, pretenders to Christianity,) treat us more cruel and barbarous than any Heathen nation did any people whom it had subjected, or reduced to the same condition, that the Americans (who are, notwithstanding, looking for the Millennial day) have us. All I ask is, for a candid and careful perusal of this the third and last edition of my Appeal, where the world may see that we, the Blacks or Coloured People, are treated more cruel by the white Christians of America, than devils themselves ever treated a set of men, women and children on this earth.

It is expected that all coloured men, women and children, of every nation, language and tongue under heaven, will try to procure a copy of this Appeal and read it, or get some one to read it to them, for it is designed more particularly for them. **Let them remember, that though our cruel oppressors and murderers, may (if possible) treat us more cruel, as Pharoah did the children of Israel, yet the God of the Etheopeans, has been pleased to hear our moans in consequence of oppression; and the day of our redemption from abject wretchedness draweth near, when we shall be enabled, in the most extended sense of the word, to stretch forth our hands to the LORD our GOD, but there must be a willingness on our part, for GOD to do these things for us, for we may be assured that he will not take us by the hairs of our head against our will and desire, and drag us from our very, mean, low and abject condition.**

Walker posits blacks as the New Israel. This rhetorical move is one that many black writers employed and is significant because it places them within the context of sacred time. There is a purpose for their lives and suffering, they argued, because they are God's Chosen People. After the end of slavery this notion provided the foundation for black missionary and evangelical activity within the United States and abroad. In saying that blacks will be able to "stretch forth our hands to the Lord our God," Walker referenced Psalm 68:31, a prophecy stating that "Princes shall come out of Egypt; Ethiopia shall soon stretch out her hands unto God."

APPEAL, &c
PREAMBLE

My dearly beloved Brethren and Fellow Citizens.

HAVING travelled over a considerable portion of these United States, and having, in the course of my travels, taken the most accurate observations of things as they exist—the result of my observations has warranted the full and unshaken conviction, that we, (coloured people of these United States,) are the most degraded, wretched, and abject set of beings that ever lived since the world began; and I pray God that none like us ever may live again until time shall be no more. They tell us of the Israelites in Egypt, the Helots in Sparta, and of the Roman Slaves, which last were made up from almost every nation under heaven, whose sufferings under those ancient and heathen nations, were, in comparison with ours, under this enlightened and Christian nation, no more than a cypher—or, in other words, **those heathen nations of antiquity, had but little more among them than the name and form of slavery; while wretchedness and endless miseries were reserved, apparently in a phial, to be poured out upon our fathers, ourselves and our children, by *Christian* Americans!**

Walker argues that American slavery is uniquely harsh compared to slavery in the ancient world. While Thomas Jefferson unfavorably compared American slaves to their Roman counterparts in antiquity, Walker argues in effect that the comparison is not a valid one.

These positions I shall endeavour, by the help of the Lord, to demonstrate in the course of this *Appeal,* to the satisfaction of the most incredulous mind—and may God Almighty, who is the Father of our Lord Jesus Christ, open your hearts to understand and believe the truth.

Josephus and Plutarch were among some of the first and most prominent historians in the ancient world. By referencing them, Walker was partially showing off his extensive education.

The *causes*, my brethren, which produce our wretchedness and miseries, are so very numerous and aggravating, that I believe the pen only of a Josephus or a Plutarch, can well enumerate and explain them.

Upon subjects, then, of such incomprehensible magnitude, so impenetrable, and so notorious, I shall be obliged to omit a large class of, and content myself with giving you an exposition of a few of those, which do indeed rage to such an alarming pitch, that they cannot but be a perpetual source of terror and dismay to every reflecting mind.

I am fully aware, in making this appeal to my much afflicted and suffering brethren, that I shall not only be assailed by those whose greatest earthly desires are, to keep us in abject ignorance and wretchedness, and who are of the firm conviction that Heaven has designed us and our children to be slaves and *beasts of burden* to them and their children. I say, I do not only expect to be held up to the public as an ignorant, impudent and restless disturber of the public peace, by such avaricious creatures, as well as a mover of insubordination—and perhaps put in prison or to death, for giving a superficial exposition of our miseries, and exposing tyrants. **But I am persuaded, that many of my brethren, particularly those who are ignorantly in league with slave-holders or tyrants, who acquire their daily bread by the blood and sweat of their more ignorant brethren—and not a few of those too, who are too ignorant to see an inch beyond their noses, will rise up and call me cursed—Yea, the jealous ones among us will perhaps use more abject subtlety, by affirming that this work is not worth perusing, that we are well situated, and there is no use in trying to better our condition, for we cannot.**

Walker highlights the important divisions within the antebellum black community. While most blacks opposed slavery, there were some who supported the institution for personal gain, he notes, and there were also numerous black slaveholders, a phenomenon that he does not discuss.

I will ask one question here.—Can our condition be any worse?—Can it be more mean and abject? If there are any changes, will they not be for the better, though they may appear for the worst at first? Can they get us any lower? Where can they get us? They are afraid to treat us worse, for they know well, the day they do it they are gone. **But against all accusations which may or can be preferred against me, I appeal to Heaven for my motive in writing—who knows that my object is, if possible, to awaken in the breasts of my afflicted, degraded and slumbering brethren, a spirit of inquiry and investigation respecting our miseries and wretchedness in this *Republican Land of Liberty*!!!!!!**

By mentioning the "Republican Land of Liberty," Walker was not referencing the Republican Party, which had yet to be organized, but was instead referring to the ideology of republicanism on which the nation was founded, an ideology that stressed equality, freedom, and individual sacrifice for the common good.

The sources from which our miseries are derived, and on which I shall comment, I shall not combine in one, but shall put them under distinct heads and expose them in their turn; in doing which, keeping truth on my side, and not departing from the strictest rules of morality, I shall endeavour to penetrate, search out, and lay them open for your inspection. If you cannot or will not profit by them, I shall have done *my* duty to you, my country and my God.

And as the inhuman system of *slavery,* is the *source* from which most of our miseries proceed, I shall begin with that *curse to nations,* which has spread terror and devastation through so many nations of antiquity, and which is raging to such a pitch at the present day in Spain and in Portugal. It had one tug in England, in France, and in the United States of America; yet the inhabitants thereof, do not learn wisdom, and erase it entirely from their dwellings and from all with whom they have to do. The fact is, the labour of slaves comes so cheap to the avaricious usurpers, and is (as they think) of such great utility to the country where it exists, that those who are actuated by sordid avarice only, overlook the evils, which will as sure as the Lord lives, follow after the good. **In fact, they are so happy to keep in ignorance and degradation, and to receive the homage and the labour of the slaves, they forget that God rules in the armies of heaven and among the inhabitants of the earth, having his ears continually open to the cries, tears and groans of his oppressed people; and being a just and holy Being will at one day appear fully in behalf of the oppressed, and arrest the progress of the avaricious oppressors; for although the destruction of the oppressors God may not effect by the oppressed, yet the Lord our God will bring other destructions upon them—for not unfrequently will he cause them to rise up one against another, to be split and divided, and to**

Walker makes a similar claim to Jefferson, who noted that a just God would likely be on the side of the slaves in a racial war. Walker also anticipates the formation of liberation theology in the 20th century, a theology that would argue that God is on the side of the oppressed. Finally, in one of the most prescient statements of this text, Walker predicted that slavery would likely cause a civil war in the United States, not unlike what occurred in the French colony of Saint Domingue (later known as Haiti) in the late 18th century.

oppress each other, and sometimes to open hostilities with sword in hand.

Some may ask, what is the matter with this united and happy people?—Some say it is the cause of political usurpers, tyrants, oppressors, &c. But has not the Lord an oppressed and suffering people among them? Does the Lord condescend to hear their cries and see their tears in consequence of oppression? Will he let the oppressors rest comfortably and happy always? Will he not cause the very children of the oppressors to rise up against them, and oftimes put them to death? "God works in many ways his wonders to perform."

I will not here speak of the destructions which the Lord brought upon Egypt, in consequence of the oppression and consequent groans of the oppressed—of the hundreds and thousands of Egyptians whom God hurled into the Red Sea for afflicting his people in their land—of the Lord's suffering people in Sparta or Lacedemon, the land of the truly famous Lycurgus—nor have I time to comment upon the cause which produced the fierceness with which Sylla usurped the title, and absolutely acted as dictator of the Roman people—the conspiracy of Cataline— the conspiracy against, and murder of Cæsar in the Senate house—the spirit with which Marc Antony made himself master of the commonwealth—his associating Octavius and Lipidus with himself in power—their dividing the provinces of Rome among themselves—their attack and defeat, on the plains of Phillippi, of the last defenders of their liberty, (Brutus and Cassius)—the tyranny of Tiberius, and from him to the final overthrow of Constantinople by the Turkish Sultan, Mahomed II. A. D. 1453. I say, I shall not take up time to speak of the *causes* which produced so much wretchedness and massacre among

At the time Walker wrote there had been multiple revolutions in Latin American nations, and many of these revolutions were intimately tied to slavery. Referencing them was another threat of the fate that would befall America unless it heeded the examples of the Spanish and the Portuguese.

those heathen nations, for I am aware that you know too well, that God is just, as well as merciful!—**I shall call your attention a few moments to that** *Christian* **nation, the Spaniards—while I shall leave almost unnoticed, that avaricious and cruel people, the Portuguese, among whom all true hearted Christians and lovers of Jesus Christ, must evidently see the judgments of God displayed. To show the judgments of God upon the Spaniards, I shall occupy but a little time, leaving a plenty of room for the candid and unprejudiced to reflect.**

All persons who are acquainted with history, and particularly the Bible, who are not blinded by the God of this world, and are not actuated solely by avarice—who are able to lay aside prejudice long enough to view candidly and impartially, things as they were, are, and probably will be—who are willing to admit that God made man to serve Him *alone,* and that man should have no other Lord or Lords but Himself—that God Almighty is the *sole proprietor* or *master* of the WHOLE human family, and will not on any consideration admit of a colleague, being unwilling to divide his glory with another—and who can dispense with prejudice long enough to admit that we are *men,* notwithstanding our *improminent noses* and *woolly heads,* and believe that we feel for our fathers, mothers, wives and children, as well as the whites do for theirs.—I say, all who are permitted to see and believe these things, can easily recognize the judgments of God among the Spaniards. Though others may lay the cause of the fierceness with which they cut each other's throats, to some other circumstance, yet they who believe that God is a God of justice, will believe that SLAVERY *is the principal cause.*

While the Spaniards are running about upon the field of battle cutting each other's throats, has not the Lord an afflicted and suffering people in the midst of them, whose cries and groans in consequence of oppression are continually pouring into the ears of the God of justice? Would they not cease to cut each other's throats, if they could? But how can they? The very support which they draw from government to aid them in perpetrating such enormities, does it not arise in a great degree from the wretched victims of oppression among them? And yet they are calling for *Peace!—Peace! !* Will any peace be given unto them? Their destruction may indeed be procrastinated awhile, but can it continue long, while they are oppressing the Lord's people? Has He not the hearts of all men in His hand? Will he suffer one part of his creatures to go on oppressing another like brutes always, with impunity? And yet, those avaricious wretches are calling for *Peace! ! ! !* I declare, it does appear to me, as though some nations think God is asleep, or that he made the Africans for nothing else but to dig their mines and work their farms, or they cannot believe history, sacred or profane. I ask every man who has a heart, and is blessed with the privilege of believing—Is not God a God of justice to *all* his creatures? Do you say he is? Then if he gives peace and tranquillity to tyrants, and permits them to keep our fathers, our mothers, ourselves and our children in eternal ignorance and wretchedness, to support them and their families, would he be to us a God of *justice?* I ask, O ye *Christians! ! !* who hold us and our children in the most abject ignorance and degradation, that ever a people were afflicted with since the world began—I say, if God gives you peace and tranquillity, and suffers you thus to go on afflicting us, and our children, who have never given you the least provocation—would he be to us *a God of justice?* If you will allow that we are MEN, who feel for each other, does not the blood of our fathers and of us their children,

"I ask every man who has a heart, and is blessed with the privilege of believing—Is not God a God of justice to all *his creatures?"*

cry aloud to the Lord of Sabaoth against you, for the cruelties and murders with which you have, and do continue to afflict us. But it is time for me to close my remarks on the suburbs, just to enter more fully into the interior of this system of cruelty and oppression.

ARTICLE I
OUR WRETCHEDNESS IN CONSEQUENCE
OF SLAVERY

My beloved brethren:—The Indians of North and of South America—the Greeks—the Irish, subjected under the king of Great Britain—the Jews, that ancient people of the Lord—the inhabitants of the islands of the sea—in fine, all the inhabitants of the earth, (except however, the sons of Africa) are called *men,* and of course are, and ought to be free. But we, (coloured people) and our children are *brutes! !* and of course are, and *ought to be* SLAVES to the American people and their children forever! ! to dig their mines and work their farms; and thus go on enriching them, from one generation to another with our *blood* and our *tears! ! ! !*

By "heathen nation," Walker likely had in mind Greece and Rome. Both countries were societies with slaves, yet most historians recognize that they gave slaves rights and privileges that American blacks would never enjoy. The irony, in Walker's estimation, is that these nations were supposedly pagan and heathen, while America called itself a Christian nation.

I promised in a preceding page to demonstrate to the satisfaction of the most incredulous, that we, (coloured people of these United States of America) are the *most wretched, degraded* and *abject* set of beings that *ever lived* since the world began, and that the white Americans having reduced us to the wretched state of *slavery,* treat us in that condition *more cruel* (they being an enlighted and Christian people), than any heathen nation did any people whom it had reduced to our condition.

These affirmations are so well confirmed in the minds of all unprejudiced men, who have taken the trouble to read histories, that they need no elucidation from me. But to put them beyond all doubt, I refer you in the first place to the children of Jacob, or of Israel in Egypt, under Pharaoh and his people. Some of my brethren do not know who Pharaoh and the Egyptians were—I know it to be a fact, that some of them take the Egyptians to have been a gang of *devils,* not knowing any better, and that they (Egyptians) having got possession of the Lord's people, treated them *nearly* as cruel as *Christian Americans* do us, at the present day. For the information of such, I would only mention that the Egyptians, were Africans or coloured people, such as we are—some of them yellow and others dark—a mixture of Ethiopians and the natives of Egypt—about the same as you see the coloured people of the United States at the present day.—I say, I call your attention then, to the children of Jacob, while I point out particularly to you his son Joseph, among the rest, in Egypt.

"And Pharaoh, said unto Joseph, thou shalt be over my house, and according unto thy word shall all my people be ruled: only in the throne will I be greater than thou."

"And Pharaoh said unto Joseph, see, I have set thee over all the land of Egypt."

"And Pharaoh said unto Joseph, I am Pharaoh, and without thee shall no man lift up his hand or foot in all the land of Egypt."

Now I appeal to heaven and to earth, and particularly to the American people themselves, who cease not to declare that our condition is not *hard*, and that we are comparatively satisfied to rest in wretchedness and misery, under them and their children. Not, indeed, to show me a coloured President, a Governor, a Legislator, a Senator, a Mayor, or an Attorney

"Now I appeal to heaven and to earth, and particularly to the American people themselves, who cease not to declare that our condition is not hard, *and that we are comparatively satisfied to rest in wretchedness and misery, under them and their children."*

Walker notes that blacks in the United States were by and large viewed solely as property and were barred from participation in the courts specifically and American civic life more broadly.

at the Bar.—**But to show me a man of colour, who holds the low office of a Constable, or one who sits in a Juror Box, even on a case of one of his wretched brethren, throughout this great Republic! !**

But let us pass Joseph the son of Israel a little farther in review, as he existed with that heathen nation.

"And Pharaoh called Joseph's name Zaphnath-paaneah; and he gave him to wife Asenath the daughter of Potipherah priest of On. And Joseph went out over all the land of Egypt."

Virginia passed a law in 1705 barring blacks from marrying whites in the colony, while Massachusetts passed a similar statute in the 1780s, even after the period in which northern states began to emancipate their slaves.

Compare the above, with the American institutions. Do they not institute laws to prohibit us from marrying among the whites? I would wish, candidly, however, before the Lord, to be understood, that I would not give a *pinch of snuff* to be married to any white person I ever saw in all the days of my life. And I do say it, that the black man, or man of colour, who will leave his own colour (provided he can get one, who is good for any thing) and marry a white woman, to be a double slave to her, just because she is *white,* ought to be treated by her as he surely will be, viz: as a NIGGER! ! ! ! It is not, indeed, what I care about inter-marriages with the whites, which induced me to pass this subject in review; for the Lord knows, that there is a day coming when they will be glad enough to get into the company of the blacks, notwithstanding, we are, in this generation, levelled by them, almost on a level with the brute creation: and some of us they treat even worse than they do the brutes that perish. I only made this extract to show how much lower we are held, and how much more cruel we are treated by the Americans, than were the children of Jacob, by the Egyptians.—We will notice the sufferings of Israel some further, under *heathen Pharaoh,* compared with ours under the *enlightened Christians of America.*

"And Pharaoh spake unto Joseph, saying, thy father and thy brethren are come unto thee:"

"The land of Egypt is before thee: in the best of the land make thy father and brethren to dwell; in the land of Goshen let them dwell: and if thou knowest any men of activity among them, then make them rulers over my cattle."

I ask those people who treat us so *well,* Oh! I ask them, where is the most barren spot of land which they have given unto us? Israel had the most fertile land in all Egypt. Need I mention the very notorious fact, that I have known a poor man of colour, who laboured night and day, to acquire a little money, and having acquired it, he vested it in a small piece of land, and got him a house erected thereon, and having paid for the whole, he moved his family into it, where he was suffered to remain but nine months, when he was cheated out of his property by a white man, and driven out of door! And is not this the case generally? Can a man of colour buy a piece of land and keep it peaceably? Will not some white man try to get it from him, even if it is in a *mud hole?* I need not comment any farther on a subject, which all, both black and white, will readily admit. **But I must, really, observe that in this very city, when a man of colour dies, if he owned any real estate it most generally falls into the hands of some white person. The wife and children of the deceased may weep and lament if they please, but the estate will be kept snug enough by its white possessor.**

But to prove farther that the condition of the Israelites was better under the Egyptians than ours is under the whites. **I call upon the professing Christians, I call upon the philanthropist, I call upon the very tyrant himself, to show me a page of history, either sacred or profane, on which a verse can be found, which maintains, that**

Walker brings up an important point, namely that even though northern states such as Massachusetts had abolished slavery long ago, racism was still very prevalent throughout the North. Indeed, just as states such as Massachusetts and Pennsylvania abolished slavery, they also passed laws restricting black migration to their states.

the Egyptians heaped the *insupportable insult* upon the children of Israel, by telling them that they were not of the *human family.* Can the whites deny this charge? Have they not, after having reduced us to the deplorable condition of slaves under their feet, held us up as descending originally from the tribes of *Monkeys* or *Orang-Outangs?* O! my God! I appeal to every man of feeling—is not this insupportable? Is it not heaping the most gross insult upon our miseries, because they have got us under their feet and we cannot help ourselves? Oh! pity us we pray thee, Lord Jesus, Master.—Has Mr. Jefferson declared to the world, that we are inferior to the whites, both in the endowments of our bodies and of minds? It is indeed surprising, that a man of such great learning, combined with such excellent natural parts, should speak so of a set of men in chains. I do not know what to compare it to, unless, like putting one wild deer in an iron cage, where it will be secured, and hold another by the side of the same, then let it go, and expect the one in the cage to run as fast as the one at liberty. So far, my brethren, were the Egyptians from heaping these insults upon their slaves, that Pharoah's daughter took Moses, a son of Israel for her own, as will appear by the following.

"And Pharoah's daughter said unto her, [Moses' mother] take this child away, and nurse it for me, and I will pay thee thy wages. And the woman took the child [Moses] and nursed it."

"And the child grew, and she brought him unto Pharoah's daughter and he became her son. And she called his name Moses: and she said because I drew him out of the water."

In all probability, Moses would have become Prince Regent to the throne, and no doubt, in process of time but he would have been seated on the throne of Egypt. But he had rather suffer shame, with the people of God, than to enjoy pleasures with that wicked people for a season. **O! that the coloured people were long since of Moses' excellent disposition, instead of courting favour with, and telling news and lies to our *natural enemies,* against each other—aiding them to keep their hellish chains of slavery upon us. Would we not long before this time, have been respectable men, instead of such wretched victims of oppression as we are?**

Would they be able to drag our mothers, our fathers, our wives, our children and ourselves, around the world in chains and hand-cuffs as they do, to dig up gold and silver for them and theirs? This question, my brethren, I leave for you to digest; and may God Almighty force it home to your hearts. Remember that unless you are united, keeping your tongues within your teeth, you will be afraid to trust your secrets to each other, and thus perpetuate our miseries under the *Christians ! ! ! ! !* ADDITION.—Remember, also to lay humble at the feet of our Lord and Master Jesus Christ, with prayers and fastings. Let our enemies go on with their butcheries, and at once fill up their cup. Never make an attempt to gain our freedom of *natural right,* from under our cruel oppressors and murderers, until you see your way clear—when that hour arrives and you move, be not afraid or dismayed; for be you assured that Jesus Christ the King of heaven and of earth who is the God of justice and of armies, will surely go before you. And those enemies who have for hundreds of years stolen our *rights,* and kept us ignorant of Him and His divine worship, he will remove. Millions of whom, are this day, so ignorant and avaricious, that they cannot conceive how God can have an attribute of justice, and show mercy to us because it pleased Him to make us black—which colour, Mr. Jefferson calls unfortunate! ! ! ! ! !

Walker again points to the disunity in the black community, or more accurately in the black communities of the United States. While he does not mention this explicitly, many 19th-century slave rebellions were thwarted when fellow slaves informed on the plot to their masters or other whites. This was the case with Gabriel Prosser's planned insurrection in 1800 as well as the Denmark Vesey conspiracy in Charleston in 1822.

"They think because they hold us in their infernal chains of slavery, that we wish to be white, or of their color—but they are dreadfully deceived—we wish to be just as it pleased our Creator to have made us, and no avaricious and unmerciful wretches, have any business to make slaves of, or hold us in slavery."

As though we are not as thankful to our God, for having made us as it pleased himself, as they, (the whites,) are for having made them white. They think because they hold us in their infernal chains of slavery, that we wish to be white, or of their color—but they are dreadfully deceived—we wish to be just as it pleased our Creator to have made us, and no avaricious and unmerciful wretches, have any business to make slaves of, or hold us in slavery How would they like for us to make slaves of, and hold them in cruel slavery, and murder them as they do us?—But is Mr. Jefferson's assertions true? viz. "that it is unfortunate for us that our Creator has been pleased to make us *black.*" We will not take his say so, for the fact. The world will have an opportunity to see whether it is unfortunate for us, that our Creator *has made us* darker than the *whites.*

Fear not the number and education of our *enemies,* against whom we shall have to contend for our lawful right; guaranteed to us by our Maker; for why should we be afraid, when God is, and will continue, (if we continue humble) to be on our side?

The man who would not fight under our Lord and Master Jesus Christ, in the glorious and heavenly cause of freedom and of God—to be delivered from the most wretched, abject and servile slavery, that ever a people was afflicted with since the foundation of the world, to the present day—ought to be kept with all of his children or family, in slavery, or in chains, to be butchered by his *cruel enemies.*

I saw a paragraph, a few years since, in a South Carolina paper, which, speaking of the barbarity of the Turks, it said: "The Turks are the most barbarous people in the world—they treat the Greeks more like *brutes* than human beings." And in the same paper was an advertisement, which said: "Eight well built Virginia and Maryland *Negro fellows* and four *wenches* will positively be *sold* this day, *to the highest bidder!*" And what astonished me still more was, to see in this same *humane* paper! ! the cuts of three men, with clubs and budgets on their backs, and an advertisement offering a considerable sum of money for their apprehension and delivery. I declare, it is really so amusing to hear the Southerners and Westerners of this country talk about *barbarity,* that it is positively, enough to make a man *smile.*

The sufferings of the Helots among the Spartans, were somewhat severe, it is true, but to say that theirs, were as severe as ours among the Americans, I do most strenuously deny—for instance, can any man show me an article on a page of ancient history which specifies, that, the Spartans chained, and hand-cuffed the Helots, and dragged them from their wives and children, children from their parents, mothers from their suckling babes, wives from their husbands, driving them from one end of the country to the other?

Walker continues to build his case for the unique harshness of American slavery. At the top of his list is the internal slave trade, which took off after the abolition of the international slave trade in 1808. The internal slave trade saw approximately 1 million slaves relocated from Upper South states such as Virginia to new lands acquired in the Southwest—Alabama, Mississippi, and Texas. This process separated families, many for the rest of their lives.

Notice the Spartans were heathens, who lived long before our Divine Master made his appearance in the flesh. Can Christian Americans deny these barbarous cruelties? Have you not, Americans, having subjected us under you, added to these miseries, by insulting us in telling us to our face, because we are helpless, that we are not of the human family? I ask you, O! Americans, I ask you, in the name of the Lord, can you deny these charges? Some perhaps may deny, by saying, that they never thought or said that we were not men. But do not actions speak louder than words?—have they not made provisions for the Greeks, and Irish? Nations who have never done the least thing for them, while *we,* who have enriched their country with our blood and tears—have dug up gold and silver for them and their children, from generation to generation, and are in more miseries than any other people under heaven, are not seen, but by comparatively, a handful of the American people? There are indeed, more ways to kill a dog, besides choking it to death with butter. Further—The Spartans or Lacedaemonians, had some frivolous pretext, for enslaving the Helots, for they (Helots) while being free inhabitants of Sparta, stirred up an intestine commotion, and were, by the Spartans subdued, and made prisoners of war. Consequently they and their children were condemned to perpetual slavery.

I have been for years troubling the pages of historians, to find out what our fathers have done to the *white Christians of America,* to merit such condign punishment as they have inflicted on them, and do continue to inflict on us their children. But I must aver, that my researches have hitherto been to no effect. I have therefore, come to the immoveable conclusion, that they (Americans) have, and do continue to punish us for nothing else, but for enriching them and their country. For I cannot conceive of any thing else. Nor will I ever believe otherwise, until the Lord shall convince me.

The world knows, that slavery as it existed among the Romans, (which was the primary cause of their destruction) was, comparatively speaking, no more than a *cypher,* when compared with ours under the Americans. Indeed I should not have noticed the Roman slaves, had not the very learned and penetrating Mr. Jefferson said, "when a master was murdered, all his slaves in the same house, or within hearing, were condemned to death."—**Here let me ask Mr. Jefferson, (but he is gone to answer at the bar of God, for the deeds done in his body while living,) I therefore**

In his critique of Thomas Jefferson, Walker offers a scathing critique of the American Revolutionary tradition. At the same time, however, he draws from that tradition—including Patrick Henry's famous slogan "Give me liberty or give me death"—to argue for the right of resistance by slaves. In this argument, Walker was outside the mainstream of American abolitionism for his time, as the overwhelming majority of antislavery activists were advocates of nonviolent resistance to slavery.

ask the whole American people, had I not rather die, or be put to death, than to be a slave to any tyrant, who takes not only my own, but my wife and children's lives by the inches?

Yea, would I meet death with avidity far! far! ! in preference to such *servile submission* to the murderous hands of tyrants. Mr. Jefferson's very severe remarks on us have been so extensively argued upon by men whose attainments in literature, I shall never be able to reach, that I would not have meddled with it, were it not to solicit each of my brethren, who has the spirit of a man, to buy a copy of Mr. Jefferson's "Notes on Virginia," and put it in the hand of his son. For let no one of us suppose that the refutations which have been written by our white friends are enough—they are *whites*— we are *blacks*. We, and the world wish to see the charges of Mr. Jefferson refuted by the blacks *themselves,* according to their chance; for we must remember that what the whites have written respecting this subject, is other men's labours, and did not emanate from the blacks. I know well, that there are some talents and learning among the coloured people of this country, which we have not a chance to develop, in consequence of oppression; but our oppression ought not to hinder us from acquiring all we can. For we will have a chance to develop them by and by. God will not suffer us, always to be oppressed. Our sufferings will come to an *end,* in spite of all the Americans this side of *eternity.* Then we will want all the learning and talents among ourselves, and perhaps more, to govern ourselves.—"Every dog must have its day," the American's is coming to an end.

But let us review Mr. Jefferson's remarks respecting us some further. Comparing our miserable fathers, with the learned philosophers of Greece, he says: "Yet notwithstanding these and other discouraging circumstances among the Romans,

"For let no one of us suppose that the refutations which have been written by our white friends are enough— they are whites—*we are* blacks.*"*

their slaves were often their rarest artists. They excelled too, in science, insomuch as to be usually employed as tutors to their master's children; Epictetus, Terence and Phædrus, were slaves,—but they were of the race of whites. It is not their *condition* then, but *nature,* which has produced the distinction."

See this, my brethren! ! Do you believe that this assertion is swallowed by millions of the whites? Do you know that Mr. Jefferson was one of as great characters as ever lived among the whites? See his writings for the world, and public labours for the United States of America. Do you believe that the assertions of such a man, will pass away into oblivion unobserved by this people and the world? If you do you are much mistaken—See how the American people treat us— have we souls in our bodies? Are we men who have any spirits at all? I know that there are many *swell-bellied* fellows among us, whose greatest object is to fill their stomachs. Such I do not mean—I am after those who know and feel, that we are MEN, as well as other people; to them, I say, that unless we try to refute Mr. Jefferson's arguments respecting us, we will only establish them.

> *"Every body who has read history, knows, that as soon as a slave among the Romans obtained his freedom, he could rise to the greatest eminence in the State, and there was no law instituted to hinder a slave from buying his freedom."*

But the slaves among the Romans. Every body who has read history, knows, that as soon as a slave among the Romans obtained his freedom, he could rise to the greatest eminence in the State, and there was no law instituted to hinder a slave from buying his freedom. Have not the Americans instituted laws to hinder us from obtaining our freedom? Do any deny this charge? Read the laws of Virginia, North Carolina, &c. Further: have not the Americans instituted laws to prohibit a man of colour from obtaining and holding any office whatever, under the government of the United States of America? Now, Mr. Jefferson tells us, that our condition is not so hard, as the slaves were under the Romans! ! ! ! ! !

It is time for me to bring this article to a close. But before I close it, I must observe to my brethren that at the close of the first Revolution in this country, with Great Britain, there were but thirteen States in the Union, now there are twenty-four, most of which are slave-holding States, and the whites are dragging us around in chains and in hand-cuffs, to their new States and Territories to work their mines and farms, to enrich them and their children—and millions of them believing firmly that we being a little darker than they, were made by our Creator to be an inheritance to them and their children for ever—the same as a parcel of *brutes*.

This great expansion of slave territory in the nation was due largely to the Louisiana Purchase of 1803, engineered during Thomas Jefferson's administration. Jefferson argued that the purchase, which doubled the territory of the United States, would create an "Empire for Liberty," but Walker instead claims that it has done the opposite, creating an empire for slavery.

Are we MEN! !—I ask you, O my brethren! are we MEN? Did our Creator make us to be slaves to dust and ashes like ourselves? Are they not dying worms as well as we? Have they not to make their appearance before the tribunal of Heaven, to answer for the deeds done in the body, as well as we? Have we any other Master but Jesus Christ alone? Is he not their Master as well as ours?—What right then, have we to obey and call any other Master, but Himself? How we could be so *submissive* to a gang of men, whom we cannot tell whether they are *as good* as ourselves or not, I never could conceive. However, this is shut up with the Lord, and we cannot precisely tell—but I declare, we judge men by their works.

The whites have always been an unjust, jealous, unmerciful, avaricious and blood-thirsty set of beings, always seeking after power and authority.—We view them all over the confederacy of Greece, where they were first known to be any thing, (in consequence of education) we see them there, cutting each other's throats—trying to subject each other to wretchedness and misery—to effect which, they used all kinds of deceitful, unfair, and unmerciful means.

We view them next in Rome, where the spirit of tyranny and deceit raged still higher. We view them in Gaul, Spain, and in Britain.—In fine, we view them all over Europe, together with what were scattered about in Asia and Africa, as heathens, and we see them acting more like devils than accountable men. But some may ask, did not the blacks of Africa, and the mulattoes of Asia, go on in the same way as did the whites of Europe. I answer, no—they never were half so avaricious, deceitful and unmerciful as the whites, according to their knowledge.

But we will leave the whites or Europeans as heathens, and take a view of them as Christians, in which capacity we see them as cruel, if not more so than ever. In fact, take them as a body, they are ten times more cruel, avaricious and unmerciful than ever they were; for while they were heathens, they were bad enough it is true, but it is positively a fact that they were not quite so audacious as to go and take vessel loads of men, women and children, and in cold blood, and through devilishness, throw them into the sea, and murder them in all kind of ways. While they were heathens, they were too ignorant for such barbarity. But being Christians, enlightened and sensible, they are completely prepared for such hellish cruelties. Now suppose God were to give them more sense, what would they do? If it were possible, would they not *dethrone* Jehovah and seat themselves upon his throne? **I therefore, in the name and fear of the Lord God of Heaven and of earth, divested of prejudice either on the side of my colour or that of the whites, advance my suspicion of them, whether they are *as good by nature* as we are or not. Their actions, since they were known as a people, have been the reverse, I do indeed suspect them, but this, as I before oberved, is shut up with the Lord, we cannot exactly tell, it will be proved in succeeding generations.—The whites have had the essence**

Walker turns the table on Jefferson and posits his suspicion that whites are morally inferior to blacks. While blacks are supposedly heathens, white Christians engage in some of the greatest barbarities the world has ever known, in Walker's opinion. His statement speaks to an important development in black intellectual history, namely African Americans' own racial conceptions. During this period most blacks would posit an equality between the races, but Walker goes further to claim that blacks are likely racially superior to whites. As with his views on violence in the antislavery movement, Walker was outside the mainstream of abolitionist thought in his conceptions of race.

of the gospel as it was preached by my master and his apostles—the Ethiopians have not, who are to have it in its meridian splendor—the Lord will give it to them to their satisfaction.

I hope and pray my God, that they will make good use of it, that it may be well with them.

ARTICLE II
OUR WRETCHEDNESS IN CONSEQUENCE
OF IGNORANCE

Ignorance, my brethren, is a mist, low down into the very dark and almost impenetrable abyss in which, our fathers for many centuries have been plunged. The Christians, and enlightened of Europe, and some of Asia, seeing the ignorance and consequent degradation of our fathers, instead of trying to enlighten them, by teaching them that religion and light with which God had blessed them, they have plunged them into wretchedness ten thousand times more intolerable, than if they had left them entirely to the Lord, and to add to their miseries, deep down into which they have plunged them tell them, that they are an *inferior* and *distinct race* of beings, which they will be glad enough to recall and swallow by and by. Fortune and misfortune, two inseparable companions, lay rolled up in the wheel of events, which have from the creation of the world, and will continue to take place among men until God shall dash worlds together.

When we take a retrospective view of the arts and sciences—the wise legislators—the Pyramids, and other magnificent buildings—the turning of the channel of the river Nile, by the sons of Africa or of Ham, among whom learning originated, and was carried thence into Greece, where it was improved upon and refined. Thence among the Romans, and all over the then enlightened parts of the world, and it has been enlightening the dark and benighted minds of men from then, down to this day. I say, when I view retrospectively, the renown of that once mighty people, the children of our great progenitor I am indeed cheered. Yea further, when I view that mighty son of Africa, HANNIBAL, one of the greatest generals of antiquity, who defeated and cut off so many thousands of the white Romans or murderers, and who carried his victorious arms, to the very gate of Rome, and I give it as my candid opinion, that had Carthage been well united and had given him good support, he would have carried that cruel and barbarous city by storm. But they were dis-united, as the coloured people are now, in the United States of America, the reason our natural enemies are enabled to keep their feet on our throats.

Walker draws on the long tradition in African American literature stretching back to Phillis Wheatley that argues that God will have his vengeance on America for the institution of slavery. During Walker's own time, countless writers invoked both the example of Haiti at the time as well as the historical example of Africa and Africans in making their arguments for equality and an end to slavery. Africa was once a great civilization and Haiti threw off the power of their oppressors, the argument went; thus, American blacks could likewise become a great people and see satisfaction for the troubles endured in bondage.

Beloved brethren—here let me tell you, and believe it, that the Lord our God, as true as he sits on his throne in heaven, and as true as our Saviour died to redeem the world, will give you a Hannibal, and when the Lord shall have raised him up, and given him to you for your possession, O my suffering brethren! remember the divisions and consequent sufferings of *Carthage* and of *Hayti*. Read the history particularly of Hayti, and see how they were butchered by the whites, and do you take warning. The person whom God shall give you, give him your support and let him go his length, and behold in him the salvation of your God. God will indeed, deliver you through him from your deplorable and wretched condition under the Christians of America. I charge you this day before my God to lay no obstacle in his way, but let him go.

The whites want slaves, and want us for their slaves, but some of them will curse the day they ever saw us. As true as the sun ever shone in its meridian splendor, my colour will root some of them out of the very face of the earth. They shall have enough of making slaves of, and butchering, and murdering us in the manner which they have. No doubt some may say that I write with a bad spirit, and that I being a black, wish these things to occur. Whether I write with a bad or a good spirit, I say if these things do not occur in their proper time, it is because the world in which we live does not exist, and we are deceived with regard to its existence.—It is immaterial however to me, who believe, or who refuse—though I should like to see the whites repent peradventure God may have mercy on them, some however, have gone so far that their cup must be filled.

But what need have I to refer to antiquity, when Hayti, the glory of the blacks and terror of tyrants, is enough to convince the most avaricious and stupid of wretches—which is at this time, and I am sorry to say it, plagued with that scourge of nations, the Catholic religion; but I hope and pray God that she may yet rid herself of it, and adopt in its stead the Protestant faith; also, I hope that she may keep peace within her borders and be united, keeping a strict look out for tyrants, for if they get the least chance to injure her, they will avail themselves of it, as true as the Lord lives in heaven.

Anti-Catholic animus in American culture stretches back to the first settlement of the colonies by England in the 17th century, and blacks were just as susceptible to it as whites. For many African Americans, this hostility to Catholicism had important ramifications for their future and for the course of abolitionism in general. In the 1810s and 1820s, a desire to immigrate to either Africa or Haiti was widespread among the black populace, many of whom were more involved in the emigration movement than the antislavery one. The Haitian Emigration Society was formed in Philadelphia to encourage such efforts, and thousands of American blacks decided to settle in the new republic. Upon arrival, however, many Americans had trouble getting land, and they found the Catholicism of the Haitians to be backward. This religious animus is one factor that led most blacks to move back to the United States and focus their attention on the antislavery movement.

But one thing which gives me joy is, that they are men who would be cut off to a man, before they would yield to the combined forces of the whole world—in fact, if the whole world was combined against them, it could not do any thing with them, unless the Lord delivers them up.

Ignorance and treachery one against the other—a grovelling servile and abject submission to the lash of tyrants,

The primary argument that Walker makes in this section of the book is that lack of education is a critical factor in blacks' current situation. In this belief he was not alone. Activists such as Prince Hall began pushing for increased access to education for blacks in the late 18th century, and Walker's friend and intellectual disciple, Maria Stewart, would likewise focus on this issue in her speeches and writings during the early 1830s.

we see plainly, my brethren, are not the natural elements of the blacks, as the Americans try to make us believe; but these are misfortunes which God has suffered our fathers to be enveloped in for many ages, no doubt in consequence of their disobedience to their Maker, and which do, indeed, reign at this time among us, almost to the destruction of all other principles: for I must truly say, that ignorance, the mother of treachery and deceit, gnaws into our very vitals.

Ignorance, as it now exists among us, produces a state of things, Oh my Lord! too horrible to present to the world. Any man who is curious to see the full force of ignorance developed among the coloured people of the United States of America, has only to go into the southern and western states of this confederacy, where, if he is not a tyrant, but has the feelings of a human being, who can feel for a fellow creature, he may see enough to make his very heart bleed! He may see there, a son take his mother, who bore almost the pains of death to give him birth, and by the command of a tyrant, strip her as naked as she came into the world, and apply the cow-hide to her, until she falls a victim to death in the road! He may see a husband take his dear wife, not unfrequently in a pregnant state, and perhaps far advanced, and beat her for an unmerciful wretch, until his infant falls a lifeless lump at her feet! Can the Americans escape God Almighty? If they do, can he be to us a God of Justice? God is just, and I know it—for he has convinced me to my satisfaction—I cannot doubt him. My observer may see fathers beating their sons, mothers their daughters, and children their parents, all to pacify the passions of unrelenting tyrants. He may also, see them telling news and lies, making mischief one upon another. These are some of the productions of ignorance, which he will see practised among my dear brethren, who are held in unjust slavery and wretchedness, by avaricious and unmerciful tyrants, to whom, and their hellish deeds, I would suffer my life to be taken before I would submit. And when my curious observer comes to take notice of those who are said to be free, (which assertion I deny) and who are making some frivolous pretentions to common sense, he will see that branch of ignorance among the slaves assuming a more cunning and deceitful course of procedure.—He may see some of my brethren in league with tyrants, selling their own brethren into *hell upon earth,* not dissimilar to the exhibitions in Africa, but in a more secret, servile and abject manner. Oh Heaven! I am full! ! ! I can hardly move my pen! ! ! and as I expect some will try to put me to death, to strike terror into others, and to obliterate from their minds the notion of freedom, so as to keep my brethren the more secure in wretchedness, where they will be permitted to stay but a short time (whether tyrants believe it or not)—I shall give the world a development of facts, which are already witnessed in the courts of heaven. My observer may see some of those ignorant and treacherous creatures (coloured people) sneaking about in the large cities, endeavouring to find out all strange coloured people, where they work and where they reside, asking them questions, and trying to ascertain whether they are runaways or not, telling them, at the same time, that they always have been, are, and always will be, friends to their brethren; and, perhaps, that they themselves are absconders, and a thousand such treacherous lies to get the better information of the more ignorant! ! ! There have been and are at this day in Boston, New-York, Philadelphia, and Baltimore, coloured men, who are in league with tyrants, and who receive a great portion of their daily bread, of the moneys which they acquire from the blood and tears of their more miserable brethren, whom they scandalously delivered into the hands of our *natural enemies! ! ! ! ! !*

"There have been and are at this day in Boston, New-York, Philadelphia, and Baltimore, coloured men, who are in league with tyrants, and who receive a great portion of their daily bread, of the moneys which they acquire from the blood and tears of their more miserable brethren, whom they scandalously delivered into the hands of our natural enemies! ! ! ! ! !"

To show the force of degraded ignorace and deceit among us some farther, I will give here an extract from a paragraph, which may be found in the Columbian Centinel of this city, for September 9, 1829, on the first page of which, the curious may find an article, headed

"AFFRAY AND MURDER."
"Portsmouth, (Ohio) Aug." 22, 1829.

"A most shocking outrage was committed in Kentucky, about eight miles from this place, on 14th inst. A negro driver, by the name of Gordon, who had purchased in Mayland about sixty negroes, was taking them, assisted by an associate named Allen, and the wagoner who conveyed the baggage, to the Mississippi. The men were hand-cuffed and chained together, in the usual manner for driving those poor wretches, while the women and children were suffered to proceed without incumbrance. It appears that, by means of a file the negroes, unobserved, had succeeded in separating the iron which bound their hands, in such a way as to be able to throw them off at any moment. About 8 o'clock in the morning, while proceeding on the state road leading from Greenup to Vanceburg, two of them dropped their shackles and commenced a fight, when the wagoner (Petit) rushed in with his whip to compel them to desist. At this moment, every negro was found to be perfectly at liberty; and one of them seizing a club, gave Petit a violent blow on the head, and laid him dead at his feet; and Allen, who came to his assistance, met a similar fate, from the contents of a pistol fired by another of the gang. Gordon was then attacked, seized and held by one of the negroes, whilst another fired twice at him with a pistol, the ball of which each time grazed his head, but not proving effectual, he was beaten with clubs, and left for dead. They then commenced pillaging the wagon, and with an axe split open the trunk of

Gordon, and rifled it of the money, about $2,400. Sixteen of the negroes then took to the woods; Gordon, in the mean time, not being materially injured, was enabled, by the assistance of one of the women, to mount his horse and flee; pursued, however, by one of the gang on another horse, with a drawn pistol; fortunately he escaped with his life barely, arriving at a plantation, as the negro came in sight; who then turned about and retreated."

"The neighbourhood was immediately rallied, and a hot pursuit given—which, we understand, has resulted in the capture of the whole gang and the recovery of the greatest part of the money. Seven of the negro men and one woman, it is said were engaged in the murders, and will be brought to trial at the next cours in Greenupsburg."

Here my brethren, I want you to notice particularly in the above article, the *ignorant* and *deceitful actions* of this coloured woman. I beg you to view it candidly, as for ETER-NITY! ! ! ! Here a *notorious wretch,* with two other confederates had SIXTY of them in a gang, driving them like *brutes*—the men all in chains and hand-cuffs, and by the help of God they got their chains and hand-cuffs thrown off, and caught two of the wretches and put them to death, and beat the other until they thought he was dead, and left him for dead; however, he deceived them, and rising from the ground, this *servile woman* helped him upon his horse, and he made his escape. Brethren, what do you think of this? Was it the natural *fine feelings* of this woman, to save such a wretch alive? I know that the blacks, take them half enlightened and ignorant, are more humane and merciful than the most enlightened and refined European that can be found in all the earth. Let no one say that I assert this because I am prejudiced on the side of my colour, and against the whites or Europeans. For what I write, I do it candidly, for

> "I know that the blacks, take them half enlightened and ignorant, are more humane and merciful than the most enlightened and refined European that can be found in all the earth."

my God and the good of both parties: Natural observations have taught me these things; there is a solemn awe in the hearts of the blacks, as it respects *murdering* men: whereas the whites, (though they are great cowards) where they have the advantage, or think that there are any prospects of getting it, they murder all before them, in order to subject men to wretchedness and degradation under them. This is the natural result of pride and avarice. But I declare, the actions of this black woman are really insupportable. For my own part, I cannot think it was any thing but servile deceit, combined with the most gross ignorance: for we must remember that *humanity, kindness* and the *fear of the Lord,* does not consist in protecting *devils.* Here is a set of wretches, who had SIXTY of them in a gang, driving them around the country like *brutes,* to dig up gold and silver for them, (which they will get enough of yet.) Should the lives of such creatures be spared? Are God and Mammon in league? What has the Lord to do with a gang of desperate wretches, who go *sneaking about the country like robbers*—light upon his people wherever they can get a chance, binding them with chains and hand-cuffs, beat and murder them as they would *rattle-snakes?* Are they not the Lord's enemies? Ought they not to be destroyed? Any person who will save such wretches from destruction, is fighting against the Lord, and will receive his just recompense. The black men acted like *blockheads.* Why did they not make sure of the wretch? He would have made sure of them, if he could. It is just the way with black men—eight white men can frighten fifty of them; whereas, if you can only get courage into the blacks, I do declare it, that one good black man can put to death six white men; and I give it as a fact, let twelve black men get well armed for battle, and they will kill and put to flight fifty whites.—The reason is, the blacks, once you get them started, they glory in death. **The whites have had us under them for more than three centuries, murdering, and**

William Lloyd Garrison certainly represented a new direction in the antislavery movement with his harsh, uncompromising rhetoric. Garrison, however, was a pacifist, whereas Walker here is one of the first blacks to openly advocate violence against slaveholders. This too represents a new and important direction in American abolitionism, which until the late 1820s had been focused largely on working through the legal system. While Walker's call for violence against slaveholders would not have a big impact in his own time, an 1843 convention of blacks took up the question, and a resolution promoting violent resistance fell short by just one vote. While the advocates of nonviolence at this convention, led by Frederick Douglass, ended up carrying the day, Walker's ideas would continue to gain influence and would be put into action with the formation of vigilance committees throughout northern cities, committees that were aimed at resisting the reenslavement of fugitives by any necessary means.

treating us like brutes; and, as Mr. Jefferson wisely said, they have never *found us out*—they do not know, indeed, that there is an unconquerable disposition in the breasts of the blacks, which, when it is fully awakened and put in motion, will be subdued, only with the destruction of the animal existence. Get the blacks started, and if you do not have a gang of tigers and lions to deal with, I am a deceiver of the blacks and of the whites. How sixty of them could let that wretch escape unkilled, I cannot conceive—they will have to suffer as much for the two whom, they secured, as if they had put one hundred to death: if you commence, make sure work—do not trifle, for they will not trifle with you—they want us for their slaves, and think nothing of murdering us in order to subject us to that wretched condition—therefore, if there is an *attempt* made by us, kill or be killed. Now, I ask you, had you not rather be killed than to be a slave to a tyrant, who takes the life of your mother, wife, and dear little children? Look upon your mother, wife and children, and answer God Almighty; and believe this, that it is no more harm for you to kill a man, who is trying to kill you, than it is for you to take a drink of water when thirsty; in fact, the man who will stand still and let another murder him, is worse than an infidel, and, if he has common sense, ought not to be pitied. The actions of this deceitful and ignorant coloured woman, in saving the life of a desperate wretch, whose avaricious and cruel object was to drive her, and her companions in miseries, through the country like cattle, to make his fortune on their carcasses, are but too much like that of thousands of our brethren in these states: if any thing is whispered by one, which has any allusion to the melioration of their dreadful condition, they run and tell tyrants, that they may be enabled to keep them the longer in wretchedness and miseries. Oh! coloured people of these United States, I ask you, in the

"How can the slaveholders but say that they can bribe the best coloured person in the country, to sell his brethren for a trifling sum of money, and take that atrocity to confirm them in their avaricious opinion, that we were made to be slaves to them and their children?"

name of that God who made us, have we, in consequence of oppression, nearly lost the spirit of man, and, in no very trifling degree, adopted that of brutes? Do you answer, no?—I ask you, then, what set of men can you point me to, in all the world, who are so abjectly employed by their oppressors, as we are by our *natural enemies?* How can, Oh! how can those enemies but say that we and our children are not of the HUMAN FAMILY, but were made by our Creator to be an inheritance to them and theirs for ever? How can the slaveholders but say that they can bribe the best coloured person in the country, to sell his brethren for a trifling sum of money, and take that atrocity to confirm them in their avaricious opinion, that we were made to be slaves to them and their children? How could Mr. Jefferson but say, "I advance it therefore as a suspicion only, that the blacks, whether originally a distinct race, or made distinct by time and circumstances, are *inferior* to the whites in the endowments both of body and mind?"—"It," says he, "is not against experience to suppose, that different species of the same genius, or varieties of the same species, may possess different qualifications." [Here, my brethren, listen to him.] "Will not a lover of natural history, then, one who views the gradations in all the races of *animals* with the eye of philosophy, excuse an effort to keep those in the department of MAN as *distinct* as nature has formed them?"—I hope you will try to find out the meaning of this verse—its widest sense and all its bearings: whether you do or not, remember the whites do. This very verse, brethren, having emanated from Mr. Jefferson, a much greater philosopher the world never afforded, has in truth injured us more, and has been as great a barrier to our emancipation as any thing that has ever been advanced against us. I hope you will not let it pass unnoticed. He goes on further, and says: "This *unfortunate* difference of colour, and *perhaps* of *faculty,* is a powerful obstacle to the emancipation of these people.

Many of their advocates, while they wish to vindicate the liberty of human nature are anxious also to preserve its *dignity* and *beauty*. Some of these, embarrassed by the question, 'What further is to be done with them?' join themselves in opposition with those who are actuated by sordid avarice only." Now I ask you candidly, my suffering brethren in time, who are candidates for the eternal worlds, how could Mr. Jefferson but have given the world these remarks respecting us, when we are so submissive to them, and so much servile deceit prevail among ourselves—when we so *meanly* submit to their murderous lashes, to which neither the Indians nor any other people under Heaven would submit? No, they would die to a man, before they would suffer such things from men who are no better than themselves, and *perhaps not so good.* Yes, how can our friends but be embarrassed, as Mr. Jefferson says, by the question, "What further is to be done with these people?" For while they are working for our emancipation, we are, by our treachery, wickedness and deceit, working against ourselves and our children—helping ours, and the enemies of God, to keep us and our dear little children in their infernal chains of slavery! ! ! Indeed, our friends cannot but relapse and join themselves "with those who are actuated by *sordid avarice* only! ! ! !" For my own part, I am glad Mr. Jefferson has advanced his positions for your sake; for you will either have to contradict or confirm him by your own actions, and not by what our friends have said or done for us; for those things are other men's labours, and do not satisfy the Americans, who are waiting for us to prove to them ourselves, that we are MEN, before they will be willing to admit the fact; for I pledge you my sacred word of honour, that Mr. Jefferson's remarks respecting us, have sunk deep into the hearts of millions of the whites, and never will be removed this side of eternity.—For how can they, when we are confirming him every day, by our *groveling submissions* and *treachery?* I

"I pledge you my sacred word of honour, that Mr. Jefferson's remarks respecting us, have sunk deep into the hearts of millions of the whites, and never will be removed this side of eternity."

aver, that when I look over these United States of America, and the world, and see the ignorant deceptions and consequent wretchedness of my brethren, I am brought oftimes solemnly to a stand, and in the midst of my reflections I exclaim to my God, "Lord didst thou make us to be slaves to our brethren, the whites?" But when I reflect that God is just, and that millions of my wretched brethren would meet death with glory—yea, more, would plunge into the very mouths of cannons and be torn into particles as minute as the atoms which compose the elements of the earth, in preference to a mean submission to the lash of tyrants, I am with streaming eyes, compelled to shrink back into nothingness before my Maker, and exclaim again, thy will be done, O Lord God Almighty.

"Men of colour, who are also of sense, for you particularly is my APPEAL designed. Our more ignorant brethren are not able to penetrate its value."

Men of colour, who are also of sense, for you particularly is my APPEAL designed. Our more ignorant brethren are not able to penetrate its value. I call upon you therefore to cast your eyes upon the wretchedness of your brethren, and to do your utmost to enlighten them—*go to work and enlighten your brethren!*—Let the Lord see you doing what you can to rescue them and yourselves from degradation. Do any of you say that you and your family are free and happy, and what have you to do with the wretched slaves and other people? So can I say, for I enjoy as much freedom as any of you, if I am not quite as well off as the best of you. Look into our freedom and happiness, and see of what kind they are composed! ! They are of the very lowest kind—they are the very *dregs!*—they are the most servile and abject kind, that ever a people was in possession of! If any of you wish to know how FREE you are, let one of you start and go through the southern and western States of this country, and unless you travel as a slave to a white man (a servant is a *slave* to the man whom he serves) or have your free papers, (which if you are not careful they will get from you) if they do not take you up and put you in jail, and if you cannot give good evidence of your freedom, sell you into eternal slavery, I am not a living man: or any man of colour, immaterial who he is, or where he came from, if he is not *the fourth from the negro race! !* (as we are called) the white Christians of America will serve him the same they will sink him into wretchedness and degradation for ever while he lives. And yet some of you have the hardihood to say that you are free and happy! May God have mercy on your freedom and happiness! ! **I met a coloured man in the street a short time since, with a string of boots on his shoulders; we fell into conversation, and in course of which, I said to him, what a miserable set of people we are! He asked, why?—Said I, we are so subjected under the whites, that we cannot obtain the comforts of life, but by cleaning their boots and shoes, old clothes, waiting on them, shaving them &c. Said he, (with the boots on his shoulders) "I am completely happy! ! ! I never want to live any better or happier than when I can get a plenty of boots and shoes to clean! ! !" Oh! how can those who are actuated by avarice only, but think, that our Creator made us to be an inheritance to them for ever, when they see that our greatest glory is centered in such mean and low objects?** Understand me, brethren, I do not mean to speak against the occupations by which we acquire enough and sometimes scarcely that, to render ourselves and families comfortable through life. I am subjected to the same inconvenience, as you all.—My objections are, to our *glorying* and being *happy* in such low employments; for if we are men, we ought to be thankful to the Lord for the past, and for the future. Be looking forward with thankful hearts to higher attainments than *wielding the razor* and *cleaning boots and shoes.* The man whose aspirations are not *above,* and even *below* these, is indeed, ignorant and wretched enough. I advance it therefore to you, not as a *problematical,* but as an unshaken and for ever immoveable *fact,* that

At this time the economic position of African Americans was precarious, to say the least. Under slavery, blacks worked in all types of professions in the North, including as blacksmiths, coopers, and furniture makers and in other skilled jobs. Most of these positions, however, would be denied to free blacks and given to whites instead. Thus, African Americans often had to settle for menial employment. Walker and other black leaders deplored this situation and called for economic independence, which would best be achieved through education and black unity.

your full glory and happiness, as well as all other coloured people under Heaven, shall never be fully consummated, but with the *entire emancipation of your enslaved brethren all over the world*. You may therefore, go to work and do what you can to rescue, or join in with tyrants to oppress them and yourselves, until the Lord shall come upon you all like a thief in the night. For I believe it is the will of the Lord that our greatest happiness shall consist in working for the salvation of our whole body. When this is accomplished a burst of glory will shine upon you, which will indeed astonish you and the world. Do any of you say this never will be done? I assure you that God will accomplish it—if nothing else will answer, he will hurl tyrants and devils into *atoms* and make way for his people. But O my brethren! I say unto you again, you must go to work and prepare the way of the Lord.

In blacks' writing stretching back to the 1790s, there is the constant imperative to prove their equality to whites in various ways. For some this would be through educational attainments, as a principal justification for black inferiority was the idea that they could not reason. For others, it was living morally upright lives. This imperative would come to be known as the "politics of respectability." Leaders such as Walker, Richard Allen, and others argued that if blacks were seen as intelligent, morally upright individuals, it would reflect well on the entire race and convince whites that blacks should not be enslaved and treated as if they were inferior.

There is a great work for you to do, as trifling as some of you may think of it. You have to prove to the Americans and the world, that we are MEN, and not *brutes*, as we have been represented, and by millions treated. Remember, to let the aim of your labours among your brethren, and particularly the youths, be the dissemination of education and religion. It is lamentable, that many of our children go to school, from four until they are eight or ten, and sometimes fifteen years of age, and leave school knowing but a little more about the grammar of their language than a horse does about handling a musket—and not a few of them are really so ignorant, that they are unable to answer a person correctly, general questions in geography, and to hear them read, would only be to disgust a man who has a taste for reading; which, to do well, as trifling as it may appear to some, (to the ignorant in particular) is a great part of learning. Some few of them, may make out to scribble tolerably well, over a half sheet of paper, which I believe has hitherto been a powerful obstacle in our way, to keep us from acquiring knowledge.

An ignorant father, who knows no more than what nature has taught him, together with what little he acquires by the senses of hearing and seeing, finding his son able to write a neat hand, sets it down for granted that he has as good learning as any body; the young, ignorant gump, hearing his father or mother, who perhaps may be ten times more ignorant, in point of literature, than himself, extolling his learning, struts about, in the full assurance, that his attainments in literature are sufficient to take him through the world, when, in fact, he has scarcely any learning at all! ! ! !

I promiscuously fell in conversation once, with an elderly coloured man on the topics of education, and of the great prevalency of ignorance among us: Said he, "I know that our people are very ignorant but my son has a good education: I spent a great deal of money on his education: he can write as well as any white man, and I assure you that no one can fool him," &c. Said I, what else can your son do, besides writing a good hand? Can he post a set of books in a mercantile manner? Can he write a neat piece of composition in prose or in verse? To these interrogations he answered in the negative. Said I, did your son learn, while he was at school, the width and depth of English Grammar? To which he also replied in the negative, telling me his son did not learn those things. Your son, said I, then, has hardly any learning at all—he is almost as ignorant, and more so, than many of those who never went to school one day in all their lives. My friend got a little put out, and so walking off, said that his son could write as well as any white man. Most of the coloured people, when they speak of the education of one among us who can write a neat hand, and who perhaps knows nothing but to scribble and puff pretty fair on a small scrap of paper, immaterial whether his words are grammatical, or spelt

The issue that Walker addresses here was one that was common among both blacks and whites. In the late 1820s when this book was first published, the United States was still primarily an agricultural nation, which meant that once children were old enough to work on the family farm they were pulled out of school or were only allowed to go to school when there was no harvest to collect. This situation was especially pronounced in the South, which was less industrialized than the North and did not have a common school system for all citizens until after the Civil War.

correctly, or not; if it only looks beautiful, they say he has as good an education as any white man—he can write as well as any white man, &c. The poor, ignorant creature, hearing, this, he is ashamed, forever after, to let any person see him humbling himself to another for knowledge but going about trying to deceive those who are more ignorant than himself, he at last falls an ignorant victim to death in wretchedness. I pray that the Lord may undeceive my ignorant brethren, and permit them to throw away pretensions, and seek after the substance of learning. I would crawl on my hands and knees through mud and mire, to the feet of a learned man, where I would sit and humbly supplicate him to instill into me, that which neither devils nor tyrants could remove, only with my life—for colored people to acquire learning in this country, makes tyrants quake and tremble on their sandy foundation. Why, what is the matter? Why, they know that their infernal deeds of cruelty will be made known to the world. Do you suppose one man of good sense and learning would submit himself, his father, mother, wife and children, to be slaves to a wretched man like himself, who, instead of compensating him for his labours, chains, hand-cuffs and beats him and family almost to death, leaving life enough in them, however, to work for, and call him master? No! no! he would cut his devilish throat from ear to ear, and well do slave-holders know it. The bare name of educating the coloured people, scares our cruel oppressors almost to death. But if they do not have enough to be frightened for yet, it will be, because they can always keep us ignorant, and because God approbates their cruelties, with which they have been for centuries murdering us. The whites shall have enough of the blacks, yet, as true as God sits on his throne in Heaven.

Some of our brethren are so very full of learning, that you cannot mention any thing to them which they do not know better than yourself! !—nothing is strange to them! !—they knew every thing years ago!—if any thing should be mentioned in company where they are, immaterial how important it is respecting us or the world, if they had not divulged it; they make light of it, and affect to have known it long before it was mentioned and try to make all in the room, or wherever you may be, believe that your conversation is nothing! !—not worth hearing! All this is the result of ignorance and ill-breeding; for a man of good-breeding, sense and penetration, if he had heard a subject told twenty times over, and should happen to be in company where one should commence telling it again, he would wait with patience on its narrator, and see if he would tell it as it was told in his presence before—paying the most strict attention to what is said, to see if any more light will be thrown on the subject: for all men are not gifted alike in telling, or even hearing the most simple narration. These ignorant, vicious, and wretched men, contribute almost as much injury to our body as tyrants themselves, by doing so much for the promotion of ignorance amongst us; for they, making such pretensions to knowledge, such of our youth as are seeking after knowledge, and can get access to them, take them as criterions to go by, who will lead them into a channel, where, unless the Lord blesses them with the privilege of seeing their folly, they will be irretrievably lost forever, while in time! ! !

I must close this article by relating the very heart-rending fact, that I have examined school-boys and young men of colour in different parts of the country, in the most simple parts of Murray's English Grammar, and not more than one in thirty was able to give a correct answer to my interrogations. If any one contradicts me, let him step out of his door into the streets of Boston, New-York, Philadelphia, or Baltimore, (no use to mention any other, for the Christians are too charitable further south or west!)—I say, let him who disputes me, step out of his door into the streets of either of those four cities, and promiscuously collect one hundred school-boys, or young men of colour, *who have been to school,* and who are considered by the coloured people to have received an excellent education, because, perhaps, some of them can write a good hand, but who, notwithstanding their neat writing, may be almost as ignorant, in comparison, as a horse.—And, I say it, he will hardly find (in this enlightened day, and in the midst of this *charitable* people) five in one hundred, who, are able to correct the false grammar of their language.— The cause of this almost universal ignorance among us, I appeal to our school-masters to declare. Here is a fact, which I this very minute take from the mouth of a young coloured man, who has been to school in this state (Massachusetts) nearly nine years, and who knows grammar this day, *nearly* as well as he did the day he first entered the school-house, under a white master. This young man says: "My master would never allow me to study grammar." I asked him, why? "The school committee," said he "forbid the coloured children learning grammar"—they would not allow any but the white children "to study grammar." It is a notorious fact, that the major part of the white Americans, have, ever since we have been among them, tried to keep us ignorant, and make us believe that God made us and our children to be slaves to them and theirs. *Oh! my God, have mercy on Christian Americans! ! !*

ARTICLE III
OUR WRETCHEDNESS IN CONSEQUENCE OF THE PREACHERS OF THE RELIGION OF JESUS CHRIST

Religion, my brethren, is a substance of deep consideration among all nations of the earth. The Pagans have a kind, as well as the Mahometans, the Jews and the Christians. But pure and undefiled religion, such as was preached by Jesus Christ and his apostles, is hard to be found in all the earth. God, through his instrument, Moses, handed a dispensation of his Divine will, to the children of Israel after they had left Egypt for the land of Canaan or of Promise, who through hypocrisy, oppression and unbelief, departed from the faith.—He then, by his apostles, handed a dispensation of his, together with the will of Jesus Christ, to the Europeans in Europe, who, in open violation of which, have made *merchandise* of us, and it does appear as though they take this very dispensation to aid them in their *infernal* depredations upon us. Indeed, the way in which religion was and is conducted by the Europeans and their descendants, one might believe it was a plan fabricated by themselves and the *devils* to oppress us. But hark! My master has taught me better than to believe it—he has taught me that his gospel as it was preached by himself and his apostles remains the same, notwithstanding Europe has tried to mingle blood and opression with it.

It is well known to the Christian world, that Bartholomew Las Casas, that very very notoriously avaricious Catholic priest or preacher, and adventurer with Columbus in his second voyage, proposed to his countrymen, the Spaniards in Hispaniola to import the Africans from the Portuguese settlement in Africa, to dig up gold and silver, and work their plantations for them, to effect which, he made a voyage thence to Spain, and opened the subject to his master, Ferdinand then in declining health, who listened to the plan: but who died soon after, and left it in the hand of his successor, Charles V.

This wretch, ("Las Casas, the Preacher,") succeeded so well in his plans of oppression, that in 1503, the first

While much of Walker's animus is pointed toward American slavery, here he places that institution in its larger Atlantic context, noting correctly that the African slave trade from its inception had the justification and support of religious figures such as Las Casas. Walker's discussion of this combined with numerous references throughout the text to "Christian Americans" is meant to highlight the hypocrisy of those in Europe and the United States who support slavery while claiming a Christian identity.

blacks had been imported into the new world. Elated with this success, and stimulated by sordid avarice only, he importuned Charles V. in 1511, to grant permission to a Flemish merchant, to import 4000 blacks at one time. Thus we see, through the instrumentality of a pretended preacher of the gospel of Jesus Christ our common master, our wretchedness first commenced in America—where it has been continued from 1503, to this day, 1829. A period of three hundred and twenty-six years. But two hundred and nine, from 1620—when twenty of our fathers were brought into Jamestown, Virginia, by a Dutch man of war, and sold off like brutes to the highest bidders; and there is not a doubt in my mind, but that tyrants are in hope to perpetuate our miseries under them and their children until the final consumation of all things.—But if they do not get dreadfully deceived, it will be because God has forgotten them.

The Pagans, Jews and Mahometans try to make proselytes to their religions, and whatever human beings adopt their religions they extend to them their protection. But Christian Americans, not only hinder their fellow creatures, the Africans, but thousands of them *will absolutely beat a coloured person nearly to death, if they catch him on his knees, supplicating the throne of grace.* This barbarous cruelty was by all the heathen nations of antiquity, and is by the Pagans, Jews and Mahometans of the present day, left entirely to Christian Americans to inflict on the Africans and their descendants, that their cup which is nearly full may be completed. I have known tyrants or usurpers of human liberty in different parts of this country to take their fellow creatures, the coloured people, and beat them until they would scarcely leave life in them; what for? Why they say "The black devils had the audacity to be found *making prayers and supplications to the God who made them! ! ! !"*

Yes, I have known small collections of coloured people to have convened together, for no other purpose than to worship God Almighty, in spirit and in truth, to the best of their knowledge; when tyrants, calling themselves *patrols*, would also convene and wait almost in breathless silence for the poor coloured people to commence singing and praying to the Lord our God, as soon as they had commenced, the wretches would burst in upon them and drag them out and commence beating them as they would rattle-snakes—many of whom, they would beat so unmercifully, that they would hardly be able to crawl for weeks and sometimes for months. Yet the American minister send out missionaries to convert the heathen, while they keep us and our children sunk at their feet in the most abject ignorance and wretchedness that ever a people was afflicted with since the world began. Will the Lord suffer this people to proceed much longer? Will he not stop them in their career? Does he regard the heathens abroad, more than the heathens among the Americans? Surely the Americans must believe that God is partial, notwithstanding his Apostle Peter, declared before Cornelius and others that he has no respect to persons, but in every nation he that feareth God and worketh righteousness is accepted with him.—"The word," said he, which God sent unto the children of Israel, preaching peace, "by Jesus Christ, (he is Lord of all.") Have not the Americans the Bible in their hands? Do they believe it? Surely they do not. See how they treat us in open violation of the Bible! ! They no doubt will be greatly offended with me, but if God does not awaken them, it will be, because they are superior to other men, as they have represented themselves to be. Our divine Lord and Master said, "all things whatsoever ye would that men should do unto you, do ye even so unto them." But an American minister, with the Bible in his hand, holds us and our children in the most abject slavery and wretchedness. Now I ask them, would they like for us to hold them and their

With many masters opposed to the Christianization of slaves, there arose a phenomenon that historians have referred to as the "invisible institution," namely the black church that operated outside of the knowledge of whites. In the North and some parts of the South there were sanctioned black churches such as the African Methodist Episcopal denomination, but many slaves did not have access to this type of religious instruction and could not stomach the preaching that some masters exposed their slaves to, as these sermons usually just told slaves not to steal or lie to their masters. Slaves would take to the "hush arbors," fields, cabins, or any other place where they could escape the gaze of their masters and overseers, and there the slaves would worship God in their own way.

children in abject slavery and wretchedness? No says one, that never can be done—your are too abject and ignorant to do it—you are not men—your were made to be slaves to us, to dig up gold and silver for us and our children. Know this, my dear sirs, that although you treat us and our children now, as you do your domestic beast—yet the final result of all future events are known but to God Almighty alone, who rules in the armies of heaven and among the inhabitants of the earth, and who dethrones one earthly king and sits up another, as it seemeth good in his holy sight. We may attribute these vicissitudes to what we please, but the God of armies and of justice rules in heaven and in earth, and the whole American people shall see and know it yet, to their satisfaction. I have known pretended preachers of the gospel of my Master, who not only held us as their natural inheritance, but treated us with as much rigor as any Infidel or Deist in the world—just as though they were intent only on taking our blood and groans to glorify the Lord Jesus Christ. The wicked and ungodly, seeing their preachers treat us with so much cruelty, they say: our preachers, who must be right, if any body are, treat them like brutes, and why cannot we?—They think it is no harm to keep them in slavery and put the whip to them, and why cannot we do the same!—**They being preachers of the gospel of Jesus Christ, if it were any harm, they would surely preach against their oppression and do their utmost to erase it from the country; not only in one or two cities, but one continual cry would be raised in all parts of this confederacy, and would cease only with the complete overthrow of the system of slavery, in every part of the country. But how far the American preachers are from preaching against slavery and oppression, which have carried their country to the brink of a precipice; to save them from plunging down the side of which, will hardly be affected, will appear in the sequel of this paragraph, which I shall narrate just as it transpired.** I

Evangelical Christians, those emphasizing the born-again experience, started coming to the South in the 1740s and 1750s. Initially, evangelicals such as the Baptists and later the Methodists had little success in the South because their message seemed to undermine the system of slavery, as many welcomed blacks into their congregations as equals. In 1784 the Methodist Episcopal Church banned its members from holding slaves, a move that also did not resonate well with southerners at all. By the 1790s, however, evangelicals started to gain more traction in the region by compromising on the issue of slavery, first retreating from their ban and then arguing that slavery and Christianity were compatible. By the 1840s, evangelical Christianity in the South fully supported the institution of slavery, and national denominations had split along regional lines over the issue.

remember a Camp Meeting in South Carolina, for which I embarked in a Steam Boat at Charleston, and having been five or six hours on the water, we at last arrived at the place of hearing, where was a very great concourse of people, who were no doubt, collected together to hear the word of God, (that some had collected barely as spectators to the scene, I will not here pretend to doubt, however, that is left to themselves and their God.) Myself and boat companions, having been there a little while, we were all called up to hear; **I among the rest went up and took my seat—being seated, I fixed myself in a complete position to hear the word of my Saviour and to receive such as I thought was authenticated by the Holy Scriptures; but to my no ordinary astonishment, our Reverend gentleman got up and told us (coloured people) that slaves must be obedient to their masters—must do their duty to their masters or be whipped—the whip was made for the backs of fools, &c.** Here I pause for a moment, to give the world time to consider what was my surprise, to hear such preaching from a minister of my Master, whose very gospel is that of peace and not of blood and whips, as this pretended preacher tried to make us believe. What the American preachers can think of us, I aver this day before my God, I have never been able to define. They have newspapers and monthly periodicals, which they receive in continual succession, but on the pages of which, you will scarcely ever find a paragraph respecting slavery, which is ten thousand times more injurious to this country than all the other evils put together; and which will be the final overthrow of its government, unless something is very speedily done; for their cup is nearly full.—Perhaps they will laugh at or make light of this; but I tell you Americans! that unless you speedily alter your course, *you* and your *Country are gone! ! ! ! ! !* For God Almighty will tear up the very face of the earth! ! ! Will not that very remarkable passage of Scripture be fulfilled on Christian

Southern ministers who were allowed to preach to slaves often drew from a few key biblical passages in their messages, one of them being Ephesians 6:5—"Slaves, be obedient to those who are your masters according to the flesh, with fear and trembling, in the sincerity of your heart, as to Christ; not by way of eyeservice, as men-pleasers, but as slaves of Christ, doing the will of God from the heart."

"Do you think that our blood is hidden from the Lord, because you can hide it from the rest of the world, by sending out missionaries, and by your charitable deeds to the Greeks, Irish, &c.?"

Americans? Hear it Americans! ! "He that is unjust, let him be unjust still:—and he which is filthy, let him be filthy still: and he that is righteous, let him be righteous still: and he that is holy, let him be holy still." I hope that the Americans may hear, but I am afraid that they have done us so much injury, and are so firm in the belief that our Creator made us to be an inheritance to them for ever, that their hearts will be hardened, so that their destruction may be sure. This language, perhaps is too harsh for the American's delicate ears. But Oh Americans! Americans! ! I warn you in the name of the Lord, (whether you will hear, or forbear,) to repent and reform, or you are ruined! ! ! Do you think that our blood is hidden from the Lord, because you can hide it from the rest of the world, by sending out missionaries, and by your charitable deeds to the Greeks, Irish, &c.? Will he not publish your secret crimes on the house top? Even here in Boston, pride and prejudice have got to such a pitch, that in the very houses erected to the Lord, they have built little places for the reception of coloured people, where they must sit during meeting, or keep away from the house of God, and the preachers say nothing about it—much less go into the hedges and highways seeking the lost sheep of the house of Israel, and try to bring them in to their Lord and Master. There are not a more wretched, ignorant, miserable, and abject set of beings in all the world, than the blacks in the Southern and Western sections of this country, under tyrants and devils. The preachers of America cannot see them, but they can send out missionaries to convert the heathens, notwithstanding. Americans! unless you speedily alter your course of proceeding, if God Almighty does not stop you, I say it in his name, that you may go on and do as you please for ever, both in time and eternity—never fear any evil at all! ! ! ! ! ! ! !

ADDITION.—The preachers and people of the United States form societies against Free Masonry and Intemperance, and write against Sabbath breaking, Sabbath mails, Infidelity, &c. &c. But the fountain head, compared with which, all those other evils are comparatively nothing, and from the bloody and murderous head of which, they receive no trifling support, is hardly noticed by the Americans. This is a fair illustration of the state of society in this country—it shows what a bearing *avarice* has upon a people, when they are nearly given up by the Lord to a hard heart and a reprobate mind, in consequence of afflicting their fellow creatures. God suffers some to go on until they are ruined for ever! ! ! ! ! Will it be the case with the whites of the United States of America?—We hope not—we would not wish to see them destroyed notwithstanding, they have and do now treat us more cruel than any people have treated another, on this earth since it came from the hands of its Creator (with the exceptions of the French and the Dutch, they treat us nearly as bad as the Americans of the United States). The will of God must however, in spite of us, *be done.*

The English are the best friends the coloured people have upon earth. Though they have oppressed us a little and have colonies now in the West Indies, which oppress us *sorely.*— Yet notwithstanding they (the English) have done one hundred times more for the melioration of our condition, than all the other nations of the earth put together. The blacks cannot but respect the English as a nation, notwithstanding they have treated us a little cruel.

There is no intelligent *black man* who knows any thing, but esteems a real Englishman, let him see him in what part of the world he will—for they are the greatest benefactors we have upon earth. We have here and there, in other nations, good friends. But as a nation, the English are our friends.

How can the preachers and people of America believe the Bible? Does it teach them any distinction on account of a

"The English are the best friends the coloured people have upon earth."

man's colour? Hearken, Americans! to the injunctions of our Lord and Master, to his humble followers.

"And Jesus came and spake unto them, saying, all power is given unto me in Heaven and in earth.

"Go ye, therefore, and teach all nations, baptizing them in the name of the Father, and of the Son, and of the Holy Ghost.

"Teaching them to observe all things whatsoever I have commanded you; and lo, I am with you always, even unto the end of the world. Amen."

I declare, that the very face of these injunctions appear to be of God and not of man. They do not show the slightest degree of distinction. "Go ye therefore," (says my divine Master) "and teach all nations," (or in other words, all people) "baptizing them in the name of the Father, and of the Son, and of the Holy Ghost." Do you understand the above, Americans? We are a people, notwithstanding many of you doubt it. You have the Bible in your hands, with this very injunction.— Have you been to Africa, teaching the inhabitants thereof the words of the Lord Jesus? "Baptizing them in the name of the Father, and of the Son, and of the Holy Ghost." **Have you not, on the contrary, entered among us, and learnt us the art of throat-cutting, by setting us to fight, one against another, to take each other as prisoners of war, and sell to you for small bits of calicoes, old swords, knives, &c. to make slaves for you and your children?**

This being done, have you not brought us among you, in chains and hand-cuffs, like brutes, and treated us with all the cruelties and rigour your ingenuity could invent, consistent with the laws of your country, which (for the blacks) are tyrannical enough? Can the American preachers appeal

The slave trade was made possible partly by the prevalence of warfare among different African nations, as Europeans would sell guns and other products of war to countries in return for slaves. But the slave trade, while it was made possible by warfare, also helped to promote even more conflicts among various African peoples, and this became one of the chief arguments against slavery by peace advocates such as the Quakers.

unto God, the Maker and Searcher of hearts, and tell him, with the Bible in their hands, that they make no distinction on account of men's colour? Can they say, O God! thou knowest all things—thou knowest that we make no distinction between thy creatures, to whom we have to preach thy Word? Let them answer the Lord; and if they cannot do it in the affirmative, have they not departed from the Lord Jesus Christ, their master? But some may say, that they never had, or were in possession of a religion, which made no distinction, and of course they could not have departed from it. I ask you then, in the name of the Lord, of what kind can your religion be? Can it be that which was preached by our Lord Jesus Christ from Heaven? I believe you cannot be so wicked as to tell him that his Gospel was that of *distinction*. What can the American preachers and people take God to be? Do they believe his words? If they do, do they believe that he will be mocked? Or do they believe, because they are whites and we blacks, that God will have respect to them? Did not God make us all as it seemed best to himself? What right, then, has one of us, to despise another, and to treat him cruel, on account of his colour, which none, but the God who made it can alter? Can there be a greater absurdity in nature, and particularly in a free republican country? But the Americans, having introduced slavery among them, their hearts have become almost seared, as with an hot iron, and God has nearly given them up to believe a lie in preference to the truth! ! ! And I am awfully afraid that pride, prejudice, avarice and blood, will, before long prove the final ruin of this happy republic, or land of *liberty! ! ! !* Can any thing be a greater mockery of religion than the way in which it is conducted by the Americans? It appears as though they are bent only on daring God Almighty to do his best—they chain and handcuff us and our children and drive us around the country like brutes, and go into the house of the God of justice to return him thanks for having aided them in their infernal

"Can any thing be a greater mockery of religion than the way in which it is conducted by the Americans?"

cruelties inflicted upon us. Will the Lord suffer this people to go on much longer, taking his holy name in vain? Will he not stop them, PREACHERS and all? O Americans! Americans! ! I call God—I call angels—I call men, to witness, that your DESTRUCTION *is at hand,* and will be speedily consummated unless you REPENT.

Source: David Walker, *Walker's Appeal, in Four Articles: Together with a Preamble, to the Coloured Citizens of the World, but in Particular, and Very Expressly, to Those of the United States of America, Written in Boston, State of Massachusetts, September 28, 1829* (Boston, 1830).

"I Will Be Heard"

William Lloyd Garrison, "To the Public"

1831

INTRODUCTION

William Lloyd Garrison was the most prominent abolitionist in the United States from the early 1830s through the end of the Civil War. Born in Newburyport, Massachusetts, in 1805, Garrison was apprenticed to the printing trade in 1818 and would become involved in the antislavery movement during the mid-1820s. He began his career as a colonizationist, arguing that the solution to slavery was the removal of blacks from the United States. Garrison quickly retreated from this position and by 1830 was an immediatist, or one who believed that slavery was a sin and should be immediately abolished. In switching his antislavery allegiance, Garrison also switched his methods for abolishing slavery. He started publishing *The Liberator* in 1831 and immediately pronounced his intention to be "as harsh as truth, and as uncompromising as justice." This newspaper would be the longest-running antislavery publication and would play a key role in the movement for close to 35 years. Along with editing *The Liberator*, Garrison was an important strategist who helped organize both the New England Anti-Slavery Society and the American Anti-Slavery Society.

January 1, 1831

In the month of August, I issued proposals for publishing "THE LIBERATOR" in Washington city; but the enterprise, though hailed in different sections of the country, was palsied by public indifference. Since that time, the removal of the Genius of Universal Emancipation to the Seat of Government has rendered less imperious the establishment of a similar periodical in that quarter.

Before moving to Boston, Garrison worked with Benjamin Lundy, the editor of the *Genius of Universal Emancipation,* an antislavery newspaper published in Baltimore. Garrison was arrested for libel while working for that paper and after the incident decided to try a city with a larger and more supportive free black population, which he found in Boston.

During my recent tour for the purpose of exciting the minds of the people by a series of discourses on the subject of slavery, every place that I visited gave fresh evidence of the fact, that a greater revolution in public sentiment was to be effected in the free states—and particularly in New-England—than at the south. I found contempt more bitter, opposition more active, detraction more relentless, prejudice more stubborn, and apathy more frozen, than among slave owners themselves. Of course, there were individual exceptions to the contrary. This state of things afflicted, but did not dishearten me.

I determined, at every hazard, to lift up the standard of emancipation in the eyes of the nation, within sight of Bunker Hill and in the birth place of liberty. That standard is now unfurled; and long may it float, unhurt by the spoliation of time or the missiles of a desperate foe—yea, till every chain be broken, and every bondman set free! Let southern oppressors tremble—let their secret abettors tremble—let their northern apologists tremble—let all the enemies of the persecuted blacks tremble.

I deem the publication of my original Prospectus unnecessary, as it has obtained a wide circulation. **The principles therein inculcated will be steadily pursued in this paper, excepting that I shall not array myself as the political partisan of any man. In defending the great cause of human rights, I wish to derive the assistance of all religions and of all parties.**

Assenting to the "self-evident truth" maintained in the American Declaration of Independence, "that all men are created equal, and endowed by their Creator with certain inalienable rights—among which are life, liberty and the pursuit of happiness," I shall strenuously contend for the immediate enfranchisement of our slave population. In Park-street Church, on the Fourth of July, 1829, in an address on slavery, I unreflectingly assented to the popular but pernicious doctrine of gradual abolition. I seize this opportunity to make a full and unequivocal recantation, and thus publicly to ask pardon of my God, of my country, and of my brethren the poor slaves, for having uttered a sentiment so full of timidity,

The city of Boston is known as the "cradle of liberty" for its role in the American Revolution. Garrison and countless other abolitionists of his generation played on this reputation of Boston in order to advance the antislavery agenda. If Boston wanted to remain true to its Revolutionary heritage, they argued, then its citizens must now support abolitionism.

Garrison here foreshadowed what would come to be central themes of his antislavery agenda. Throughout his abolitionist career he rejected participation in politics because he felt that the U.S. Constitution was "a covenant with death, and an agreement with hell." He would likewise denounce American churches and ministers who remained on the sidelines of the movement or advocated gradual emancipation instead of the immediate emancipation he called for. Garrison's ideas were so influential to the movement that they are collectively referred to as Garrisonianism.

injustice and absurdity. A similar recantation, from my pen, was published in the Genius of Universal Emancipation at Baltimore, in September, 1829. My conscience is now satisfied.

I am aware, that many object to the severity of my language; but is there not cause for severity? I will be as harsh as truth, and as uncompromising as justice. On this subject, I do not wish to think, or speak, or write, with moderation. No! no! Tell a man whose house is on fire, to give a moderate alarm; tell him to moderately rescue his wife from the hands of the ravisher; tell the mother to gradually extricate her babe from the fire into which it has fallen;—but urge me not to use moderation in a cause like the present. I am in earnest—I will not equivocate—I will not excuse—I will not retreat a single inch—AND I WILL BE HEARD. The apathy of the people is enough to make every statue leap from its pedestal, and to hasten the resurrection of the dead.

With these words, Garrison announces the rhetorical style that his paper would follow. For the next 34 years *The Liberator* would condemn slaveholders as thieves, rapists, and murderers, a move that was not generally followed by his abolitionist predecessors.

It is pretended, that I am retarding the cause of emancipation by the coarseness of my invective, and the precipitancy of my measures. The charge is not true. On this question my influence,—humble as it is,—is felt at this moment to a considerable extent, and shall be felt in coming years—not perniciously, but beneficially—not as a curse, but as a blessing; and posterity will bear testimony that I was right. I desire to thank God, that he enables me to disregard "the fear of man which bringeth a snare," and to speak his truth in its simplicity and power. And here I close with this fresh dedication:

Oppression! I have seen thee, face to face,
And met thy cruel eye and cloudy brow;
But thy soul-withering glance I fear not now—
For dread to prouder feelings doth give place

Of deep abhorrence! Scorning the disgrace
Of slavish knees that at thy footstool bow,
I also kneel—but with far other vow
Do hail thee and thy hord of hirelings base:—
I swear, while life-blood warms my throbbing veins,
Still to oppose and thwart, with heart and hand,
Thy brutalising sway—till Afric's chains
Are burst, and Freedom rules the rescued land,—
Trampling Oppression and his iron rod:
Such is the vow I take—SO HELP ME GOD!

Source: William Lloyd Garrison, "To the Public," *The Liberator,* January 1, 1831.

Female Prophets of Abolition

Maria Stewart, "Address Delivered at the African Masonic Hall, Boston"

1833

INTRODUCTION

Like her friend and mentor David Walker, Maria Stewart was a self-educated woman living in Boston during the late 1820s and early 1830s. Stewart was involved in the social life of Boston's black community, becoming a member of Thomas Paul's African Baptist Church. After the death of her husband in 1829, she underwent a conversion experience that led to her involvement in the antislavery cause. Stewart published her first tract, titled "Religion and the Pure Principles of Morality," in William Lloyd Garrison's *The Liberator* in 1831. In the tract, she called for black unity and self-improvement. Stewart achieved many firsts in just a few short years. She became the first woman to speak publicly to mixed audiences of men and women and was indeed the first American woman to lecture publicly about the antislavery movement. Stewart's activism combined a focus on racial equality with a focus on gender equality, and she became one of the first women's rights activists in the nation. While she was a bright light in Boston's black community, many leaders did not appreciate her unconventional approach to activism. In her speech at the African Masonic Hall, she called the black men of Boston to account for the degraded situation in which blacks in general found themselves and was heavily ostracized for her efforts. Stewart soon moved to New York, where she became a teacher and continued her involvement in the antislavery movement.

African rights and liberty is a subject that ought to fire the breast of every free man of color in these United States, and excite in his bosom a lively, deep, decided and heart-felt interest. When I cast my eyes on the long list of illustrious names that are enrolled on the bright annals of fame among the whites, I turn my eyes within, and ask my thoughts, "Where are the names of our illustrious ones?" It must certainly have been for the want of energy on the part of the free people of color, that they have been long willing to bear the yoke of oppression. It must have been the want of ambition and force that has given the whites occasion to say, that our natural abilities are not as good, and our capacities by nature inferior to theirs. They boldly assert, that, did we possess a natural independence of soul, and feel a love for liberty within our breasts, some one of our sable race, long before this, would have testified it, notwithstanding the disadvantages under which we labor. We have made ourselves appear altogether unqualified to speak in our own defense, and are therefore looked upon as objects of pity and commiseration. We have been imposed upon, insulted and derided on every side; and now, if we complain, it is considered as the height of impertinence. We have suffered ourselves to be considered as Bastards, cowards, mean, faint-hearted wretches; and on this account, (not because of our complexion) many despise us, and would gladly spurn us from their presence.

Stewart likens herself to a prophet, as did her friend and mentor David Walker, by saying that she was compelled to come forward. This statement justifies her very act of speaking and giving advice to men, which was not something that women did in public during America's earliest years. Indeed, Stewart was a pioneer in that she was one of the first women to speak to audiences of men in public. Her work on behalf of blacks also contributed to the emerging women's rights movement of the 1830s and 1840s.

These things have fired my soul with a holy indignation, and compelled me thus to come forward; and endeavor to turn their attention to knowledge and improvement; for knowledge is power.

This was perhaps the most radical and controversial part of Stewart's speech, which would not win her any friends in Boston. Here she questions the manhood of the assembled Masons and calls for them to prove that manhood to whites. Rather than settling for menial jobs, she suggests, blacks should seize the chance to meaningfully contribute to society.

I would ask, is it blindness of mind, or at stupidity of soul, or the want of education, that has caused our men who are 60 to 70 years of age, never to let their voices be heard, or nor their hands be raised in behalf of their color? Or has it been for the fear of offending the whites? If it has, O ye fearful ones, throw of your fearfulness, and come forth in the name of the Lord, and in the strength of the God of Justice, and make yourselves useful and active members in society; for they admire a noble and patriotic spirit in others; and should they not admire it in us? If you are men, convince them that you possess the spirit of men; and as your day, so shall your strength be.

Have the sons of Africa no souls? feel they no ambitious desires? shall the chains of ignorance forever confine them? shall the insipid appellation of "clever negroes," or "good creatures," any longer content them? **Where can we find among ourselves the man of science, or a philosopher, or an able statesman, or a counsellor at law? Show me our fearless and brave, our noble and gallant ones. Where are our lecturers on natural history, and our critics in useful knowledge? There may be a few such men among us, but they are rare.**

In advocating for the advancement of blacks, writers such as Stewart sometimes adopted the same mental framework as thinkers such as Thomas Jefferson. Recall his own critiques of blacks for their lack of accomplishments in America, critiques based largely on intellectual achievements. Stewart in a sense accepts the logic of Jefferson and calls for blacks to prove their humanity through intellectual achievement.

It is true, our fathers bled and died in the revolutionary war, and others fought bravely under the command of Jackson, in defense of liberty. But where is the man that has distinguished himself in these modern days by acting wholly in the defense of African rights and liberty? **There was one, although he sleeps, his memory lives.**

Stewart is most likely referring to David Walker, an important source of inspiration for her writings and lectures.

I am sensible that there are many highly intelligent gentlemen of color in those United States, in the force of whose arguments, doubtless, I should discover my inferiority; but if they are blest with wit and talent, friends and fortune, why have they not made themselves men of eminence, by striving to take all the reproach that is cast upon the people of color, and in endeavoring to alleviate the woes of their brethren in bondage? Talk, without effort, is nothing; you are abundantly capable, gentlemen, of making yourselves men of distinction; and this gross neglect, on your part, causes my blood to boil within me. Here is the grand cause which hinders the rise and progress of the people of color. It is their want of laudable ambition and requisite courage.

Individuals have been distinguished according to their genius and talents, ever since the first formation of man,

Stewart here combines two intellectual trends in antebellum America. The first is the use of African history as an argument for racial equality. Egypt, Ethiopia, and other African nations, the argument went, contributed immensely to the rise of civilization, proving that skin color is not a badge of inferiority. The second intellectual trend that she draws from is providentialism, the notion that God repays nations and peoples according to their works. Blacks have fallen from their past glory because of sin, she suggests, but will soon return, as Psalm 68:31 argues.

and will continue to be while the world stands. The different grades rise to honor and respectability as their merits may deserve. **History informs us that we sprung from one of the most learned nations of the whole earth; from the seat, if not the parent of science; yes, poor, despised Africa was once the resort of sages and legislators of other nations, was esteemed the school for learning, and the most illustrious men in Greece flocked thither for instruction. But it was our gross sins and abominations that provoked the Almighty to frown thus heavily upon us, and give our glory unto others. Sin and prodigality have caused the downfall of nations, kings and emperors; and were it not that God in wrath remembers mercy; we might indeed despair; but a promise is left us; "Ethiopia shall again stretch forth her hands unto God."**

But it is of no use for us to boast that we sprung from this learned and enlightened nation, for this day a thick mist of moral gloom hangs over millions of our race. Our condition as a people has been low for hundreds of years, and it will continue to be so, unless, by true piety and virtue, we strive to regain that which we have lost. White Americans, by their prudence, economy and exertions, have sprung up and become one of the most flourishing nations in the world, distinguished for their knowledge of the arts and sciences, for their polite literature. While our minds are vacant, and starving for want of knowledge, theirs are filled to overflowing. Most of our color have been taught to stand in fear of the white man, from their earliest infancy, to work as soon as they could walk, and call "master," before they scarce could lisp the name of mother. Continual fear and laborious servitude have in some degree lessened in us that natural force and energy which belong to man; or else, in defiance of opposition, our men, before this, would have nobly and boldly contended for their rights. **But give the man of color an equal opportunity with the white from the cradle to manhood, and from manhood to the grave, and you would discover the dignified statesman, the man of science, and the philosopher. But there is no such opportunity for the sons of Africa, and I fear that our powerful one's are fully determined that there never shall be.**

Stewart posits her environmental theory of race. Drawing from thinkers such as Princeton theologian Samuel Stanhope Smith, environmentalists such as Stewart argued that one's surroundings—not one's natural characteristics—determined one's place in life. Any perceived racial differences were the result of environmental influences and could be changed.

For bid, ye Powers on high, that it should any longer be said that our men possess no force. O ye sons of Africa, when will your voices be heard in our legislative halls, in defiance of your enemies, contending for equal rights and liberty? How can you, when you reflect from what you have fallen, refrain from crying mightily unto God, to turn away from us the fierceness of his anger, and remember our transgressions against us no more forever. But a God of infinite purity will not regard the prayers of those who hold religion in one hand, and prejudice, sin and pollution in the other; he will not regard the prayers of self-righteousness and hypocrisy. Is it possible, I exclaim, that for the want of knowledge, we have labored for hundreds of years to support others, and been content to receive what they chose to give us in return? Cast your eyes about, look as far as you can see; all, all is owned by the lordly white, except here and there a lowly dwelling which the man of color, midst deprivations, fraud and opposition, has been scarce able to procure. Like king Solomon, who put neither nail nor hammer to the temple, yet received the praise; so also have the white Americans gained themselves a name, like the names of the great men that are in the earth, while in reality we have been their principal foundation and support. We have pursued the shadow, they have obtained the substance; we have performed the labor they have received the profits; we have planted the vines, they have eaten the fruits of them.

Stewart's position is known as the politics of respectability. From the late 18th century onward, many black leaders argued that it was vice and sin that held blacks in their inferior place. If they emulated the perceived values of middle-class whites—thrift, temperance, and hard work—then whites would recognize their humanity and equality, it was believed. The politics of respectability has remained an important strain of black intellectual life to the present day.

I would implore our men, and especially our rising youth, to flee from the gambling board and the dance-hall; for we are poor, and have no money to throw away. I do not consider dancing as criminal in itself, but it is astonishing to me that our young men are so blind to their own interest and the future welfare of their children, as to spend their hard earnings for this frivolous amusement; for it has been carried on among us to such an unbecoming extent, that it has became absolutely disgusting. "Faithful are the wounds of a friend, but the kisses of an enemy are deceitful." Had those men among us, who have had an opportunity, turned their attention as assiduously to mental and moral improvement as they have to gambling and dancing, I might have remained quietly at home, and they stood contending in my place.

These polite accomplishments will never enroll your names on the bright annals of tune, who admire the belle void of intellectual knowledge, or applaud the dandy that talks largely on politics, without striving to assist his fellow in the revolution, when the nerves and muscles of every other man forced him into the field of action. You have a right to rejoice, and to let your hearts cheer you in the days of your youth; yet remember that for all these things, God will bring you into judgment. Then, O ye sons of Africa, turn your mind from these perishable objects, and contend for the cause of God and the rights of man. **Form yourselves into temperance societies. There are temperate men among you; then why will you any longer neglect to strive, by your example, to suppress vice in all its abhorrent forms? You have been told repeatedly of the glorious results arising from temperance, and can you bear to see the whites arising in honor and respectability, without endeavoring to grasp after that honor and respectability also?**

Aside from the abolitionist movement, temperance was the largest social movement of 19th-century America. Alcoholism was rampant in the first half of the century and was blamed for a host of social problems, including prostitution, poverty, and domestic abuse. Stewart argues that the temperance and antislavery movements are interconnected, as whites will never respect blacks who are mired in drunkenness.

But I forbear. Let our money, instead of being thrown away as heretofore, be appropriated for schools and seminaries of learning for our children and youth. We ought to follow the example of the whites in this respect. Nothing would raise our respectability, add to our peace and happiness, and reflect so much honor upon us, as to be ourselves the promoters of temperance, and the supporters, as far as we are able, of useful and scientific knowledge. The rays of light and knowledge have been hid from our view; we have been taught to consider ourselves as scarce superior to the brute creation; and have performed the most laborious part of American drudgery. Had we as a people received, one half the early advantages the whites have received, I would defy the government of these United States to deprive us any longer of our rights.

I am informed that the agent of the Colonization Society has recently formed an association of young men, for the purpose of influencing those of us to go to Liberia who may feel disposed. The colonizationists are blind to their own interest, for should the nations of the earth make war with America, they would find their forces much weakened by our absence; or should we remain here, can our "brave soldiers," and "fellow-citizens," as they were termed in time of calamity, condescend to defend the rights of the whites, and be again deprived of their own, or sent to Liberia in return? Or, if the colonizationists are real friends to Africa, let them expend the money which they collect, in erecting a college to educate her injured sons in this land of gospel light and liberty; for it would be most thankfully received on our part, and convince us of the truth of their professions, and save time, expense and anxiety. Let them place before us noble objects, worthy of pursuit, and see if we prove ourselves to be those unambitious negroes they term us. But ah! methinks their hearts are so frozen towards us, they had rather their money should be sunk in the ocean than to administer it to our relief; and I fear, if they dared, like Pharaoh, king of Egypt, they would order every male child among us to be drowned. But the most high God is still as able to subdue the lofty pride of these white Americans, as He was the heart of that ancient rebel. They say, though we are looked upon as things, yet we sprang from a scientific people. Had our men the requisite force and energy, they would soon convince them by their efforts both in public and private, that they were men, or things in the shape of men. Well may the colonizationists laugh us to scorn for our negligence; well may they cry, "Shame to the sons of Africa." As the burden of the Israelites was too great for Moses to bear, so also is our burden too great for Moses to bear, so also is our burden too great for our noble advocate to bear. You must feel interested, my brethren, in what he undertakes, and hold up his hands by your good works, or in spite of himself, his soul will become discouraged, and his heart will die within him; for he has, as it were, the strong bulls of Bashan to contend with.

The 1830s was a period of an increased sense of urgency among antislavery reformers. The movement had begun in the North during the American Revolutionary era, but slavery continued to grow in the southern states. Stewart, Walker, Garrison, and others began to argue for immediate action to end slavery now as opposed to some distant time in the future.

It is of no use for us to wait any longer for a generation of well educated men to arise. We have slumbered and slept too long already; the day is far spent; the night of death approaches; and you have sound sense and good judgement sufficient to begin with, if you feel disposed to make a right use of it. Let every man of color throughout the United States, who possesses the spirit and principles of a man, sign a petition to Congress, to abolish slavery in the District of Columbia, and grant you the rights and privileges of common free citizens; for if you had had faith as a grain of mustard seed, long before this the mountains of prejudice might have been removed.

We are all sensible that the Anti-Slavery Society has taken hold of the arm of our whole population, in order to raise

them out of the mire. Now all we have to do is, by a spirit
of virtuous ambition to strive to raise ourselves; and I am
happy to have it in my power thus publicly to say, that the
colored inhabitants of this city, in some respects, are beginning to improve. Had the free people of color in these United
States nobly and boldly contended for their rights, and
showed a natural genius and talent, although not so brilliant
as some; had they help up, encouraged and patronized each
other, nothing could have hindered us from being a thriv-
ing and flourishing people. There has been a fault among
us. The reason why our distinguished men have not made
themselves more influential is, because they fear that the
strong current of opposition through which they must pass,
would cause their downfall and prove their overthrew. And
what gives rise to this opposition? Envy. And what has it
amounted to? Nothing. And who are the cause of it? Our
whited sepulchers, who want to be great, and don't know
how; who love to be called of men 'Rabbi, Rabbi,' who put
on false sanctity, and humble themselves to their brethren,
for the sake of acquiring the highest place in the synagogue,
and the uppermost seats at the feast. You, dearly beloved,
who are the genuine followers of our Lord Jesus Christ, the
salt of the earth and the light of the world, are not so culpable. As I told you, in the very first of my writing, I tell you
again, I am but as a drop in the bucket—as one particle of the
small dust of the earth. God will surely raise up those among
us who will plead the cause of virtue, and the pure principles
of morality, more eloquently than I am able to do.

It appears to me that America has become like the great city
of Babylon, for she has boasted in her heart,—I sit a queen,
and am no widow, and shall see no sorrow? She is indeed
a seller of slaves and the souls of men; she has made the
Africans drunk with the wine of her fornication; she has put
them completely beneath her feet, and she means to keep

them there; her right hand supports the reins of government, and her left hand the wheel of power, and she is determined not to let go her grasp. But many powerful sons and daughters of Africa will shortly arise, who will put down vice and immorality among us, and declare by Him that sitteth upon the throne, that they will have their rights; and if refused, I am afraid they will spread horror and devastation around. I believe that the oppression of injured Africa has come up before the Majesty of Heaven; and when our cries shall have reached the ears of the Most High, it will be a tremendous day for the people of this land; for strong is the arm of the Lord God Almighty.

Life has almost lost its charms for me; death has lost its sting and the grave its terrors; and at times I have a strong desire to depart and dwell with Christ, which is far better. Let me entreat my white brethren to awake and save our sons from dissipation, and our daughters from ruin. Lend the hand of assistance to feeble merit, plead the cause of virtue among our sable race; so shall our curses upon you be turned into blessings; and though you should endeavor to drive us from these shores, still we will cling to you the more firmly; nor will we attempt to rise above you: we will presume to be called your equals only.

The unfriendly whites first drove the native American from his much loved home. Then they stole our fathers from their peaceful and quiet dwellings, and brought them hither, and made bond-men and bond-women of them and their little ones; they have obliged our brethren to labor, kept them in utter ignorance, nourished them in vice, and raised them in degradation; and now that we have enriched their soil, and filled their coffers, they say that we are not capable of becoming like white men, and that we never can rise to respectability in this country. They would drive us to a strange land.

But before I go, the bayonet shall pierce me through. African rights and liberty is a subject that ought to fire the breast of every free man of color in these United States, and excite in his bosom a lively, deep, decided and heart-felt interest.

Source: Maria Stewart, "Address Delivered at the African Masonic Hall, Boston," *The Liberator,* May 4, 1833, 72.

Southern Abolitionists

Angelina Grimké, *An Appeal to the Christian Women of the South*

1836

INTRODUCTION

Angelina Grimké followed the example set by Maria Stewart in combining abolitionism with women's rights activism. Grimké was born on a slave plantation in Charleston, South Carolina, and converted from her father's Episcopalian faith to Presbyterianism in 1826. When she offered a resolution that her church should condemn slavery in 1829 it was declined, and she soon converted to the Quaker faith. Since the time of the Germantown petition in 1688, Quakers had been at the forefront of American abolitionism, and while the entire religious body was not as involved in the cause by the 1830s, individuals such as Grimké remained prominent activists. She moved to Philadelphia in 1827 and along with her sister became one of the most prominent female activists in the nation, traveling the country on speaking tours, writing books and articles, and helping organize antislavery societies. Here Grimké writes to southern women urging them to take action and do what they can to abolish slavery.

Many female activists in the antislavery movement and other reform efforts justified their work by appealing to biblical examples of women who had achieved greatness in their day. These women included Esther, Abraham's wife Sarah, and the Virgin Mary.

"Then Mordecai commanded to answer Esther, Think not within thyself that thou shalt escape in the king's house more than all the Jews. For if thou altogether holdest thy peace at this time, then shall there enlargement and deliverance arise to the Jews from another place: but thou and thy father's house shall be destroyed: and who knoweth whether thou art come to the kingdom for such a time as this. And Esther bade them return Mordecai this answer: and so will I go in unto the king, which is not according to law, and if I perish, I perish."
Esther IV. 13–16.

RESPECTED FRIENDS,

It is because I feel a deep and tender interest in your present and eternal welfare that I am willing thus publicly to address

121

you. Some of you have loved me as a relative, and some have felt bound to me in Christian sympathy, and Gospel fellowship; and even when compelled by a strong sense of duty, to break those outward bonds of union which bound us together as members of the same community, and members of the same religious denomination, you were generous enough to give me credit, for sincerity as a Christian, though you believed I had been most strangely deceived. I thanked you then for your kindness, and I ask you now, for the sake of former confidence and former friendship, to read the following pages in the spirit of calm investigation and fervent prayer. It is because you have known me, that I write thus unto you.

But there are other Christian women scattered over the Southern States, a very large number of whom have never seen me, and never heard my name, and who feel no interest whatever in me. But I feel an interest in you, as branches of the same vine from whose root I daily draw the principle of spiritual vitality—Yes! Sisters in Christ I feel an interest in you, and often has the secret prayer arisen on your behalf, Lord "open thou their eyes that they may see wondrous things out of thy Law"—It is then, because I do feel and do pray for you, that I thus address you upon a subject about which of all others, perhaps you would rather not hear any thing; but, "would to God ye could bear with me a little in my folly, and indeed bear with me, for I am jealous over you with godly jealousy." **Be not afraid then to read my appeal; it is not written in the heat of passion or prejudice, but in that solemn calmness which is the result of conviction and duty. It is true, I am going to tell you unwelcome truths, but I mean to speak those truths in love, and remember Solomon says, "faithful are the wounds of a friend." I do not believe the time has yet come when Christian women**

Both Angelina Grimké and her sister Sarah grew up in the South and left because of their distaste for the institution of slavery. So while Angelina here writes as a northern abolitionist, she is still claiming the status of an insider, both religiously and as one who has roots in the South.

Grimké may have been setting herself up as a counterpoint to abolitionists such as William Lloyd Garrison. While Garrison had no qualms about using harsh language to depict slaveholders, Grimké means to speak her arguments "in tenderness and love."

"will not endure sound doctrine," even on the subject of Slavery, if it is spoken to them in tenderness and love, therefore I now address you.

To all of you then, known or unknown, relatives or strangers, (for you are all one in Christ,) I would speak. **I have felt for you at this time, when unwelcome light is pouring in upon the world on the subject of slavery; light which even Christians would exclude, if they could, from our country, or at any rate from the southern portion of it, saying, as its rays strike the rock bound coasts of New England and scatter their warmth and radiance over her hills and valleys and from thence travel onward over the Palisades of the Hudson, and down the soft flowing waters of the Delaware and gild the waves of the Potomac, "hitherto shalt thou come and no further;" I know that even professors of His name who has been emphatically called the "Light of the world" would, if they could, build a wall of adamant around the Southern States whose top might reach unto heaven, in order to shut out the light which is bounding from mountain to mountain and from the hills to the plains and valleys beneath, through the vast extent of our Northern States.**

The light that Grimké refers to is a metaphor for increasing antislavery sentiment. She could mean that the country is being enlightened about slavery in the scientific sense, referring to the Age of Enlightenment, or she could just as easily be referring to the Inner Light that Quaker theology posits as being present in all people, a light that provides a direct connection to God's will.

But believe me, when, I tell you, their attempts will be as utterly fruitless as were the efforts of the builders of Babel; and why? Because moral, like natural light, is so extremely subtle in its nature as to overleap all human barriers, and laugh at the puny efforts of man to control it. All the excuses and palliations of this system must inevitably be swept away, just as other "refuges of lies" have been, by the irresistible torrent of a rectified public opinion. "The supporters of the slave system," says Jonathan Dymond in his admirable work on the Principles of Morality, "will hereafter be regarded with the same public feeling, as he who was an advocate for the slave trade now is." It will be, and that very soon, clearly perceived and fully acknowledged by all the virtuous and the candid, that in principle it is as sinful to hold a human being in bondage who has been born in Carolina, as one who has been born in Africa. All that sophistry of argument which has been employed to prove, that although it is sinful to send to Africa to procure men and women as slaves, who, have never been in slavery, that still, it is not sinful to keep those in bondage who have come down by inheritance, will be utterly overthrown. **We must come back to the good old doctrine of our fore fathers who declared to the world, "this self evident truth that all men are created equal, and that they have certain inalienable rights among which are, life, liberty, and the pursuit of happiness." It is even a greater absurdity to suppose a man can be legally born a slave under our free Republican Government, than under the petty despotisms of barbarian Africa. If then, we have no right to enslave an African, surely we can have none to enslave an American; if a self evident truth that all men every where and of every color are born equal, and have an inalienable right to liberty, then it is equally true that no man can be born a slave, and no man can ever rightfully be reduced to involuntary bondage and held as a slave, however fair may be the claim of his master or mistress through wills and title-deeds.**

By the mid-1830s, the transatlantic slave trade had been abolished for about 30 years. While public opinion in both the North and South seemed to be against slave trading, slavery was still widely accepted. Grimké believes that in due time the nation will feel the same disgust for slavery that it now feels for slave trading.

But after all, it may be said, our fathers were certainly mistaken, for the Bible sanctions Slavery, and that is the highest authority. Now the Bible is my ultimate appeal in all matters of faith and practice, and it is to this test I am anxious to bring the subject at issue between us. Let us then begin with Adam and examine the charter of privileges which was given to him. "Have dominion over the fish of the sea, and over the fowl of the air, and over every living thing that moveth upon the earth." In the eighth Psalm we have a still fuller description of this charter which through Adam was given to all mankind. "Thou madest him to have dominion over the works of thy hands; thou hast put all things under his feet. All sheep and oxen, yea, and the beasts of the field, the fowl of the air, the fish of the sea, and whatsoever passeth through the paths of the seas." And after the flood when this charter of human rights was renewed, we find no additional power vested in man. "And the fear of you and the dread of you shall be upon every beast of the earth, and every fowl of the air, and upon all that moveth upon the earth, and upon all the fishes of the sea, into your hand are they delivered." In this charter, although the different kinds of irrational beings are so particularly enumerated, and supreme dominion over all of them is granted, yet man is never vested with this dominion over his fellow man; he was never told that any of the human species were put under his feet; it was only all things, and man, who was created in the image of his Maker, never can properly be termed a thing, though the laws of Slave States do call him "a chattel personal;" Man then, I assert never was put under the feet of man, by that first charter of human rights which was given by God, to the Fathers of the Antediluvian and Postdiluvian worlds, therefore this doctrine of equality is based on the Bible.

But it may be argued, that in the very chapter of Genesis from which I have last quoted, will be found the curse pronounced upon Canaan, by which his posterity was consigned to servitude under his brothers Shem and Japheth. **I know this prophecy was uttered, and was most fearfully and wonderfully fulfilled, through the immediate descendants of Canaan, i.e. the Canaanites, and I do not know but it has been through all the children of Ham, but I do**

Grimké starts by attempting to undermine two of the most prominent religious justifications for slavery, namely that it is sanctioned in the Bible and covered by the Curse of Ham. The Curse of Ham was a prophecy, she notes, and thus was not so much a call for action as a prediction that would not excuse any sins committed, sins such as man stealing and enslaving others.

know that prophecy does not tell us what ought to be, but what actually does take place, ages after it has been delivered, and that if we justify America for enslaving the children of Africa, we must also justify Egypt for reducing the children of Israel to bondage, for the latter was foretold as explicitly as the former. I am well aware that prophecy has often been urged as an excuse for Slavery, but be not deceived, the fulfilment of prophecy will not cover one sin in the awful day of account.

Hear what our Saviour says on this subject; "it must needs be that offences come, but woe unto that man through whom they come"—Witness some fulfilment of this declaration in the tremendous destruction of Jerusalem, occasioned by that most nefarious of all crimes the crucifixion of the Son of God. Did the fact of that event having been foretold, exculpate the Jews from sin in perpetrating it; No—for hear what the Apostle Peter says to them on this subject, "Him being delivered by the determinate counsel and foreknowledge of God ye have taken, and by wicked hands have crucified and slain." Other striking instances might be adduced, but these will suffice.

But it has been urged that the patriarchs held slaves, and therefore, slavery is right. Do you really believe that patriarchal servitude was like American slavery? Can you believe it? If so, read the history of these primitive fathers of the church and be undeceived. Look at Abraham, though so great a man, going to the herd himself and fetching a calf from thence and serving it up with his own hands, for the entertainment of his guests. Look at Sarah, that princess as her name signifies, baking cakes upon the hearth. If the servants they had were like Southern slaves, would they have performed such comparatively menial offices for themselves? Hear too the plaintive lamentation of Abraham

"But it has been urged that the patriarchs held slaves, and therefore, slavery is right. Do you really believe that patriarchal servitude was like American slavery?"

"Such was the footing upon which Abraham was with his servants, that he trusted them with arms. Are slaveholders willing to put swords and pistols into the hands of their slaves?"

when he feared he should have no son to bear his name down to posterity. "Behold thou hast given me no seed, &c, one born in my house is mine heir." From this it appears that one of his servants was to inherit his immense estate. Is this like Southern slavery? I leave it to your own good sense and candor to decide. Besides, such was the footing upon which Abraham was with his servants, that he trusted them with arms. Are slaveholders willing to put swords and pistols into the hands of their slaves? He was as a father among his servants; what are planters and masters generally among theirs? When the institution of circumcision was established, Abraham was commanded thus; "He that is eight days old shall be circumcised among you, every man-child in your generations; he that is born in the house, or bought with money of any stranger which is not of thy seed." And to render this command with regard to his servants still more impressive it is repeated in the very next verse; and herein we may perceive the great care which was taken by God to guard the rights of servants even under this "dark dispensation." What too was the testimony given to the faithfulness of this eminent patriarch. "For I know him that he will command his children and his household after him, and they shall keep the way of the Lord to do justice and judgment." Now my dear friends many of you believe that circumcision has been superseded by baptism in the Church; Are you careful to have all that are born in your house or bought with money of any stranger, baptized? Are you as faithful as Abraham to command your household to keep the way of the Lord? I leave it to your own consciences to decide. Was patriarchal servitude then like American Slavery?

But I shall be told, God sanctioned Slavery, yea commanded Slavery under the Jewish Dispensation. Let us examine this subject calmly and prayerfully. I admit that a species of servitude was permitted to the Jews, but in studying the subject

I have been struck with wonder and admiration at perceiving how carefully the servant was guarded from violence, injustice and wrong. I will first inform you how these servants became servants, for I think this a very important part of our subject. From consulting Horne, Calmet and the Bible, I find there were six different ways by which the Hebrews became servants legally.

1. If reduced to extreme poverty, a Hebrew might sell himself, i.e. his services, for six years, in which case he received the purchase money himself. Lev. xxv, 39.

2. A father might sell his children as servants, i.e. his daughters, in which circumstance it was understood the daughter was to be the wife or daughter-in-law of the man who bought her, and the father received the price. In other words, Jewish women were sold as white women were in the first settlement of Virginia—as wives, not as slaves. Ex. xxi, 7.

3. Insolvent debtors might be delivered to their creditors as servants. 2 Kings iv, 1.

4. Thieves not able to make restitution for their thefts, were sold for the benefit of the injured person. Ex. xxii, 3.

5. They might be born in servitude. Ex. xxi, 4.

6. If a Hebrew had sold himself to a rich Gentile, he might be redeemed by one of his brethren at any time the money was offered; and he who redeemed him, was not to take advantage of the favor thus conferred, and rule over him with rigor. Lev. xxv, 47–55.

Before going into an examination of the laws by which these servants were protected, I would just ask whether

Grimké attempts to demolish another religious argument—namely that the Bible permits slavery—by arguing that it permitted servitude but not slavery akin to what Americans have. Slaves of the Hebrews had many legal rights and protections under biblical law, while that was not the case for American slaves, as we saw with the opinion of Thomas Ruffin where he posited that slaves must be completely under the will and control of their masters.

American slaves have become slaves in any of the ways in which the Hebrews became servants. Did they sell themselves into slavery and receive the purchase money into their own hands? No! Did they become insolvent, and by their own imprudence subject themselves to be sold as slaves? No! Did they steal the property of another, and were they sold to make restitution for their crimes? No! Did their present masters, as an act of kindness, redeem them from some heathen tyrant to whom they have sold themselves in the dark hour of adversity? No! Were they born in slavery? No! No! not according to Jewish Law, for the servants who were born in servitude among them, were born of parents who had sold themselves for six years: Ex. xxi, 4.

Were the female slaves of the South sold by their fathers? How shall I answer this question? Thousands and tens of thousands never were, their fathers never have received the poor compensation of silver or gold for the tears and toils, the suffering, and anguish, and hopeless bondage of their daughters. They labor day by day, and year by year, side by side, in the same field, if haply their daughters are permitted to remain on the same plantation with them, instead of being as they often are, separated from their parents and sold into distant states, never again to meet on earth. But do the fathers of the South ever sell their daughters? My heart beats, and my hand trembles, as I write the awful affirmative, Yes! The fathers of this Christian land often sell their daughters, not as Jewish parents did, to be the wives and daughters-in-law of the man who buys them, but to be the abject slaves of petty tyrants and irresponsible masters. Is it not so, my friends? I leave it to your own candor to corroborate my assertion. Southern slaves then have not become slaves in any of the six different ways in which Hebrews became servants, and I hesitate not to say that American masters cannot according to Jewish law substantiate their claim to the men, women, or children they now hold in bondage.

But there was one way in which a Jew might illegally be reduced to servitude; it was this, he might be stolen and afterwards sold as a slave, as was Joseph. To guard most effectually against this dreadful crime of mansteal-ing, God enacted this severe law. 'He that stealeth a man and selleth him, or if he be found in his hand, he shall surely be put to death.' As I have tried American Slavery by legal Hebrew servitude, and found, (to your surprise, perhaps,) that Jewish law cannot justify the slaveholder's claim, let us now try it by illegal Hebrew bondage. Have the Southern slaves then been stolen? If they did not sell themselves into bondage; if they were not sold as insolvent debtors or as thieves; if they were not redeemed from a heathen master to whom they had sold themselves; if they were not born in servitude according to Hebrew law; and if the females were not sold by their fathers as wives and daughters-in-law to those who purchased them; then what shall we say of them? What can we say of them? But that according to Hebrew Law they have been stolen.

But I shall be told that the Jews had other servants who were absolute slaves. Let us look a little into this also. They had other servants who were procured in two different ways.

1. Captives taken in war were reduced to bondage instead of being killed but we are not told that their children were enslaved Deut. xx, 14.

2. Bondmen and bond maids might be bought from the heathen round about them; these were left by fathers to their children after them, but it does not appear that the

> *"To guard most effectually against this dreadful crime of manstealing, God enacted this severe law. 'He that stealeth a man and selleth him, or if he be found in his hand, he shall surely be put to death.'"*

children of these servants ever were reduced to servitude. Lev. xxv, 44.

I will now try the right of the southern planter by the claims of Hebrew masters over their heathen slaves. Were the southern slaves taken captive in war? No! Were they bought from the heathen? No! for surely, no one will now vindicate the slave-trade so far as to assert that slaves were bought from the heathen who were obtained by that system of piracy. The only excuse for holding southern slaves is that they were born in slavery, but we have seen that they were not born in servitude as Jewish servants were, and that the children of heathen slaves were not legally subjected to bondage even under the Mosaic Law. How then have the slaves of the South been obtained?

I will next proceed to an examination of those laws which were enacted in order to protect the Hebrew and the Heathen servant; for I wish you to understand that both are protected by Him, of whom it is said "his mercies are over all his works." I will first speak of those which secured the rights of Hebrew servants. This code was headed thus:

1. Thou shalt not rule over him with rigor, but shalt fear thy God.

2. If thou buy a Hebrew servant, six years shall he serve, and in the seventh year he shall go out free for nothing. Ex. xxi, 2.

3. If he come in by himself, he shall go out by himself; if he were married, then his wife shall go out with him.

4. If his master have given him a wife and she have borne him sons and daughters, the wife and her children shall be his master's, and he shall go out by himself.

"The only excuse for holding southern slaves is that they were born in slavery, but we have seen that they were not born in servitude as Jewish servants were, and that the children of heathen slaves were not legally subjected to bondage even under the Mosaic Law."

5. If the servant shall plainly say, I love my master, my wife, and my children; I will not go out free; then his master shall bring him unto the Judges, and he shall bring him to the door, or unto the door-post, and his master shall bore his car through with an awl, and he shall serve him forever. Ex. xxi, 5–6.

6. If a man smite the eye of his servant, or the eye of his maid, that it perish, he shall let him go free for his eye's sake. And if he smite out his man servant's tooth or his maid servant's tooth he shall let him go free for his tooth's sake. Ex. xxi, 26, 27.

7. On the Sabbath rest was secured to servants by the fourth commandment. Ex. xx, 10.

8. Servants were permitted to unite with their masters three times in every year in celebrating the Passover, the feast of Pentecost, and the feast of Tabernacles; every male throughout the land was to appear before the Lord at Jerusalem with a gift; here the bond and the free stood on common ground. Deut. xvi.

9. If a man smite his servant or his maid with a rod, and he die under his hand, he shall be surely punished. Notwithstanding, if he continue a day or two, he shall not be punished, for he is his money. Ex. xxi, 20, 21.

From these laws we learn that Hebrew men servants were bound to serve their masters only six years, unless their attachment to their employers, their wives and children, should induce them to wish to remain in servitude, in which case, in order to prevent the possibility of deception on the part of the master, the servant was first taken before the magistrate, where he openly declared

Another major argument against American slavery is that since American slaves are in bondage for life, their condition vastly differs from that of biblical slaves, who were not enslaved for life and whose children were not considered slaves. Since the two differ in this important respect, Grimké suggests, American slavery cannot be justified with recourse to the Bible.

his intention of continuing in his master's service, (probably a public register was kept of such) he was then conducted to the door of the house, (in warm climates doors are thrown open,) and there his ear was publicly bored and by submitting to this operation he testified his willingness to serve him forever, i.e. during his life, for Jewish Rabbins who must have understood Jewish slavery, (as it is called,) "affirm that servants were set free at the death of their masters and did not descend to their heirs:" or that he was to serve him until the year of Jubilee, when all servants were set at liberty.

To protect servants from violence, it was ordained that if a master struck out the tooth or destroyed the eye of a servant, that servant immediately became free, for such an act of violence evidently showed he was unfit to possess the power of a master, and therefore that power was taken from him. All servants enjoyed the rest of the Sabbath and partook of the privileges and festivities of the three great Jewish Feasts; and if a servant died under the infliction of chastisement, his master was surely to be punished. As a tooth for a tooth and life for life was the Jewish law, of course he was punished with death. I know that great stress has been laid upon the following verse: "Notwithstanding, if he continue a day or two, he shall not be punished, for he is his money."

Slaveholders, and the apologists of slavery, have eagerly seized upon this little passage of scripture, and held it up as the masters' Magna Charta, by which they were licensed by God himself to commit the greatest outrages upon the defenceless victims of their oppression. But, my friends, was it designed to be so? If our Heavenly Father would protect by law the eye and the tooth of a Hebrew servant, can we for a moment believe that he would abandon, that same servant to the brutal rage of a master who would destroy even life itself. Do we not rather see in this, the only law which protected masters, and was it not right that in case of the death of a servant, one or two days after chastisement was inflicted, to which other circumstances might have contributed, that the master should be protected when, in all probability, he never intended to produce so fatal a result? But the phrase "he is his money" has been adduced to show that Hebrew servants were regarded as mere things, "chattels personal;" if so, why were so many laws made to secure their rights as men, and to ensure their rising into equality and freedom? If they were mere things, why were they regarded as responsible beings, and one law made for them as well as for their masters? But I pass on now to the consideration of how the female Jewish servants were protected by law.

1. If she please not her master, who hath betrothed her to himself, then shall he let her be redeemed: to sell her unto another nation he shall have no power, seeing he hath dealt deceitfully with her.

2. If he have betrothed her unto his son, he shall deal with her after the manner of daughters.

3. If he take him another wife, her food, her raiment, and her duty of marriage, shall he not diminish.

4. If he do not these three unto her, then shall she go out free without money.

On these laws I will give you Calmet's remarks; "A father could not sell his daughter as a slave, according to the Rabbins, until she was at the age of puberty, and unless he were reduced to the utmost indigence. Besides when

"If they were mere things, why were they regarded as responsible beings, and one law made for them as well as for their masters?"

"Thus were the rights of female servants carefully secured by law under the Jewish Dispensation; and now I would ask, are the rights of female slaves at the South thus secured?"

a master bought an Israelitish girl, it was always with the presumption that he would take her to wife. Hence Moses adds, 'if she please not her master, and he does not think fit to marry her, he shall set her at liberty,' or according to the Hebrew, 'he shall let her be redeemed.' 'To sell her to another nation he shall have no power, seeing he hath dealt deceitfully with her;' as to the engagement implied, at least of taking her to wife. 'If he have betrothed her unto his son, he shall deal with her after the manner of daughters, i.e. he shall take care that his son uses her as his wife, that he does not despise, or maltreat her. If he make his son marry another wife, he shall give her dowry, her clothes and compensation for her virginity; if he does none of these three, she shall go out free without money." Thus were the rights of female servants carefully secured by law under the Jewish Dispensation; and now I would ask, are the rights of female slaves at the South thus secured? Are they sold only as wives and daughters-in-law, and when not treated as such, are they allowed to go out free? No! They have all not only been illegally obtained as servants according to Hebrew law, but they are also illegally held in bondage. Masters at the South and West have all forfeited their claims, (if they ever had any,) to their female slaves.

We come now to examine the case of those servants who were "of the heathen round about;" Were they left entirely unprotected by law? Horne in speaking of the law, "Thou shalt not rule over him with rigor, but shalt fear thy God," remarks, "this law Lev. xxv, 43, it is true speaks expressly of slaves who were of Hebrew descent; but as alien born slaves were ingrafted into the Hebrew Church by circumcision, there is no doubt but that it applied to all slaves;" if so, then we may reasonably suppose that the other protective laws extended to them also; and that the only difference between Hebrew and Heathen servants lay in this, that the former served but six years unless they chose to remain longer, and were always freed at the death of their masters; whereas the latter served until the year of Jubilee, though that might include a period of forty-nine years,—and were left from father to son.

There are however two other laws which I have not yet noticed. The one effectually prevented all involuntary servitude, and the other completely abolished Jewish servitude every fifty years. They were equally operative upon the Heathen and the Hebrew.

1. **"Thou shall not deliver unto his master the servant that is escaped from his master unto thee. He shall dwell with thee, even among you, in that place which he shall choose, in one of thy gates where it liketh him best: thou shall not oppress him." Deut. xxiii, 15, 16.**

2. **"And ye shall hallow the fiftieth year, and proclaim Liberty throughout all the land, unto all the inhabitants thereof: it shall be a jubilee unto you." Lev. xxv, 10.**

Here, then, we see that by this first law, the door of Freedom was opened wide to every servant who had any cause whatever for complaint; if he was unhappy with his master, all he had to do was to leave him, and no man had a right to deliver him back to him again, and not only so, but the absconded servant was to choose where lie should live, and no Jew was permitted to oppress him.

Even with the gradual abolition laws of the 1780s and 1790s, slavery still existed in some northern states into the 1820s and beyond. As slavery became scarcer in northern states, however, southern slaves started running away in greater numbers, a phenomenon that Grimké speaks to in discussing runaway slaves during biblical times.

He left his master just as our Northern servants leave us; we have no power to compel them to remain with us, and no man has any right to oppress them; they go and dwell in that place where it chooseth them, and live just where they like. Is it so at the South? Is the poor runaway

In 1793 Congress passed a fugitive slave law, which the 1787 Constitution provided for. When slaves escaped to northern states, legal entities such as justices of the peace and the courts were expected to help secure their return to their masters.

slave protected by law from the violence of that master whose oppression and cruelty has driven him from his plantation or his house? No! no! Even the free states of the North are compelled to deliver unto his master the servant that is escaped from his master into them.

"By human law, under the Christian Dispensation, in the nineteenth century we are commanded to do, what God more than three thousand years ago, under the Mosaic Dispensation, positively commanded the Jews not to do."

By human law, under the Christian Dispensation, in the nineteenth century we are commanded to do, what God more than three thousand years ago, under the Mosaic Dispensation, positively commanded the Jews not to do. In the wide domain even of our free states, there is not one city of refuge for the poor runaway fugitive; not one spot upon which he can stand and say, I am a free man—I am protected in my rights as a man, by the strong arm of the law; no! not one. How long the North will thus shake hands with the South in sin, I know not. How long she will stand by like the persecutor Saul, consenting unto the death of Stephen, and keeping the raiment of them that slew him. I know not; but one thing I do know, the guilt of the North is increasing in a tremendous ratio as light is pouring in upon her on the subject and the sin of slavery. As the sun of righteousness climbs higher and higher in the moral heavens, she will stand still more and more abashed as the query is thundered down into her ear, "Who hath required this at thy hand?" It will be found no excuse then that the Constitution of our country required that persons bound to service escaping from their masters should be delivered up; no more excuse than was the reason which Adam assigned for eating the forbidden fruit. He was condemned and punished because he hearkened to the voice of his wife, rather than to the command of his Maker; and we will assuredly be condemned and punished for obeying Man rather than God, if we do not speedily repent and bring forth fruits meet for repentance. Yea, are we not receiving chastisement even now?

But by the second of these laws a still more astonishing fact is disclosed. If the first effectually prevented all
involuntary servitude, the last absolutely forbade even
voluntary servitude being perpetual. On the great day
of atonement every fiftieth year the Jubilee trumpet was
sounded throughout the land of Judea, and Liberty was
proclaimed to all the inhabitants thereof. I will not say that
the servants' chains fell off and their manacles were burst,
for there is no evidence that Jewish servants ever felt the
weight of iron chains, and collars, and handcuffs; but I do
say that even the man who had voluntarily sold himself
and the heathen who had been sold to a Hebrew master,
were set free, the one as well as the other. This law was
evidently designed to prevent the oppression of the poor,
and the possibility of such a thing as perpetual servitude
existing among them.

Where, then, I would ask, is the warrant, the justification, or the palliation of American Slavery from Hebrew
servitude? How many of the southern slaves would now
be in bondage according to the laws of Moses; Not one.
You may observe that I have carefully avoided using the
term slavery when speaking of Jewish servitude; and
simply for this reason, that no such thing existed among
that people; the word translated servant does not mean
slave, it is the same that is applied to Abraham, to Moses,
to Elisha and the prophets generally. Slavery then never
existed under the Jewish Dispensation at all, and I cannot
but regard it as an aspersion on the character of Him who
is "glorious in Holiness" for any one to assert that "God
sanctioned, yea commanded slavery under the old dispensation." I would fain lift my feeble voice to vindicate
Jehovah's character from so foul a slander. If slaveholders are determined to hold slaves as long as they can, let
them not dare to say that the God of mercy and of truth

*"Where, then, I would ask, is
the warrant, the justification,
or the palliation of American
Slavery from Hebrew
servitude?"*

ever sanctioned such a system of cruelty and wrong. It is blasphemy against Him.

We have seen that the code of laws framed by Moses with regard to servants was designed to protect them as men and women, to secure to them their rights as human beings, to guard them from oppression and defend them from violence of every kind. Let us now turn to the Slave laws of the South and West and examine them too. I will give you the substance only, because I fear I shall trespass too much on you, time, were I to quote them at length.

1. Slavery is hereditary and perpetual, to the last moment of the slave's earthly existence, and to all his descendants to the latest posterity.

2. The labor of the slave is compulsory and uncompensated while the kind of labor, the amount of toil, the time allowed for rest, are dictated solely by the master. No bargain is made, no wages given. A pure despotism governs the human brute; and even his covering and provender, both as to quantity and quality, depend entirely on the master's discretion.

3. The slave being considered a personal chattel may be sold or pledged, or leased at the will of his master. He may be exchanged for marketable commodities, or taken in execution for the debts or taxes either of a living or dead master. Sold at auction, either individually, or in lots to suit the purchaser, he may remain with his family, or be separated from them forever.

4. Slaves can make no contracts and have no legal right to any property, real or personal. Their own honest earnings and the legacies of friends belong in point of law to their masters.

5. Neither a slave nor a free colored person can be a witness against any white, or free person, in a court of justice, however atrocious may have been the crimes they have seen him commit, if such testimony would be for the benefit of a slave; but they may give testimony against a fellow slave, or free colored man, even in cases affecting life, if the master is to reap the advantage of it.

6. The slave may be punished at his master's discretion—without trial—without any means of legal redress; whether his offence be real or imaginary; and the master can transfer the same despotic power to any person or persons, he may choose to appoint.

7. The slave is not allowed to resist any free man under any circumstances, his only safety consists in the fact that his owner may bring suit and recover the price of his body, in case his life is taken, or his limbs rendered unfit for labor.

8. Slaves cannot redeem themselves, or obtain a change of masters, though cruel treatment may have rendered such a change necessary for their personal safety.

9. The slave is entirely unprotected in his domestic relations.

10. **The laws greatly obstruct the manumission of slaves, even where the master is willing to enfranchise them.**

A concerted antislavery movement never developed in the South, but during the American Revolutionary era there was a movement among many individual masters to manumit their slaves, and state legislatures accordingly relaxed laws on manumission. After Gabriel Prosser's attempted rebellion in 1800, however, this movement was stamped out, and manumission laws were strengthened, as masters believed that having a large contingent of free blacks in a slave society would be detrimental.

11. The operation of the laws tends to deprive slaves of religious instruction and consolation.

12. The whole power of the laws is exerted to keep slaves in a state of the lowest ignorance.

13. There is in this country a monstrous inequality of law and right. What is a trifling fault in the white man, is considered highly criminal in the slave; the same offences which cost a white man a few dollars only, are punished in the negro with death.

14. The laws operate most oppressively upon free people of color.

Shall I ask you now my friends, to draw the parallel between Jewish servitude and American slavery? No! For there is no likeness in the two systems; I ask you rather to mark the contrast. **The laws of Moses protected servants in their rights as men and women, guarded them from oppression and defended them from wrong. The Code Noir of the South robs the slave of all his rights as a man, reduces him to a chattel personal, and defends the master in the exercise of the most unnatural and unwarrantable power over his slave.**

"Code Noir" refers to so-called Black Codes, or laws that were specific to slaves and free blacks. Americans adopted some of these from the French Code Noir, instituted in their slave territories during the 17th century.

They each bear the impress of the hand which formed them. The attributes of justice and mercy are shadowed out in the Hebrew code; those of injustice and cruelty, in the Code Noir of America. Truly it was wise in the slave-holders of the South to declare then slaves to be "chattels personal;" for before they could be robbed of wages, wives, children, and friends, it was absolutely necessary to deny they were human beings. It is wise in them, to keep them in abject ignorance, for the strong man armed must be bound before we can spoil his house—the powerful intellect of man must be bound down with the iron chains of nescience before we can rob him of his rights as a man; we must reduce him to a thing before we can claim the right to set our feet upon his neck, because it was only all things which were originally put under the feet of man by the Almighty and Beneficent Father of all, who has declared himself to be no respecter of persons, whether red, white or black.

But some have even said that Jesus Christ did not condemn slavery. To this I reply that our Holy Redeemer lived and preached among the Jews only. The laws which Moses had enacted fifteen hundred years previous to his appearance among them, had never been annulled, and these laws protected every servant in Palestine. If then He did not condemn Jewish servitude this does not prove that he would not have condemned such a monstrous system as that of American slavery, if that had existed among them. But did not Jesus condemn slavery? Let us examine some of his precepts. "Whatsoever ye would that men should do to you, do ye even so to them," Let every slaveholder apply these queries to his own heart; Am I willing to be a slave—Am I willing to see my wife the slave of another—Am I willing to see my mother a slave, or my father, my sister or my brother? If not, then in holding others as slaves, I am doing what I would not wish to be done to me or any relative I have; and thus have I broken this golden rule which was given me to walk by.

But some slaveholders have said, "we were never in bondage to any man," and therefore the yoke of bondage would be insufferable to us, but slaves are accustomed to it, their backs are fitted to the burden. Well, I am willing to admit that you who have lived in freedom would find slavery even more oppressive than the poor slave does, but then you may try this question in another form—Am I willing to reduce my little child to slavery? You know that if it is brought up a slave it will never know any contrast, between freedom and bondage, its back will become fitted to the burden just as the negro child's does—not by

"Some have even said that Jesus Christ did not condemn slavery."

"I appeal to you, my friends, as mothers; Are you willing to enslave your children?"

nature—but by daily, violent pressure, in the same way that the head of the Indian child becomes flattened by the boards in which it is bound. It has been justly remarked that "God never made a slave," he made man upright; his back was not made to carry burdens, nor his neck to wear a yoke, and the man must be crushed within him, before his back can be fitted to the burden of perpetual slavery; and that his back is not fitted to it, is manifest by the insurrections that so often disturb the peace and security of slave-holding countries. Who ever heard of a rebellion of the beasts of the field; and why not? simply because they were all placed under the feet of man, into whose hand they were delivered; it was originally designed that they should serve him, therefore their necks have been formed for the yoke, and their backs for the burden; but not so with man, intellectual, immortal man! I appeal to you, my friends, as mothers; Are you willing to enslave your children? You start back with horror and indignation at such a question. But why, if slavery is no wrong to those upon whom it is imposed? why, if as has often been said, slaves are happier than their masters, freedom the cares and perplexities of providing for themselves and their families? why not place your children in the way of being supported without your having the trouble to provide for them, or they for themselves? Do you not perceive that as soon as this golden rule of action is applied to yourselves that you involuntarily shrink from the test; as soon as your actions are weighed in this balance of the sanctuary that you are found wanting? Try yourselves by another of the Divine precepts, "Thou shalt love thy neighbor as thyself." Can we love a man as we love ourselves if we do, and continue to do unto him, what we would not wish any one to do to us? Look too, at Christ's example, what does he say of himself, "I came not to be ministered unto, but to minister." Can you for a moment imagine the meek, and lowly, and compassionate

Saviour, a slaveholder? do you not shudder at this thought as much as at that of his being a warrior? But why, if slavery is not sinful?

Again, it has been said, the Apostle Paul did not condemn Slavery, for he sent Onesimus back to Philemon. I do not think it can be said he sent him back, for no coercion was made use of. Onesimus was not thrown into prison and then sent back in chains to his master, as your runaway slaves often are—this could not possibly have been the case, because you know Paul as a Jew, was bound to protect the runaway, he had no right to send any fugitive back to his master.

The story of Onesimus and Paul was one that slaveholders often used to justify the institution and to justify fugitive slave laws. Onesimus was a runaway slave whom Paul sent back to his master. Thus, slaveholders reasoned, Paul must have approved of slavery and of sending runaways back to bondage.

The state of the case then seems to have been this. Onesimus had been an unprofitable servant to Philemon and left him—he afterwards became converted under the Apostle's preaching, and seeing that he had been to blame in his conduct, and desiring by future fidelity to atone for past error, he wished to return, and the Apostle gave him the letter we now have as a recommendation to Philemon, informing him of the conversion of Onesimus, and entreating him as "Paul the aged" "to receive him, not now as a servant, but above a servant, a brother beloved, especially to me, but how much more unto thee, both in the flesh and in the Lord. If thou count me therefore as a partner, receive him as myself." This then surely cannot be forced into a justification of the practice of returning runaway slaves back to their masters, to be punished with cruel beatings and scourgings as they often are. Besides the word δουλος here translated servant, is the same that is made use of in Matt. xviii, 27. Now it appears that this servant owed his lord ten thousand talents; he possessed property to a vast amount. Onesimus could not then have been a slave, for slaves do not own their wives, or children; no, not even their own bodies, much less property. But

"Is the daily bread of instruction provided for your slaves? are their minds enlightened, and they gradually prepared to rise from the grade of menials into that of free, independent members of the state?"

again, the servitude which the apostle was accustomed to, must have been very different from American slavery, for he says, "the heir (or son), as long as he is a child, differeth nothing from a servant, though he be lord of all. But is under tutors and governors until the time appointed of the father." From this it appears, that the means of instruction were provided for servants as well as children; and indeed we know it must have been so among the Jews, because their servants were not permitted to remain in perpetual bondage, and therefore it was absolutely necessary they should be prepared to occupy higher stations in society than those of servants. Is it so at the South, my friends? Is the daily bread of instruction provided for your slaves? are their minds enlightened, and they gradually prepared to rise from the grade of menials into that of free, independent members of the state? Let your own statute book, and your own daily experience, answer these questions.

If this apostle sanctioned slavery, why did he exhort masters thus in his epistle to the Ephesians, "and ye, masters, do the same things unto them (i.e. perform your duties to your servants as unto Christ, not unto me) forbearing threatening; knowing that your master also is in heaven, neither is there respect of persons with him." And in Colossians, "Masters give unto your servants that which is just and equal, knowing that ye also have a master in heaven." Let slaveholders only obey these injunctions of Paul, and I am satisfied slavery would soon be abolished. If he thought it sinful even to threaten servants, surely he must have thought it sinful to flog and to beat them with sticks and paddles; indeed, when delineating the character of a bishop, he expressly names this as one feature of it, "no striker." Let masters give unto their servants that which is just and equal, and all that vast system of unrequited labor would crumble into ruin. Yes, and if they once felt they had no right to the labor of their

servants without pay, surely they could not think they had
a right to their wives, their children, and their own bodies.
Again, how can it be said Paul sanctioned slavery, when,
as though to put this matter beyond all doubt, in that black
catalogue of sins enumerated in his first epistle to Timothy,
he mentions "menstealers," which word may be translated
"slavedealers." But you may say, we all despise slavedealers as much as any one can; they are never admitted
into genteel or respectable society. And why not? Is it not
because even you shrink back from the idea of associating
with those who make their fortunes by trading in the bodies and souls of men, women, and children? whose daily
work it is to break human hearts, by tearing wives from
their husbands, and children from their parents? But why
hold slavedealers as despicable, if their trade is lawful and
virtuous? and why despise them more than the gentlemen
of fortune and standing who employ them as their agents?
Why more than the professors of religion who barter their
fellow-professors to them for gold and silver? We do not
despise the land agent, or the physician, or the merchant,
and why? Simply because their professions are virtuous
and honorable; and if the trade of men-jobbers was honorable, you would not despise them either. There is no difference in principle, in Christian ethics, between the despised
slavedealer and the Christian who buys slaves from, or
sells slaves to him; indeed, if slaves were not wanted by the
respectable, the wealthy, and the religious in a community,
there would be no slaves in that community, and of course
no slavedealers. It is then the Christians and the honorable
men and women of the South, who are the main pillars
of this grand temple built to Mammon and to Moloch. It is
the most enlightened in every country who are most to blame
when any public sin is supported by public opinion, hence
Isaiah says, "When the Lord hath performed his whole work
upon mount Zion and on Jerusalem, (then) I will punish the

*"There is no difference in
principle, in Christian ethics, between the despised
slavedealer and the Christian
who buys slaves from, or
sells slaves to him; indeed,
if slaves were not wanted by
the respectable, the wealthy,
and the religious in a community, there would be no slaves
in that community, and of
course no slavedealers."*

fruit of the stout heart of the king of Assyria, and the glory of his high looks." And was it not so? Open the historical records of that age, was not Israel carried into captivity B.C. 606, Judah B.C. 588, and the stout heart of the heathen monarchy not punished until B.C. 536, fifty-two years after Judah's, and seventy years after Israel's captivity, when it was overthrown by Cyrus, king of Persia? Hence, too, the apostle Peter says, "judgment must begin at the house of God." Surely this would not be the case, if the professors of religion were not most worthy of blame.

But it may be asked, why are they most culpable? I will tell you, my friends. It is because sin is imputed to us just in proportion to the spiritual light we receive. Thus the prophet Amos says, in the name of Jehovah, "You only have I known of all the families of the earth: therefore I will punish you for all your iniquities." Hear too the doctrine of our Lord on this important subject; "The servant who knew his Lord's will and prepared not himself, neither did according to his will, shall be beaten with many stripes:" and why? "For unto whomsoever much is given, of him shall much be required; and to whom men have committed much, of him they will ask the more." Oh! then that the Christians of the south would ponder these things in their hearts, and awake to the vast responsibilities which rest upon them at this important crisis.

I have thus, I think, clearly proved to you seven propositions, viz.: First, that slavery is contrary to the declaration of our independence. Second, that it is contrary to the first charter of human rights given to Adam, and renewed to Noah. Third, that the fact of slavery having been the subject of prophecy, furnishes no excuse whatever to slavedealers. Fourth, that no such system existed under the patriarchal dispensation. Fifth, that slavery never existed under the

"Oh! then that the Christians of the south would ponder these things in their hearts, and awake to the vast responsibilities which rest upon them at this important crisis."

Jewish dispensation; but so far otherwise, that every servant was placed under the protection of law, and care taken not only to prevent all involuntary servitude, but all voluntary perpetual bondage. Sixth, that slavery in America reduces a man to a thing, a "chattel personal," robs him of all his rights as a human being, fetters both his mind and body, and protects the master in the most unnatural and unreasonable power, whilst it throws him out of the protection of law. Seventh, that slavery is contrary to the example and precepts of our holy and merciful Redeemer, and of his apostles.

But perhaps you will be ready to query, why appeal to women on this subject? We do not make the laws which perpetuate slavery. No legislative power is vested in us; we can do nothing to overthrow the system, even if we wished to do so. To this I reply, I know you do not make the laws, but I also know that you are the wives and mothers, the sisters and daughters of those who do; and if you really suppose you can do nothing to overthrow slavery, you are greatly mistaken. You can do much in every way: four things I will name. 1st. You can read on this subject. 2d. You can pray over this subject. 3d. You can speak on this subject. 4th. You can act on this subject. I have not placed reading before praying because I regard it more important, but because, in order to pray aright, we must understand what we are praying for; it is only then we can "pray with the understanding, and the spirit also."

Grimké is an example of the impact of the burgeoning women's rights movement in mid-19th-century America. She was one of a few women who spoke to mixed audiences of men and women and published books. In urging southern women to speak and later act on the subject of slavery, she is working for both the antislavery movement and contributing to the empowerment of women. While it would be decades before women could vote or run for office, this period witnessed the growing importance of women in social reform movements across the North.

1. Read then on the subject of slavery. Search the Scriptures daily, whether the things I have told you are true. Other books and papers might be a great help to you in this investigation, but they are not necessary, and it is hardly probable that your Committees of Vigilance will allow you to have any other.

"Read the Bible then, it contains the words of Jesus, and they are spirit and life. Judge for yourselves whether he sanctioned such a system of oppression and crime."

The Bible then is the book I want you to read in the spirit of inquiry, and the spirit of prayer. Even the enemies of Abolitionists, acknowledge that their doctrines are drawn from it. In the great mob in Boston, last autumn, when the books and papers of the Anti-Slavery Society, were thrown out of the windows of their office, one individual laid hold of the Bible and was about tossing it out to the ground, when another reminded him that it was the Bible he had in his hand. "O! 'tis all one," he replied, and out went the sacred volume, along with the rest. We thank him for the acknowledgment. Yes, "it is all one," for our books and papers are mostly commentaries on the Bible, and the Declaration. Read the Bible then, it contains the words of Jesus, and they are spirit and life. Judge for yourselves whether he sanctioned such a system of oppression and crime.

2. Pray over this subject. When you have entered into your closets, and shut to the doors, then pray to your father, who seeth in secret, that he would open your eyes to see whether slavery is sinful, and if it is, that he would enable you to bear a faithful, open and unshrinking testimony against it, and to do whatsoever your hands find to do, leaving the consequences entirely to him, who still says to us whenever we try to reason away duty from the fear of consequences, "What is that to thee, follow thou me." Pray also for that poor slave, that he may be kept patient and submissive under his hard lot, until God is pleased to open the door of freedom to him without violence or bloodshed. Pray too for the master that his heart may be softened. And he made willing to acknowledge, as Joseph's brethren did, "Verily we are guilty concerning our brother," before he will be compelled to add in consequence of Divine judgment, "therefore is all this evil come upon us." Pray also for all your brethren and sisters who are laboring in the righteous cause of Emancipation in the Northern States, England and the world. There is

great encouragement for prayer in these words of our Lord. "Whatsoever ye shall ask the Father in my name, he will give it to you"—Pray then without ceasing, in the closet and the social circle.

3. Speak on this subject. It is through the tongue, the pen, and the press, that truth is principally propagated. Speak then to your relatives, your friends, your acquaintances on the subject of slavery; be not afraid if you are conscientiously convinced it is sinful, to say so openly, but calmly, and to let your sentiments be known. If you are served by the slaves of others, try to ameliorate their condition as much as possible; never aggravate their faults, and thus add fuel to the fire of anger already kindled, in a master and mistress's bosom; remember their extreme ignorance, and consider them as your Heavenly Father does the less culpable on this account, even when they do wrong things. Discountenance all cruelty to them, all starvation, all corporal chastisement; these may brutalize and break their spirits, but will never bend them to willing, cheerful obedience. If possible, see that they are comfortably and seasonably fed, whether in the house or the field; it is unreasonable and cruel to expect slaves to wait for their breakfast until eleven o'clock, when they rise at five or six. Do all you can, to induce their owners to clothe them well, and to allow them many little indulgences which would contribute to their comfort. Above all, try to persuade your husband, father, brothers and sons, that slavery is a crime against God and man, and that it is a great sin to keep human beings in such abject ignorance; to deny them the privilege of learning to read and write. The Catholics are universally condemned, for denying the Bible to the common people, but, slaveholders must not blame them, for they are doing the very same thing, and for the very same reason, neither of these systems can bear the light which bursts from the pages of that Holy Book. And lastly,

"Above all, try to persuade your husband, father, brothers and sons, that slavery is a crime against God and man, and that it is a great sin to keep human beings in such abject ignorance; to deny them the privilege of learning to read and write."

endeavour to inculcate submission on the part of the slaves, but whilst doing this be faithful in pleading the cause of the oppressed.

"Will you behold unheeding,
Life's holiest feelings crushed,
Where woman's heart is bleeding,
Shall woman's voice be hushed?"

In most slave states, slaves were forbidden from reading and writing. Masters thought it dangerous for slaves to read because they could become acquainted with antislavery arguments as well as the existence of a vibrant antislavery movement in the North. Writing was dangerous as well because slaves could forge traveling passes that would allow them to run away.

4. Act on this subject. Some of you own slaves yourselves. If you believe slavery is sinful, set them at liberty, "undo the heavy burdens and let the oppressed go free." If they wish to remain with you, pay them wages, if not let them leave you. Should they remain teach them, and have them taught the common branches of an English education; they have minds and those minds ought to be improved. So precious a talent as intellect, never was given to be wrapt in a napkin and buried in the earth. It is the duty of all, as far as they can, to improve their own mental faculties, because we are commanded to love God with all our minds, as well as with all our hearts, and we commit a great sin, if we forbid or prevent that cultivation of the mind in others, which would enable them to perform this duty. Teach your servants then to read &c, and encourage them to believe it is their duty to learn, if it were only that they might read the Bible.

More than a century before Martin Luther King Jr. preached a philosophy of nonviolent resistance to the law and decades before Henry David Thoreau did so in his essay on civil disobedience, Angelina Grimké urged her readers to break unjust and immoral laws pertaining to slavery.

But some of you will say, we can neither free our slaves nor teach them to read, for the laws of our state forbid it. Be not surprised when I say such wicked laws ought to be no barrier in the way of your duty, and I appeal to the Bible to prove this position.

What was the conduct of Shiphrah and Puah, when the king of Egypt issued his cruel mandate, with regard to the Hebrew children? "They feared God, and did not as the King of Egypt commanded them, but saved the men children alive." Did these women do right in disobeying that monarch? "Therefore (says the sacred text,) God dealt well with them, and made them houses" Ex. i. What was the conduct of Shadrach, Meshach, and Abednego, when Nebuchadnezzar set up a golden image in the plain of Dura, and commanded all people, nations, and languages, to fall down and worship it? "Be it known, unto thee, (said these faithful Jews) O king, that we will not serve thy gods, nor worship the image which thou hast set up." Did these men do right in disobeying the law of their sovereign? Let their miraculous deliverance from the burning fiery furnace, answer; Dan. iii. What was the conduct of Daniel, when Darius made a firm decree that no one should ask a petition of any man or God for thirty days? Did the prophet cease to pray? No! "When Daniel knew that the writing was signed, he went into his house, and his windows being open towards Jerusalem, he kneeled upon his knees three times a day, and prayed and gave thanks before his God, as he did aforetime." Did Daniel do right thus to break the law of his king? Let his wonderful deliverance out of the mouths of the lions answer; Dan. vii. Look, too, at the Apostles Peter and John. When the rulers of the Jews, "commanded them not to speak at all, nor teach in the name of Jesus," what did they say? "Whether it be right in the sight of God, to hearken unto you more than unto God, judge ye." And what did they do "They spake the word of God with boldness, and with great power gave the Apostles witness of the resurrection of the Lord Jesus;" although this was the very doctrine, for the preaching of which, they had just been cast into prison, and further threatened. Did these men do right? I leave you to answer, who now enjoy the benefits of their labors and sufferings, in that Gospel they dared to preach when positively commanded not to teach any more in the name of Jesus; Acts iv.

"If you think slavery is sinful, all you have to do is to set your slaves at liberty, do all you can to protect them, and in humble faith and fervent prayer, commend them to your common Father."

But some of you may say, if we do free our slaves, they will be taken up and sold, therefore there will be no use in doing it. Peter and John might just as well have said, we will not preach the gospel, for if we do, we shall be taken up and put in prison, therefore there will be no use in our preaching. Consequences, my friends, belong no more to you, than they did to these apostles. Duty is ours and events are God's. If you think slavery is sinful, all you have to do is to set your slaves at liberty, do all you can to protect them, and in humble faith and fervent prayer, commend them to your common Father. He can take care of them; but if for wise purposes he sees fit to allow them to be sold, this will afford you an opportunity of testifying openly, wherever you go, against the crime of manstealing. Such an act will be clear robbery, and if exposed, might, under the Divine direction, do the cause of Emancipation more good, than any thing that could happen, for, "He makes even the wrath of man to praise him, and the remainder of wrath he will restrain."

I know that this doctrine of obeying God, rather than man, will be considered as dangerous, and heretical by many, but I am not afraid openly to avow it, because it is the doctrine of the Bible; but I would not be understood to advocate resistance to any law however oppressive, if, in obeying it, I was not obliged to commit sin. If for instance, there was a law, which imposed imprisonment or a fine upon me if I manumitted a slave, I would on no account resist that law, I would set the slave free, and then go to prison or pay the fine. If a law commands me to sin I will break it; if it calls me to suffer, I will let it take its course unresistingly. The doctrine of blind obedience and unqualified submission to any human power, whether civil or ecclesiastical, is the doctrine of despotism, and ought to have no place among Republicans and Christians.

But you will perhaps say, such a course of conduct would inevitably expose us to great suffering. Yes! my Christian friends, I believe it would, but this will not excuse you or any one else for the neglect of duty. If Prophets and Apostles, Martyrs, and Reformers had not been willing to suffer for the truth's sake, where would the world have been now? If they had said, we cannot speak the truth, we cannot do what we believe is right, because the laws of our country or public opinion are against us, where would our holy religion have been now? The Prophets were stoned, imprisoned, and killed, by the Jews. And why? Because they exposed and openly rebuked public sins; they opposed public opinion; had they held their peace, they all might have lived in ease and died in favor with a wicked generation. Why were the Apostles persecuted from city to city, stoned, incarcerated, beaten, and crucified? Because they dared to speak the truth; to tell the Jews, boldly and fearlessly, that they were the murderers of the Lord of Glory, and that, however great a stumbling block the Cross might be to them, there was no other name given under heaven by which men could be saved, but the name of Jesus. Because they declared, even at Athens, the seat of learning and refinement, the self-evident truth, that "they be no gods that are made with men's hands," and exposed to the Grecians the foolishness of worldly wisdom, and the impossibility of salvation but through Christ, whom they despised on account of the ignominious death he died. Because at Rome, the proud mistress of the world, they thundered out the terrors of the law upon that idolatrous, way-making, and slaveholding community. Why were the martyrs stretched upon the rack, gibbetted and burnt, the scorn and diversion of a Nero, whilst their tarred and burning bodies sent up a light which illuminated the Roman capital? Why were the Waldenses hunted like wild beasts upon the mountains of Piedmont, and slain with the sword of the Duke of Savoy and the proud

"If Prophets and Apostles, Martyrs, and Reformers had not been willing to suffer for the truth's sake, where would the world have been now?"

monarch of France? Why were the Presbyterians chased like the partridge over the highlands of Scotland—the Methodists pumped, and stoned, and pelted with rotten eggs—the Quakers incarcerated in filthy prisons, beaten, whipped at the cart's tail, banished and hung? Because they dared to speak the truth, to break the unrighteous laws of their country, and chose rather to suffer affliction with the people of God, "not accepting deliverance," even under the gallows. Why were Luther and Calvin persecuted and excommunicated, Cranmer, Ridley, and Latimer burnt? Because they fearlessly proclaimed the truth, though that truth was contrary to public opinion, and the authority of Ecclesiastical councils and conventions. Now all this vast amount of human suffering might have been saved. All these Prophets and Apostles, Martyrs, and Reformers, might have lived and died in peace with all men, but following the example of their great pattern, "they despised the shame, endured the cross, and are now set down on the right hand of the throne of God," having received the glorious welcome of "well done good and faithful servants, enter ye into the joy of your Lord."

But you may say we are women, how can our hearts endure persecution? And why not? Have not women stood up in all the dignity, and strength of moral courage to be the leaders of the people, and to bear a faithful testimony for the truth whenever the providence of God has called them to do so? Are there no women in that noble army of martyrs who are now singing the song of Moses and the Lamb? Who led out the women of Israel from the house of bondage, striking the timbrel, and singing the song of deliverance on the banks of that sea whose waters stood up like walls of crystal to open a passage for their escape? It was a woman; Miriam, the prophetess, the sister of Moses and Aaron. Who went up with Barak to Kadesh to fight against

"Have not women stood up in all the dignity, and strength of moral courage to be the leaders of the people, and to bear a faithful testimony for the truth whenever the providence of God has called them to do so?"

Jabin, King of Canaan, into whose hand Israel had been sold because of their iniquities? It was a woman! Deborah the wife of Lapidoth, the judge, as well as the prophetess of that backsliding people; Judges iv, 9. Into whose hands was Sisera, the captain of Jabin's host delivered? Into the hand of a woman. Jael the wife of Heber! Judges vi, 21. Who dared to speak the truth concerning those judgments which were coming upon Judea, when Josiah, alarmed at finding that his people "had not kept the word of the Lord to do after all that was written in the book of the Law," sent to enquire of the Lord concerning these things? It was a woman. Huldah the prophetess, the wife of Shallum; 2, Chron. xxxiv, 22. Who was chosen to deliver the whole Jewish nation from that murderous decree of Persia's King, which wicked Haman had obtained by calumny and fraud? It was a woman; Esther the Queen; yes, weak and trembling woman was the instrument appointed by God, to reverse the bloody mandate of the eastern monarch, and save the whole visible church from destruction. What human voice first proclaimed to Mary that she should be the mother of our Lord? It was a woman! Elizabeth, the wife of Zacharias; Luke i, 42, 43. Who united with the good old Simeon in giving thanks publicly in the temple, when the child, Jesus, was presented there by his parents, "and spake of him to all them that looked for redemption in Jerusalem?" It was a woman! Anna the prophetess. Who first proclaimed Christ as the true Messiah in the streets of Samaria, once the capital of the ten tribes? It was a woman! Who ministered to the Son of God whilst on earth, a despised and persecuted Reformer, in the humble garb of a carpenter? They were women! Who followed the rejected King of Israel, as his fainting footsteps trod the road to Calvary? "A great company of people and of women;" and it is remarkable that to them alone, he turned and addressed the pathetic language, "Daughters of Jerusalem, weep not for me, but weep for yourselves and your children." Ah! who sent unto the Roman Governor when he was set down on the judgment seat, saying unto him, "Have thou nothing to do with that just man, for I have suffered many things this day in a dream because of him?" It was a woman! the wife of Pilate. Although "he knew that for envy the Jews had delivered Christ," yet he consented to surrender the Son of God into the bands of a brutal soldiery, after having himself scourged his naked body. Had the wife of Pilate sat upon that judgment seat, what would have been the result of the trial of this "just person?"

And who last hung round the cross of Jesus on the mountain of Golgotha? Who first visited the sepulchre early in the morning on the first day of the week, carrying sweet spices to embalm his precious body, not knowing that it was incorruptible and could not be holden by the bands of death? These were women! To whom did he first appear after his resurrection? It was to a woman! Mary Magdalene; Mark xvi, 9. Who gathered with the apostles to wait at Jerusalem, in prayer and supplication, for "the promise of the Father;" the spiritual blessing, of the Great High Priest of his Church, who had entered, not into the splendid temple of Solomon, there to offer the blood of bulls, and of goats, and the smoking censer upon the golden altar, but into Heaven itself, there to present his intercessions, after having "given himself for us, an offering and a sacrifice to God for a sweet smelling savor?" Women were among that holy company; Acts i, 14. And did women wait in vain? Did those who had ministered to his necessities, followed in his train, and wept at his crucifixion, wait in vain? No! No! Did the cloven tongues of fire descend upon the heads of women as well as men? Yes, my friends, "it sat upon each one of them;" Acts ii, 73. Women as well as men were to be living stones in the temple of grace, and therefore their heads were consecrated by the descent of the Holy Ghost as well as those of men. Were women recognized as fellow laborers in the gospel field? They were! Paul says in his epistle to the Philippians, "help those women who labored with me, in the gospel;" Phil. iv, 3.

But this is not all. Roman women were burnt at the stake, their delicate limbs were torn joint from joint by the ferocious beasts of the Amphitheatre, and tossed by the wild bull in his fury, for the diversion of that idolatrous, warlike, and slaveholding people. Yes, women suffered under the ten persecutions of heathen Rome, with the most unshrinking constancy and fortitude; not all the entreaties of friends, nor the claims of new born infancy, nor the cruel threats of enemies could make them sprinkle one grain of incense upon the altars of Roman idols. Come now with me to the beautiful valleys of Piedmont. Whose blood stains the green sward, and decks the wild flowers with colors not their own, and smokes on the sword of persecuting France? It is woman's, as well as man's? Yes, women were accounted as sheep for the slaughter, and were cut down as the tender saplings of the wood.

But time would fail me, to tell of all those hundreds and thousands of women, who perished in the Low countries of Holland, when Alva's sword of vengeance was unsheathed against the Protestants, when the Catholic Inquisitions of Europe became the merciless executioners of vindictive wrath, upon those who dared to worship God, instead of bowing down in unholy adoration before "my Lord God the Pope," and when England, too, burnt her Ann Ascoes at the stake of martyrdom. Suffice it to say, that the Church, after having been driven from Judea to Rome, and from Rome to Piedmont, and from Piedmont to England, and from England

"Come now with me to the beautiful valleys of Piedmont. Whose blood stains the green sward, and decks the wild flowers with colors not their own, and smokes on the sword of persecuting France? It is woman's, as well as man's?"

to Holland, at last stretched her fainting wings over the dark bosom of the Atlantic, and found on the shores of a great wilderness, a refuge from tyranny and oppression—as she thought, but even here, (the warm blush of shame mantles my cheek as I write it,) even here, woman was beaten and banished, imprisoned, and hung upon the gallows, a trophy to the Cross.

Women played an important role in the anti-slavery movement from its inception. As early as the 1760s, women ran away from and sued their masters for their freedom, providing important precedents for freedom suits in states such as Massachusetts and Connecticut. Women such as Phillis Wheatley likewise took up their pens to write against slavery, and women's participation in black churches and schools would constitute an important part of antislavery activism until the 1830s.

And what, I would ask in conclusion, have women done for the great and glorious cause of Emancipation? Who wrote that pamphlet which moved the heart of Wilberforce to pray over the wrongs, and his tongue to plead the cause of the oppressed African? It was a woman, Elizabeth Heyrick. Who labored assiduously to keep the sufferings of the slave continually before the British public? They were women. And how did they do it? By their needles, paint brushes and pens, by speaking the truth, and petitioning Parliament for the abolition of slavery. And what was the effect of their labors? Read it in the Emancipation bill of Great Britain. Read it, in the present state of her West India Colonies. Read it, in the impulse which has been given to the cause of freedom, in the United States of America. Have English women then done so much for the negro, and shall American women do nothing? Oh no! Already are there sixty female Anti-Slavery Societies in operation.

These are doing just what the English women did, telling the story of the colored man's wrongs, praying for his deliverance, and presenting his kneeling image constantly before the public eye on bags and needle-books, card-racks, pen-wipers, pin-cushions, &c. Even the children of the north are in scribing on their handy work, "May the points of our needles prick the slaveholder's conscience." Some of the reports of these Societies exhibit not only considerable talent, but a deep sense of religious duty, and a determination to persevere through evil as well as good report, until every scourge, and every shackle, is buried under the feet of the manumitted slave.

The Ladies' Anti-Slavery Society of Boston was called last fall, to a severe trial of their faith and constancy. They were mobbed by "the gentlemen of property and standing," in that city at their anniversary meeting, and their lives were jeoparded by an infuriated crowd; but their conduct on that occasion did credit to our sex, and affords a full assurance that they will never abandon the cause of the slave. The pamphlet, Right and Wrong in Boston, issued by them in which a particular account is given of that "mob of broad cloth in broad day," does equal credit to the head and the heart of her who wrote it. I wish my Southern sisters could read it; they would then understand that the women of the North have engaged in this work from a sense of religious duty, and that nothing will ever induce them to take their hands from it until it is fully accomplished. They feel no hostility to you, no bitterness or wrath; they rather sympathize in your trials and difficulties; but they well know that the first thing to be done to help you, is to pour in the light of truth on your minds, to urge you to reflect on, and pray over the subject. This is all they can do for you, you must work out your own deliverance with fear and trembling, and with the direction and blessing of God, you can do it. Northern women may labor to produce a correct public opinion at the North, but if Southern women sit down in listless indifference and criminal idleness, public opinion cannot be rectified and purified at the South. It is manifest to every reflecting mind, that slavery must be abolished; the era in which we live, and the light which is overspreading the whole world on this subject, clearly show that the time cannot be distant when it will be done. Now there are only

"It is manifest to every reflecting mind, that slavery must be abolished; the era in which we live, and the light which is overspreading the whole world on this subject, clearly show that the time cannot be distant when it will be done."

two ways in which it can be effected, by moral power or physical force, and it is for you to choose which of these you prefer. Slavery always has, and always will produce insurrections wherever it exists, because it is a violation of the natural order of things, and no human power can much longer perpetuate it. The opposers of abolitionists fully believe this; one of them remarked to me not long since, there is no doubt there will be a most terrible over-turning at the South in a few years, such cruelty and wrong, must be visited with Divine vengeance soon. Abolitionists believe, too, that this must inevitably be the case if you do not repent, and they are not willing to leave you to perish without entreating you, to save yourselves from destruc-tion; well may they say with the apostle, "am I then your enemy because I tell you the truth," and warn you to flee from impending judgments.

But why, my dear friends, have I thus been endeavoring to lead you through the history of more than three thousand years, and to point you to that great cloud of witnesses who have gone before, "from works to rewards?" Have I been seeking to magnify the sufferings, and exalt the character of woman, that she "might have praise of men?" No! no! my object has been to arouse you, as the wives and mothers, the daughters and sisters, of the South, to a sense of your duty as women, and as Christian women, on that great subject, which has already shaken our country, from the St. Law-rence and the lakes, to the Gulf of Mexico, and from the Mississippi to the shores of the Atlantic; and will continue mightily to shake it, until the polluted temple of slavery fall and crumble into ruin. I would say unto each one of you, "what meanest thou, O sleeper! arise and call upon thy God, if so be that God will think upon us that we perish not." **Per-ceive you not that dark cloud of vengeance which hangs over our boasting Republic? Saw you not the lightnings**

The Texas Revolution had begun in October 1835 and concluded the following year. Also known as the Texas War for Independence, one of the key issues in this conflict was the refusal of the Mexican government, of which Texas was then a part, to allow American set-tlers to continue holding slaves.

of Heaven's wrath, in the flame which leaped from the Indian's torch to the roof of yonder dwelling, and lighted with its horrid glare the darkness of midnight? Heard you not the thunders of Divine anger, as the distant roar of the cannon came rolling onward, from the Texan country, where Protestant American Rebels are fighting with Mexican Republicans—for what? For the re-establishment of slavery; yes! of American slavery in the bosom of a Catholic Republic, where that system of robbery, violence, and wrong, had been legally abolished for twelve years. Yes! citizens of the United States, after plundering Mexico of her land, are now engaged in deadly conflict, for the privilege of fastening chains, and collars, and manacles—upon whom? upon the subjects of some foreign prince?

No! upon native born American Republican citizens, although the fathers of those very men declared to the whole world, while struggling to free themselves from the three penny taxes of an English king, that they believed it to, be a self-evident truth that all men were created equal, and had an unalienable right to liberty.

Well may the poet exclaim in bitter sarcasm,

*"The fustian flag that proudly waves
In solemn mockery o'er a land of slaves."*

Can you not, my friends, understand the signs of the times; do you not see the sword of retributive justice hanging over the South or are you still slumbering at your posts?—Are there no Shiphrahs, no Puahs among you, who wilt dare in Christian firmness and Christian meekness, to refuse to obey the wicked laws which require woman to enslave, to degrade and to brutalize woman? Are there no Miriams, who would rejoice to lead out the captive daughters of the Southern States to liberty and light? Are there no Huldahs there who will dare to speak the truth concerning the sins of the people and those judgments, which it requires no prophet's eye to see, must follow if repentance is not speedily sought? Is there no Esther among you, who will plead for the poor devoted slave? Read the history of this Persian queen, it is full of instruction; she at first refused to plead for the Jews; but, hear the words of Mordecai, "Think not within thyself, that thou shalt escape in the king's house more than all the Jews, for if thou altogether holdest thy peace at this time, then shalt there enlargement and deliverance arise to the Jews from another place: but thou and thy father's house shall be destroyed." Listen, too, to her magnanimous reply to this powerful appeal; "I will go in unto the king, which is not according to law, and if I perish, I perish." Yes! if there were but one Esther at the South, she might save her country from ruin; but let the Christian women there arise, as the Christian women of Great Britain did, in the majesty of moral power, and that salvation is certain. Let them embody themselves in societies, and send petitions up to their different legislatures, entreating their husbands, fathers, brothers and sons, to abolish the institution of slavery; no longer to subject woman to the scourge and the chain, to mental darkness and moral degradation; no longer to tear husbands from their wives, and children from their parents; no longer to make men, women, and children, work without wages; no longer to make their lives bitter in hard bondage; no longer to reduce American citizens to the abject condition of slaves, of "chattels personal;" no longer to barter the image of God in human shambles for corruptible things such as silver and gold.

The women of the South can overthrow this horrible system of oppression and cruelty, licentiousness and wrong. Such

"The women of the South can overthrow this horrible system of oppression and cruelty, licentiousness and wrong."

appeals to your legislatures would be irresistible, for there is something in the heart of man which will bend under moral suasion. There is a swift witness for truth in his bosom, which will respond to truth when it is uttered with calmness and dignity. If you could obtain but six signatures to such a petition in only one state, I would say, send up that petition, and be not in the least discouraged by the scoffs, and jeers of the heartless, or the resolution of the house to lay it on the table. It will be a great thing if the subject can be introduced into your legislatures in any way, even by women, and they will be the most likely to introduce it there in the best possible manner, as a matter of morals and religion, not of expediency or politics. You may petition, too, the different ecclesiastical bodies of the slave states. Slavery must be attacked with the whole power of truth and the sword of the spirit. You must take it up on Christian ground, and fight against it with Christian weapons, whilst your feet are shod with the preparation of the gospel of peace. And you are now loudly called upon by the cries of the widow and the orphan, to arise and gird yourselves for this great moral conflict, with the whole armour of righteousness upon the right hand and on the left.

There is every encouragement for you to labor and pray, my friends, because the abolition of slavery as well as its existence, has been the theme of prophecy. "Ethiopia (says the Psalmist) shall stretch forth her hands unto God."

Here Grimké refers to the biblical verse Psalm 68:31: "Princes shall come out of Egypt, and Ethiopia shall stretch forth her hands unto God." This was an important text in arguments for Christianizing slaves and freeing them as well.

And is she not now doing so? Are not the Christian negroes of the south lifting their hands in prayer for deliverance, just as the Israelites did when their redemption was drawing nigh? Are they not sighing and crying by reason of the hard bondage? And think you, that He, of whom it was said, "and God heard their groaning, and their cry came up unto him by reason of the hard bondage," think you that his ear is heavy that he cannot now hear the cries of his suffering children? Or that He who raised up a Moses, an Aaron, and a Miriam, to bring them up out of the land of Egypt from the house of bondage, cannot now, with a high hand and a stretched out arm, rid the poor negroes out of the hands of their masters? Surely you believe that his aim is not shortened that he cannot save. And would not such a work of mercy redound to his glory? But another string of the harp of prophecy vibrates to the song of deliverance: "But they shall sit every man under his vine, and under his fig-tree, and none shall make them afraid; for the mouth of the Lord of Hosts hath spoken it." The slave never can do this as long as he is a slave; whilst he is a "chattel personal" he can own no property; but the time is to come when every man is to sit under his own vine and his own fig-tree, and no domineering driver, or irresponsible master, or irascible mistress, shall make him afraid of the chain or the whip. Hear, too, the sweet tones of another string: "Many shall run to and fro, and knowledge shall be increased." Slavery is an insurmountable barrier to the increase of knowledge in every community where it exists; slavery, then, must be abolished before this prediction can be fulfilled. The last chord I shall touch, will be this, "They shall not hurt nor destroy in all my holy mountain."

Grimké is placing the antislavery movement within the larger social reform causes known collectively as the Benevolent Empire. The Benevolent Empire was an outgrowth of the Second Great Awakening, a religious movement in 19th-century America that stressed moral perfection of both the individual and society. In doing this, Grimké argues that abolitionism is God's will.

Slavery, then, must be overthrown before the prophecies can be accomplished, but how are they to be fulfilled? Will the wheels of the millennial car be rolled onward by miraculous power? No! God designs to confer this holy privilege upon man; it is through his instrumentality that the great and glorious work of reforming the world is to be done. And see you not how the mighty engine of moral power is dragging in its rear the Bible and peace societies, anti-slavery and temperance, sabbath schools, moral

reform, and missions? or to adopt another figure, do not these seven philanthropic associations compose the beautiful tints in that bow of promise which spans the arch of our moral heaven?

Who does not believe, that if these societies were broken up, their constitutions burnt, and the vast machinery with which they are laboring to regenerate mankind was stopped, that the black clouds of vengeance would soon burst over our world, and every city would witness the fate of the devoted cities of the plain! Each one of these societies is walking abroad through the earth scattering the seeds of truth over the wide field of our world, not with the hundred hands of a Briareus, but with a hundred thousand.

Another encouragement for you to labor, my friends, is, that you will have the prayers and co-operation of English and Northern philanthropists. You will never bend your knees in supplication at the throne of grace for the overthrow of slavery, without meeting there the spirits of other Christians, who will mingle their voices with yours, as the morning, or evening sacrifice ascends to God. Yes, the spirit of prayer and of supplication has been poured out upon many, many hearts; there are wrestling Jacobs who will not let go of the prophetic promises of deliverance for the captive, and the opening of prison doors to them that are bound. There are Pauls who are saying, in reference to this subject, "Lord, what wilt thou have me to do?" There are Marys sitting in the house now, who are ready to arise and go forth in this work as soon as the message is brought, "the master is come and calleth for thee." And there are Marthas, too, who have already gone out to meet Jesus, as he bends his footsteps to their brother's grave, and weeps, not over the lifeless body of Lazarus bound hand and foot in grave-clothes, but over the politically and intellectually lifeless slave, bound hand

"Yes, some may be ready to say of the colored race, how can they ever be raised politically and intellectually, they have been dead four hundred years?"

and foot in the iron chains of oppression and ignorance. Some may be ready to say, as Martha did, who seemed to expect nothing but sympathy from Jesus, "Lord, by this time he stinketh, for he hath been dead four days." She thought it useless to remove the stone and expose the loathsome body of her brother; she could not believe that so great a miracle could be wrought, as to raise that putrefied body into life; but "Jesus said, take ye away the stone;" and when they had taken away the stone where the dead was laid, and uncovered the body of Lazarus, then it was that "Jesus lifted up his eyes and said, Father, I thank thee that thou hast heard me," &c. "And when he had thus spoken, he cried with a loud voice, Lazarus come forth." Yes, some may be ready to say of the colored race, how can they ever be raised politically and intellectually, they have been dead four hundred years? But we have nothing to do with how this is to be done; our business is to take away the stone which has covered up the dead body of our brother, to expose the putrid carcass, to show how that body has been bound with the grave-clothes of heathen ignorance, and his face with the napkin of prejudice, and having done all it was our duty to do, to stand by the negro's grave, in humble faith and holy hope, waiting to hear the life-giving command of "Lazarus, come forth." This is just what Anti-Slavery Societies are doing; they are taking away the stone from the mouth of the tomb of slavery, where lies the putrid carcass of our brother. They want the pure light of heaven to shine into that dark and gloomy cave; they want all men to see how that dead body has been bound, how that face has been wrapped in the napkin of prejudice and shall they wait beside that grave in vain? Is not Jesus still the resurrection and the life? Did He come to proclaim liberty to the captive, and the opening of prison doors to them that are bound, in vain? Did He promise to give beauty for ashes, the oil of joy for mourning, and the garment of praise for the spirit of heaviness unto them that mourn in Zion, and will He refuse to beautify the mind, anoint the head, and throw around the captive negro mantle of praise for that spirit of heaviness which has so long bound him down to the ground? Or shall we not rather say with the prophet, "the zeal of the Lord of Hosts will perform this?" Yes, his promises are sure, and amen in Christ Jesus, that he will assemble her that halteth, and gather her that is driven out, and her that is afflicted.

But I will now say a few words on the subject of Abolitionism. Doubtless you have all heard Anti-Slavery Societies denounced as insurrectionary and mischievous, fanatical and dangerous.

While the antislavery movement was certainly growing in the mid-1830s, it was by no means widespread, nor did a majority of northerners participate. Many northerners had business interests with slaveholders and profited from slavery, while others simply did not care about a race of people they considered inferior. Thus, abolitionists were often portrayed as fanatics who posed a threat to the stability of society.

It has been said they publish the most abominable untruths, and that they are endeavoring to excite rebellions at the South. Have you believed these reports, my friends? Have you also been deceived by these false assertions? Listen to me, then, whilst I endeavor to wipe from the fair character of Abolitionism such unfounded accusations. You know that I am a Southerner; you know that my dearest relatives are now in a slave State. Can you for a moment believe I would prove so recreant to the feelings of a daughter and a sister, as to join a society which was seeking to overthrow slavery by falsehood, bloodshed, and murder? I appeal to you who have known and loved me in days that are passed, can you believe it? No! my friends. As a Carolinian, I was peculiarly jealous of any movements on this subject; and before I would join an Anti-Slavery Society, I took the precaution of becoming acquainted with some of the leading Abolitionists, of reading their publications and attending their meetings, at which I heard addresses both from colored and white men; and it was not until I was fully convinced that their principles were entirely pacific, and their efforts only moral, that I gave my name as a member to the Female

"I am not at all afraid to assert, that Anti-Slavery publications have not overdrawn the monstrous features of slavery at all."

Anti-Slavery Society of Philadelphia. Since that time, I have regularly taken the Liberator, and read many Anti-Slavery pamphlets and papers and books, and can assure you I never have seen a single insurrectionary paragraph, and never read any account of cruelty which I could not believe. Southerners may deny the truth of these accounts, but why do they not prove them to be false? Their violent expressions of horror at such accounts being believed, may deceive some, but they cannot deceive me, for I lived too long in the midst of slavery, not to know what slavery is. When I speak of this system, "I speak that I do know," and I am not at all afraid to assert, that Anti-Slavery publications have not overdrawn the monstrous features of slavery at all. And many a Southerner knows this as well as I do. A lady in North Carolina remarked to a friend of mine, about eighteen months since, "Northerners know nothing at all about slavery; they think it is perpetual bondage only; but of the depth of degradation that word involves, they have no conception; if they had, they would never cease their efforts until so horrible a system was overthrown." She did not know how faithfully some Northern men and Northern women had studied this subject; how diligently they had searched out the cause of "him who had none to help him," And how fearlessly they had told the story of the negro's wrongs. Yes, Northerners know every thing about slavery now. This monster of iniquity has been unveiled to the world, her frightful features unmasked, and soon, very soon will she be regarded with no more complacency by the American republic, than is the idol of Juggernaut, rolling its bloody wheels over the crashed bodies of its prostrate victims.

But you will probably ask, if Anti-Slavery societies are not insurrectionary, why do Northerners tell us they are? Why, I would ask you in return, did Northern senators and Northern representatives give their votes, at the last sitting of congress, to the admission of Arkansas Territory as a state? Take those men, one by one, and ask them in their parlours, do you approve of slavery? Ask them on Northern ground, where they will speak the truth, and I doubt not, every man of them will tell you, no! Why then, I ask, did they give their votes to enlarge the mouth of that grave which has already destroyed its tens of thousands? All our enemies tell us they are as much anti-slavery as we are. Yes, my friends, thousands who are helping you to bind the fetters of slavery on the Negro, despise you in their hearts for doing it; they rejoice that such an institution has not been entailed upon them. Why then, I would ask, do they lend you their help? I will tell you, "they love the praise of men more than the praise of God." The Abolition cause has not yet become so popular as to induce them to believe, that by advocating it in congress they shall sit still more securely in their seats there, and like the chief rulers in the days of our Saviour, though many believed on him, yet they did not confess him, lest they should be put out of the synagogue; John xii, 42, 43. Or perhaps like Pilate, thinking they could prevail nothing, and fearing a tumult, they determined to release Barabbas and surrender the just man, the poor innocent slave to be stripped of his rights and scourged. In vain will such men try to wash their hands, and say, with the Roman governor, "I am innocent of the blood of this just person." Northern American statesmen are no more innocent of the crime of slavery, than Pilate was of the murder of Jesus, or Saul of that of Stephen. These are high charges, but I appeal to their hearts; I appeal to public opinion ten years from now. Slavery then is a national sin.

But you will say, a great many other Northerners tell us so, who can have no political motives. The interests of the North, you must know, my friends, are very closely combined with those of the South.

This interest of northerners in slavery was known as the combination of the "lords of the loom" and "lords of the lash." The former referred to northern industrialists—owners of mills and factories that used the products of slave labor—while the latter referred to slaveholders, known as such because the lash is what they used to keep slaves in check.

"The Northern merchants and manufacturers are making their fortunes out of the produce of slave labor; the grocer is selling your rice and sugar; how then can these men bear a testimony against slavery without condemning themselves?"

The Northern merchants and manufacturers are making their fortunes out of the produce of slave labor; the grocer is selling your rice and sugar; how then can these men bear a testimony against slavery without condemning themselves? But there is another reason, the North is most dreadfully afraid of Amalgamation. She is alarmed at the very idea of a thing so monstrous, as she thinks. And lest this consequence might flow from emancipation, she is determined to resist all efforts at emancipation without expatriation. It is not because she approves of slavery, or believes it to be "the corner stone of our republic," for she is as much anti-slavery as we are; but amalgamation is too horrible to think of. Now I would ask you, is it right, is it generous, to refuse the colored people in this country the advantages of education and the privilege, or rather the right, to follow honest trades and callings merely because they are colored? The same prejudice exists here against our colored brethren that existed against the Gentiles in Judea. Great numbers cannot bear the idea of equality, and fearing lest, if they had the same advantages we enjoy, they would become as intelligent, as moral, as religious, and as respectable and wealthy, they are determined to keep them as low as they possibly can. Is this doing as they would be done by? Is this loving their neighbor as themselves? Oh! that such opposers of Abolitionism would put their souls in the stead of the free colored man's and obey the apostolic injunction, to "remember them that are in bonds as bound with them." I will leave you to judge whether the fear of amalgamation ought to induce men to oppose anti-slavery efforts, when they believe slavery to be sinful. Prejudice against color, is the most powerful enemy we have to fight with at the North.

You need not be surprised, then, at all, at what is said against Abolitionists by the North, for they are wielding a two-edged sword, which even here, cuts through the cords of caste, on the one side, and the bonds of interest on the other. They are only sharing the fate of other reformers, abused and reviled whilst they are in the minority; but they are neither angry nor discouraged by the invective which has been heaped upon them by slaveholders at the South and their apologists at the North. They know that when George Fox and William Edmundson were laboring in behalf of the negroes in the West Indies in 1671 that the very same slanders were propagated against them, which are now circulated against Abolitionists. Although it was well known that Fox was the founder of a religious sect which repudiated all war, and all violence, yet even he was accused of "endeavoring to excite the slaves to insurrection and of teaching the negroes to cut their master's throats." And these two men who had their feet shod with the preparation of the Gospel of Peace, were actually compelled to draw up a formal declaration that they were not trying to raise a rebellion in Barbadoes. It is also worthy of remark that these Reformers did not at this time see the necessity of emancipation under seven years, and their principal efforts were exerted to persuade the planters of the necessity of instructing their slaves; but the slaveholder saw then, just what the slaveholder sees now, that an enlightened population never can be a slave population, and therefore they passed a law that negroes should not even attend the meetings of Friends. Abolitionists know that the life of Clarkson was sought by slavetraders, and that even Wilberforce was denounced on the floor of Parliament as a fanatic and a hypocrite by the present King of England, the very man who, in 1834 set his seal to that instrument which burst the fetters of eight hundred thousand slaves in his West India colonies. They know that the first Quaker who bore a faithful testimony against the sin of slavery was cut off from religious fellowship with that society. That Quaker was a woman. On her deathbed she sent for the committee who dealt with her—she told them, the near approach of death had not altered her sentiments on the subject of slavery and waving her hand towards a very fertile and beautiful portion of country which lay stretched before her window, she said with great solemnity, "Friends, the time will come when there will not be friends enough in all this district to hold one meeting for worship, and this garden will be turned into a wilderness."

The aged friend, who with tears in his eyes, related this interesting circumstance to me, remarked, that at that time there were seven meetings of friends in that part of Virginia, but that when he was there ten years ago, not a single meeting was held, and the country was literally a desolation. Soon after her decease, John Woolman began his labors in our society, and instead of disowning a member for testifying against slavery, they have for fifty-two years positively forbidden their members to hold slaves.

"Abolitionists understand the slaveholding spirit too well to be surprised at any thing that has yet happened at the South or the North; they know that the greater the sin is, which is exposed, the more violent will be the efforts to blacken the character and impugn the motives of those who are engaged in bringing to light the hidden things of darkness."

Abolitionists understand the slaveholding spirit too well to be surprised at any thing that has yet happened at the South or the North; they know that the greater the sin is, which is exposed, the more violent will be the efforts to blacken the character and impugn the motives of those who are engaged in bringing to light the hidden things of darkness. They understand the work of Reform too well to be driven back by the furious waves of opposition, which are only foaming out their own shame. They have stood "the world's dread laugh," when only twelve men formed the first Anti-Slavery Society in Boston in 1831. They have faced and refuted the calumnies of their enemies, and proved themselves to be emphatically peace men by never resisting the violence of mobs, even when driven by them from the temple of God, and dragged by an infuriated crowd through the streets of the emporium of New-England, or subjected by slaveholders to the pain of corporal punishment. "None of these things move them;" and, by the grace of God, they are determined to persevere in this work of faith and labor of love: they mean to pray, and preach, and write, and print, until slavery is completely overthrown, until Babylon is taken up and cast into the sea, to "be found no more at all." They mean to petition Congress year after year, until the seat of our government is cleansed from the sinful traffic of "slaves and the souls of men." Although that august assembly may be like the unjust judge who "feared not God neither regarded man," yet it must yield just as he did, from the power of importunity. Like the unjust judge, Congress must redress the wrongs of the widow, lest by the continual coming up of petitions, it be wearied. This will be striking the dagger into the very heart of the monster, and once 'tis done, he must soon expire.

Abolitionists have been accused of abusing their Southern brethren. Did the prophet Isaiah abuse the Jews when he addressed to them the cutting reproofs contained in the first chapter of his prophecies, and ended by telling them, they would be ashamed of the oaks they had desired, and confounded for the garden they had chosen? **Did John the Baptist abuse the Jews when he called them "a generation of vipers," and warned them "to bring forth fruits meet for repentance?" Did Peter abuse the Jews when he told them they were the murderers of the Lord of Glory? Did Paul abuse the Roman Governor when he reasoned before him of righteousness, temperance, and judgment, so as to send conviction home to his guilty heart, and cause him to tremble in view of the crimes he was living in? Surely not. No man will now accuse the prophets and apostles of abuse, but what have Abolitionists done more than they? No doubt the Jews thought the prophets and**

By using these biblical examples, Grimké again attempts to infuse the antislavery movement with divine sanction, claiming that contemporary abolitionists are just like the biblical prophets of old, speaking the Lord's word to a skeptical people.

apostles in their day, just as harsh and uncharitable as slaveholders now, think Abolitionists; if they did not, why did they beat, and stone, and kill them?

"Until the pictures of the slave's sufferings were drawn and held up to public gaze, no Northerner had any idea of the cruelty of the system, it never entered their minds that such abominations could exist in Christian, Republican America."

Great fault has been found with the prints which have been employed to expose slavery at the North, but my friends, how could this be done so effectually in any other way? Until the pictures of the slave's sufferings were drawn and held up to public gaze, no Northerner had any idea of the cruelty of the system, it never entered their minds that such abominations could exist in Christian, Republican America; they never suspected that many of the gentlemen and ladies who came from the South to spend the summer months in travelling among them, were petty tyrants at home. And those who had lived at the South, and came to reside at the North, were too ashamed of slavery even to speak of it; the language of their hearts was, "tell it not in Gath, publish it not in the streets of Askelon;" they saw no use in uncovering the loathsome body to popular sight, and in hopeless despair, wept in secret places over the sins of oppression. To such hidden mourners the formation of Anti-Slavery Societies was as life from the dead, the first beams of hope which gleamed through the dark clouds of despondency and grief. Prints were made use of to effect the abolition of the Inquisition in Spain, and Clarkson employed them when he was laboring to break up the Slave trade, and English Abolitionists used them just as we are now doing. They are powerful appeals and have invariably done the work they were designed to do, and we cannot consent to abandon the use of these until the realities no longer exist.

With regard to those white men, who, it was said, did try to raise an insurrection in Mississippi a year ago, and who were stated to be Abolitionists, none of them were proved to be members of Anti-Slavery Societies, and it must remain a matter of great doubt whether, even they were guilty of the crimes alleged against them, because when any community is thrown into such a panic as to inflict Lynch law upon accused persons, they cannot be supposed to be capable of judging with calmness and impartiality. We know that the papers of which the Charleston mail was robbed, were not insurrectionary, and that they were not sent to the colored people as was reported, We know that Amos Dresser was no insurrectionist though he was accused of being so, and on this false accusation was publicly whipped in Nashville in the midst of a crowd of infuriated slaveholders. Was that young man disgraced by this infliction of corporal punishment? No more than was the great apostle of the Gentiles who five times received forty stripes, save one. Like him, he might have said, "henceforth I bear in my body the marks of the Lord Jesus," for it was for the truth's sake, he suffered, as much as did the Apostle Paul. Are Nelson, and Garrett, and Williams, and other Abolitionists who have recently been banished from Missouri, insurrectionists? We know they are not, whatever slaveholders may choose to call them. The spirit which now asperses the character of the Abolitionists, is the very same which dressed up the Christians of Spain in the skins of wild beasts and pictures of devils when they were led to execution as heretics. Before we condemn individuals, it is necessary, even in a wicked community, to accuse them of some crime; hence, when Jezebel wished to compass the death of Naboth, men of Belial were suborned to bear false witness against him, and so it was with Stephen, and so it ever has been, and ever will be, as long as there is any virtue to suffer on the rack, or the gallows. False witnesses must appear against Abolitionists before they can be condemned. . . .

What can I say more, my friends, to induce you to set your hands, and heads, and hearts, to this great work of justice

"The spirit which now asperses the character of the Abolitionists, is the very same which dressed up the Christians of Spain in the skins of wild beasts and pictures of devils when they were led to execution as heretics."

and mercy. Perhaps you have feared the consequences of immediate Emancipation, and been frightened by all those dreadful prophecies of rebellion, bloodshed and murder, which have been uttered. "Let no man deceive you," they are the predictions of that same "lying spirit" which spoke through the four hundred prophets of old, to Ahab king of Israel, urging, him on to destruction. Slavery may produce these horrible scenes if it is continued five years longer, but Emancipation never will.

"I can prove the safety of immediate Emancipation by history."

I can prove the safety of immediate Emancipation by history. In St. Domingo in 1793 six hundred thousand slaves were set free in a white population of forty-two thousand. That Island marched as by enchantment towards its ancient splendor, cultivation prospered, every day produced perceptible proofs of its progress, and the negroes all continued quietly to work on the different plantations, until in 1802, France determined to reduce these liberated slaves again to bondage. It was at this time that all those dreadful scenes of cruelty occurred, which we so often unjustly hear spoken of, as the effects of Abolition. They were occasioned not by Emancipation, but by the base attempt to fasten the chains of slavery on the limbs of liberated slaves.

In Gaudaloupe eighty-five thousand slaves were freed in a white population of thirteen thousand. The same prosperous effects followed manumission here, that had attended it in Hayti, every thing was quiet until Bonaparte sent out a fleet to reduce these negroes again to slavery, and in 1802 this institution was re-established in that Island. In 1834, when Great Britain determined to liberate the slaves in her West India colonies, and proposed the apprenticeship system; the planters of Bermuda and Antigua, after having joined the other planters in their representations of the bloody consequences of Emancipation, in order if possible to hold back the hand which was offering the boon of freedom to the poor negro; as soon as they found such falsehoods were utterly disregarded, and Abolition must take place, came forward voluntarily, and asked for the compensation which was due to them, saying, they preferred immediate emancipation, and were not afraid of any insurrection. And how is it with these islands now? They are decidedly more prosperous than any of those in which the apprenticeship system was adopted, and England is now trying to abolish that system, so fully convinced is she that immediate Emancipation is the safest and the best plan.

And why not try it in the Southern States, if it never has occasioned rebellion; if not a drop of blood has ever been shed in consequence of it, though it has been so often tried, why should we suppose it would produce such disastrous consequences now? "Be not deceived then, God is not mocked," by such false excuses for not doing justly and loving mercy. There is nothing to fear from immediate Emancipation, but every thing from the continuance of slavery.

Sisters in Christ, I have done. As a Southerner, I have felt it was my duty to address you. I have endeavoured to set before you the exceeding sinfulness of slavery, and to point you to the example of those noble women who have been raised up in the church to effect great revolutions, and to suffer for the truth's sake. I have appealed to your sympathies as women, to your sense of duty as Christian women. I have attempted to vindicate the Abolitionists, to prove the entire safety of immediate Emancipation, and to plead the cause of the poor and oppressed. I have done—I have sowed the seeds of truth, but I well know, that even if an Apollos were to follow in my steps to water them, "God only can give the increase." To Him then who is able to prosper the work of his servant's hand, I commend this Appeal in

"There is nothing to fear from immediate Emancipation, but every thing from the continuance of slavery."

fervent prayer, that as he "hath chosen the weak things of the world, to confound the things which are mighty," so He may cause His blessing, to descend and carry conviction to the hearts of many Lydias through these speaking pages. Farewell—Count me not your "enemy because I have told you the truth," but believe me in unfeigned affection,

Your sympathizing Friend,

ANGELINA E. GRIMKÉ

Source: Angelina Emily Grimké, *An Appeal to the Christian Women of the South* (New York: American Anti-Slavery Society, 1836).

Antislavery and Women's Rights

Elizabeth Margaret Chandler, "Am I Not a Woman and a Sister?"

1837

INTRODUCTION

Just one year after Angelina Grimké called on southern Christian women to aid in the abolitionist cause, Elizabeth Margaret Chandler produced this famous counterpoint to Josiah Wedgwood's 1787 medallion. Chandler was a poet and one of the first women in the United States to write about slavery, producing poems for Benjamin Lundy's *Genius of Universal Emancipation,* the antislavery newspaper that William Lloyd Garrison also worked for. Garrison used this image in his Liberator, which helped circulate it to thousands and ensured its lasting significance.

While Josiah Wedgwood's piece "Am I Not a Man and a Brother?" seemingly highlighted the universality of slavery, Chandler's rendering of "Am I Not a Woman and a Sister?" was aimed at highlighting the specific challenges that female slaves faced in bondage, including separation from their children and the constant threat of physical abuse, symbolized by the woman's naked upper body. Chandler, who was in charge of the Ladies Department of the *Genius of Universal Emancipation,* also wanted to appeal to the thousands of female reformers throughout the nation, some of whom may not have readily identified with the figure of the male slave. Like the work of Maria Stewart and Angelina Grimké, this image displays the intimate connection between the causes of abolitionism and women's rights in the United States.

Source: George Bourne, *Slavery Illustrated In Its Effects upon Woman and Domestic Society* (Boston: Isaac Knapp, 1837), 12.

Slave Narratives

Charles Ball, *Slavery in the United States*
1837

INTRODUCTION

Charles Ball was born enslaved in Maryland in 1780 and gained his freedom in the 1820s. Near the end of the 1830s he published his account of life in slavery. Ball described the institution as "one long waste, barren desert, of cheerless, hopeless, lifeless slavery; to be varied only by the pangs of hunger, and the stings of the lash." In the excerpt below, he reflects on the religion of slaves and the impact of the institution of slavery on that religious life. He notes that because of slavery many blacks are not Christians, as their masters fear what conversion will do to their property. This issue reflects a long-standing concern among slaveholders, dating back to the 17th century, that conversion to Christianity would undermine their property in slaves. In highlighting this issue, Ball aims to speak to the intense religiosity of the United States in the 1830s, where the Second Great Awakening, a massive religious revival, had been under way for decades. In making the case that slavery harms Christianity's spread, Ball hoped to inspire religious readers to take up the cause of the enslaved.

Ball's narrative, like all slave narratives, served the function of detailing the lives of slaves to increase support for the abolitionist movement. Many leaders of this movement—William Lloyd Garrison, Sojourner Truth, Arthur and Lewis Tappan, and Lydia Maria Child, among others—were intensely pious individuals, and thus appealing to their religious sensibilities was a strong rhetorical move likely to attract support. Ball does this by arguing that slavery hinders the Christianization of slaves, despite the arguments that it was carried on to evangelize heathen Africans.

... All over the south, the slaves are discouraged, as much as possible, and by all possible means, from going to any place of religious worship on Sunday. This is to prevent them from associating together, from different estates, and distant parts of the country; and plotting conspiracies and insurrections. On some estates, the overseers are required to prohibit the people from going to meeting off the plantation, at any time, under the severest penalties. While preachers cannot come upon the plantations, to preach to the people, without first obtaining permission of the master, and afterwards procuring the sanction of the overseer. No slave dare leave the plantation to which he belongs, a single mile, without a written pass from the overseer, or master; but by exposing himself to the danger of being taken up and flogged. Any white man who meets a slave off the plantation without a pass, has a right to take him up, and flog him at his discretion. All these causes combined, operate powerfully to keep the slave at home. But, in addition to those principles of restraint, it is a rule on every plantation, that no overseer ever departs from, to flog every slave, male or female, that leaves the estate for a single hour, by night or by day—Sunday not excepted—without a written pass.

The overseer who should permit the people under his charge to go about the neighbourhood without a pass, would soon lose his character, and no one would employ him; nor would his reputation less certainly suffer in the estimation of the planters, were he to fall into the practice of granting passes, except on the most urgent occasions; and for purposes generally to be specified in the pass.

A cotton planter has no more idea of permitting his slaves to go at will, about the neighbourhood on Sunday, than a farmer in Pennsylvania has of letting his horses out of his field on that day. Nor would the neighbours be less inclined to complain of the annoyance, in the former, than in the latter case.

In drawing this comparison between slaves and horses, Ball alludes to the dehumanization of the institution, as people are treated just like or even worse than animals.

There has always been a strong repugnance, amongst the planters, against their slaves becoming members of any religious society, Not, as I believe, because they are so maliciously disposed towards their people as to wish to deprive them of the comforts of religion—provided the principles of religion did not militate against the principles of slavery—but they fear that the slaves, by attending meetings, and listening to the preachers, may imbibe with the morality they teach, the notions of equality and liberty, contained in the gospel. This, I have no doubt, is the ground of all the dissatisfaction, that the planters express, with the itinerant preachers, who have from time to time, sought

The first slaves came to Virginia in 1619, yet it was not until the late 18th and early 19th centuries that slaves began converting to Christianity en masse. Some masters feared that baptism would free their slaves, a fear that was especially prominent during the 18th century. Later, other masters simply believed that acquiring religion and the knowledge that came with it would make for restless and discontented slaves. This was not the case for all masters, however, as many believed that religion would create better slaves.

opportunities of instructing the slaves in their religious duties.

The cotton planters have always, since I knew any thing of them, been most careful to prevent the slaves from learning to read; and such is the gross ignorance that prevails, that many of them could not name the four cardinal points.

Ball grew up in the late 18th century, a period when the Atlantic slave trade was still flourishing and continual imports of slaves came from Africa to the United States. These Africans brought their own religious beliefs. Some practiced Islam and others coming from Central Africa may have been Catholics, but most practiced traditional African religions, which emphasized practices such as ancestor worship and magic. Ball alludes to the great amount of religious diversity, which during his time was not seen as a good thing.

At the time I first went to Carolina, there were a great many African slaves in the country, and they continued to come in for several years afterwards. I became intimately acquainted with some of these men. Many of them believed there were several gods; some of whom were good, and others evil, and they prayed as much to the latter as to the former. I knew several who must have been, from what I have since learned, Mohamedans; though at that time, I had never heard of the religion of Mohamed.

There was one man on this plantation, who prayed five times every day, always turning his face to the east, when in the performance of his devotion.

There is, in general, very little sense of religious obligation, or duty, amongst the slaves on the cotton plantations; and Christianity cannot be, with propriety, called the religion of these people. They are universally subject to the grossest and most abject superstition; and uniformly believe in witchcraft, conjuration, and the agency of evil spirits in the affairs of human life. Far the greater part of them are either natives of Africa, or the descendants of those who have always, from generation to generation, lived in the south, since their ancestors were landed on this continent; and their superstition, for it does not deserve the name of religion, is no better, nor is it less ferocious, than that which oppresses the inhabitants of the wildest regions of Negro-land.

They have not the slightest religious regard for the Sabbath-day, and their masters make no efforts to impress them with the least respect for this sacred institution. . . .

Source: Charles Ball, *Slavery in the United States: A Narrative of the Life and Adventures of Charles Ball, a Black Man, Who Lived Forty Years in Maryland, South Carolina, and Georgia, as a Slave, under Various Masters, and Was One Year in the Navy with Commodore Barney, during the Late War; Containing an Account of the Manners and Usages of the Planters and Slaveholders of the South—A Description of the Condition and Treatment of the Slaves, with Observations upon the State of Morals amongst the Cotton Planters, and the Perils and Sufferings of a Fugitive Slave, Who Twice Escaped from the Cotton Country* (New York: John S. Taylor, 1837), 162–165.

"Republicanism a Sham"

Frederick Douglass, "What to the Slave Is the Fourth of July?"

1852

INTRODUCTION

Frederick Douglass, like Charles Ball, was also enslaved in Maryland and gained his freedom in 1837, the same year that Ball published his slave narrative. Douglass moved first to Newburyport, Massachusetts, where he became involved with William Lloyd Garrison and the antislavery movement. Douglass became an abolitionist speaker, writer, and eventually newspaper editor, publishing the *North Star* and *Frederick Douglass' Paper,* among others. In this speech, given at an antislavery convention in Rochester, New York, Douglass questions the meaning of the Fourth of July, and by implication American ideals, to slaves in the United States. The speech was delivered on July 5, which was the traditional day that African Americans celebrated American independence because if they attempted to do so publicly on July 4, they could be subject to racial violence. The irony of this situation is not lost on Douglass, who questions American Christianity and republicanism in this scathing attack on slavery.

Mr. President, Friends and Fellow Citizens:

He who could address this audience without a quailing sensation, has stronger nerves than I have. I do not remember ever to have appeared as a speaker before any assembly more shrinkingly, nor with greater distrust of my ability, than I do this day. A feeling has crept over me, quite unfavorable to the exercise of my limited powers of speech. The task before me is one which requires much previous thought and study for its proper performance. I know that apologies of this sort are generally considered flat and unmeaning. I trust, however, that mine will not be so considered. Should I seem at ease, my appearance would much misrepresent me. The little experience I have had in addressing public meetings, in country schoolhouses, avails me nothing on the present occasion.

The papers and placards say, that I am to deliver a 4th [of] July oration. This certainly sounds large, and out of the common way, for it is true that I have often had the privilege to speak in this beautiful Hall, and to address many who now honor me with their presence. But neither their familiar faces, nor the perfect gage I think I have of Corinthian Hall, seems to free me from embarrassment.

The fact is, ladies and gentlemen, the distance between this platform and the slave plantation, from which I escaped, is considerable—and the difficulties to be overcome in getting from the latter to the former, are by no means slight. That I am here to-day is, to me, a matter of astonishment as well as of gratitude. You will not, therefore, be surprised, if in what I have to say, I evince no elaborate preparation, nor grace my speech with any high sounding exordium. With little experience and with less learning, I have been able to throw my thoughts hastily and imperfectly together; and trusting to your patient and generous indulgence, I will proceed to lay them before you.

This, for the purpose of this celebration, is the 4th of July. It is the birthday of your National Independence, and of your political freedom. This, to you, is what the Passover was to the emancipated people of God. It carries your minds back to the day, and to the act of your great deliverance; and to the signs, and to the wonders, associated with that act, and that day. This celebration also marks the beginning of another year of your national life; and reminds you that the Republic of America is now 76 years old. I am glad, fellow-citizens, that your nation is so young. Seventy-six years, though

In these first few sentences, Douglass makes extensive use of the pronoun "your," foreshadowing his later statements that this holiday is one for whites, not blacks, and certainly not for enslaved blacks.

a good old age for a man, is but a mere speck in the life of a nation. Three score years and ten is the allotted time for individual men; but nations number their years by thousands. According to this fact, you are, even now, only in the beginning of your national career, still lingering in the period of childhood. I repeat, I am glad this is so. There is hope in the thought, and hope is much needed, under the dark clouds which lower above the horizon. The eye of the reformer is met with angry flashes, portending disastrous times; but his heart may well beat lighter at the thought that America is young, and that she is still in the impressible stage of her existence. May he not hope that high lessons of wisdom, of justice and of truth, will yet give direction to her destiny? Were the nation older, the patriot's heart might be sadder, and the reformer's brow heavier. Its future might be shrouded in gloom, and the hope of its prophets go out in sorrow. There is consolation in the thought that America is young. Great streams are not easily turned from channels, worn deep in the course of ages. They may sometimes rise in quiet and stately majesty, and inundate the land, refreshing and fertilizing the earth with their mysterious properties. They may also rise in wrath and fury, and bear away, on their angry waves, the accumulated wealth of years of toil and hardship. They, however, gradually flow back to the same old channel, and flow on as serenely as ever. But, while the river may not be turned aside, it may dry up, and leave nothing behind but the withered branch, and the unsightly rock, to howl in the abyss-sweeping wind, the sad tale of departed glory. As with rivers so with nations.

Fellow-citizens, I shall not presume to dwell at length on the associations that cluster about this day. The simple story of it is that, 76 years ago, the people of this country were British subjects. The style and title of your "sovereign people" (in which you now glory) was not then born. You were under the British Crown. Your fathers esteemed the English Government as the home government; and England as the fatherland. This home government, you know, although a considerable distance from your home, did, in the exercise of its parental prerogatives, impose upon its colonial children, such restraints, burdens and limitations, as, in its mature judgment, it deemed wise, right and proper.

But, your fathers, who had not adopted the fashionable idea of this day, of the infallibility of government, and the absolute character of its acts, presumed to differ from the home government in respect to the wisdom and the justice of some of those burdens and restraints. They went so far in their excitement as to pronounce the measures of government unjust, unreasonable, and oppressive, and altogether such as ought not to be quietly submitted to. I scarcely need say, fellow-citizens, that my opinion of those measures fully accords with that of your fathers. Such a declaration of agreement on my part would not be worth much to anybody. It would, certainly, prove nothing, as to what part I might have taken, had I lived during the great controversy of 1776. **To say now that America was right, and England wrong, is exceedingly easy. Everybody can say it; the dastard, not less than the noble brave, can flippantly discant on the tyranny of England towards the American Colonies. It is fashionable to do so; but there was a time when to pronounce against England, and in favor of the cause of the colonies, tried men's souls.** They who did so were accounted in their day, plotters of mischief, agitators and rebels, dangerous men. To side with the right, against the wrong, with the weak against the strong, and with the oppressed against the oppressor! here lies the merit, and the one which, of all others, seems unfashionable in our day. The cause of liberty may be stabbed by the men who glory in the deeds of your fathers. But, to proceed.

Douglass alludes to the writings of Thomas Paine, specifically his *American Crisis* essays, the first of which began with the line "these are the times that try men's souls." In doing so, Douglass not only displays his own learning but also shows the influence of American Revolutionary thought on his own principles.

While Douglass is speaking of the Founders, his words here have contemporary significance: Just as they petitioned and remonstrated against tyranny, so too have American slaves petitioned against their bondage. It just might be the case that slaves eventually take the same course of action as the Founders—violent rebellion against their oppressors.

Feeling themselves harshly and unjustly treated by the home government, your fathers, like men of honesty, and men of spirit, earnestly sought redress. They petitioned and remonstrated; they did so in a decorous, respectful, and loyal manner. Their conduct was wholly unexceptionable. This, however, did not answer the purpose. They saw themselves treated with sovereign indifference, coldness and scorn. Yet they persevered. They were not the men to look back.

As the sheet anchor takes a firmer hold, when the ship is tossed by the storm, so did the cause of your fathers grow stronger, as it breasted the chilling blasts of kingly displeasure. The greatest and best of British statesmen admitted its justice, and the loftiest eloquence of the British Senate came to its support. But, with that blindness which seems to be the unvarying characteristic of tyrants, since Pharaoh and his hosts were drowned in the Red Sea, the British Government persisted in the exactions complained of.

The madness of this course, we believe, is admitted now, even by England; but we fear the lesson is wholly lost on our present ruler.

Oppression makes a wise man mad. Your fathers were wise men, and if they did not go mad, they became restive under this treatment. They felt themselves the victims of grievous wrongs, wholly incurable in their colonial capacity. With brave men there is always a remedy for oppression. Just here, the idea of a total separation of the colonies from the crown was born! It was a startling idea, much more so, than we, at this distance of time, regard it. The timid and the prudent (as has been intimated) of that day, were, of course, shocked and alarmed by it.

Such people lived then, had lived before, and will, probably, ever have a place on this planet; and their course, in respect to any great change, (no matter how great the good to be attained, or the wrong to be redressed by it), may be calculated with as much precision as can be the course of the stars. They hate all changes, but silver, gold and copper change! Of this sort of change they are always strongly in favor.

These people were called Tories in the days of your fathers; and the appellation, probably, conveyed the same idea that is meant by a more modern, though a somewhat less euphonious term, which we often find in our papers, applied to some of our old politicians.

The Tories were the conservatives of their day, and at the time Douglass gave this speech, that title belonged to the Democratic Party, which was strongest in the South. The Democrats wanted to keep America a rural nation, while the Whigs, and later the Republicans, pushed for industrialization. Democrats generally resisted social reforms and called for power to be located in state governments rather than in the federal government.

Their opposition to the then dangerous thought was earnest and powerful; but, amid all their terror and affrighted vociferations against it, the alarming and revolutionary idea moved on, and the country with it.

On the 2d of July, 1776, the old Continental Congress, to the dismay of the lovers of ease, and the worshipers of property, clothed that dreadful idea with all the authority of national sanction. They did so in the form of a resolution; and as we seldom hit upon resolutions, drawn up in our day whose transparency is at all equal to this, it may refresh your minds and help my story if I read it.

Resolved, That these united colonies are, and of right, ought to be free and Independent States; that they are absolved from all allegiance to the British Crown; and that all political connection between them and the State of Great Britain is, and ought to be, dissolved.

Citizens, your fathers made good that resolution. They succeeded; and to-day you reap the fruits of their success. The freedom gained is yours; and you, therefore, may properly celebrate this anniversary. The 4th of July is the first great fact in your nation's history—the very ring-bolt in the chain of your yet undeveloped destiny.

Pride and patriotism, not less than gratitude, prompt you to celebrate and to hold it in perpetual remembrance. I have said that the Declaration of Independence is the ring-bolt to the chain of your nation's destiny; so, indeed, I regard it. The principles contained in that instrument are saving principles. Stand by those principles, be true to them on all occasions, in all places, against all foes, and at whatever cost.

From the round top of your ship of state, dark and threatening clouds may be seen. Heavy billows, like mountains in the distance, disclose to the leeward huge forms of flinty rocks! That bolt drawn, that chain broken, and all is lost. Cling to this day—cling to it, and to its principles, with the grasp of a storm-tossed mariner to a spar at midnight.

The coming into being of a nation, in any circumstances, is an interesting event. But, besides general considerations, there were peculiar circumstances which make the advent of this republic an event of special attractiveness.

The whole scene, as I look back to it, was simple, dignified and sublime.

The population of the country, at the time, stood at the insignificant number of three millions. The country was poor in the munitions of war. The population was weak and scattered, and the country a wilderness unsubdued. There were then no means of concert and combination, such as exist now. Neither steam nor lightning had then been reduced to order and discipline. From the Potomac to the Delaware was a journey of many days. Under these, and innumerable other disadvantages, your fathers declared for liberty and independence and triumphed.

Fellow Citizens, I am not wanting in respect for the fathers of this republic. The signers of the Declaration of Independence were brave men. They were great men too—great enough to give fame to a great age. It does not often happen to a nation to raise, at one time, such a number of truly great men. The point from which I am compelled to view them is not, certainly, the most favorable; and yet I cannot contemplate their great deeds with less than admiration. They were statesmen, patriots and heroes, and for the good they did, and the principles they contended for, I will unite with you to honor their memory.

They loved their country better than their own private interests; and, though this is not the highest form of human excellence, all will concede that it is a rare virtue, and that when it is exhibited, it ought to command respect. He who will, intelligently, lay down his life for his country, is a man whom it is not in human nature to despise. Your fathers staked their lives, their fortunes, and their sacred honor, on the cause of their country. In their admiration of liberty, they lost sight of all other interests.

In classical republican thought, one of the most important political philosophies upon which the nation was founded, virtue was the highest ideal of a citizen, and virtue meant the willingness to sacrifice one's individual interests for the good of the country.

They were peace men; but they preferred revolution to peaceful submission to bondage. They were quiet men; but they did not shrink from agitating against oppression. They showed forbearance; but that they knew its limits. They believed in order; but not in the order of tyranny. With them, nothing was "settled" that was not right. With them, justice, liberty and humanity were "final;" not slavery and oppression. You may well cherish the memory of such men.

They were great in their day and generation. Their solid manhood stands out the more as we contrast it with these degenerate times.

How circumspect, exact and proportionate were all their movements! How unlike the politicians of an hour! Their statesmanship looked beyond the passing moment, and stretched away in strength into the distant future. They seized upon eternal principles, and set a glorious example in their defense. Mark them!

Fully appreciating the hardship to be encountered, firmly believing in the right of their cause, honorably inviting the scrutiny of an on-looking world, reverently appealing to heaven to attest their sincerity, soundly comprehending the solemn responsibility they were about to assume, wisely measuring the terrible odds against them, your fathers, the fathers of this republic, did, most deliberately, under the inspiration of a glorious patriotism, and with a sublime faith in the great principles of justice and freedom, lay deep the corner-stone of the national superstructure, which has risen and still rises in grandeur around you.

Of this fundamental work, this day is the anniversary. Our eyes are met with demonstrations of joyous enthusiasm. Banners and pennants wave exultingly on the breeze. The din of business, too, is hushed. Even Mammon seems to have quitted his grasp on this day. The ear-piercing fife and the stirring drum unite their accents with the ascending peal of a thousand church bells. Prayers are made, hymns are sung, and sermons are preached in honor of this day; while the quick martial tramp of a great and multitudinous nation, echoed back by all the hills, valleys and mountains of a vast continent, bespeak the occasion one of thrilling and universal interest—a nation's jubilee.

Friends and citizens, I need not enter further into the causes which led to this anniversary. Many of you understand them better than I do. You could instruct me in regard to them. That is a branch of knowledge in which you feel, perhaps, a much deeper interest than your speaker. The causes which led to the separation of the colonies from the British crown have never lacked for a tongue. They have all been taught in your common schools, narrated at your firesides, unfolded from your pulpits, and thundered from your legislative halls, and are as familiar to you as household words. They form the staple of your national poetry and eloquence.

Historians of the American Revolutionary War emerged very shortly after the conflict had ended. This first generation of Revolutionary scholars are known as participant historians because in some way or another they participated in the events of the war. David Ramsay of South Carolina and Mercy Otis Warren of Massachusetts are two prime examples. Throughout the 19th century, efforts to celebrate and commemorate the founding were seen in the work of historians, memorialists, speakers, and politicians.

I remember, also, that, as a people, Americans are remarkably familiar with all facts which make in their own favor. This is esteemed by some as a national trait—perhaps a national weakness. It is a fact, that whatever makes for the wealth or for the reputation of Americans, and can be had cheap! will be found by Americans. I shall not be charged with slandering Americans, if I say I think the American side of any question may be safely left in American hands.

I leave, therefore, the great deeds of your fathers to other gentlemen whose claim to have been regularly descended will be less likely to be disputed than mine!

THE PRESENT.

My business, if I have any here to-day, is with the present. The accepted time with God and his cause is the ever-living now.

"Trust no future, however pleasant,
Let the dead past bury its dead;
Act, act in the living present,
Heart within, and God overhead."

We have to do with the past only as we can make it useful to the present and to the future. To all inspiring motives, to noble deeds which can be gained from the past, we are welcome. But now is the time, the important time. Your fathers have lived, died, and have done their work, and have done much of it well. You live and must die, and you must do your work. You have no right to enjoy a child's share in the labor of your fathers, unless your children are to be blest by your labors. You have no right to wear out and waste the hard-earned fame of your fathers to cover your indolence. Sydney Smith tells us that men seldom eulogize the wisdom and virtues of their fathers, but to excuse some folly or wickedness of their own. This truth is not a doubtful one. There are illustrations of it near and remote, ancient and modern. It was fashionable, hundreds of years ago, for the children of Jacob to boast, we have "Abraham to our father," when they had long lost Abraham's faith and spirit. That people contented themselves under the shadow of Abraham's great name, while they repudiated the deeds which made his name great. Need I remind you that a similar thing is being done all over this country to-day? Need I tell you that the Jews are not the only people who built the tombs of the prophets, and garnished the sepulchres of the righteous? **Washington could not die till he had broken the chains of his slaves. Yet his monument is built up by the price of human blood, and the traders in the bodies and souls of men shout—"We have Washington to *our father.*"—Alas! that it should be so; yet so it is.**

Construction on the Washington Monument commenced in 1848, just four years before his speech, and it was opened in 1885 (lack of funds and the Civil War halted construction between 1854 and 1877). In its earliest years the monument was built with slave labor, as slavery was legal in Washington, D.C., although the slave trade in the nation's capital had been abolished with the Compromise of 1850.

The evil that men do, lives after them,
The good is oft' interred with their bones.

Fellow-citizens, pardon me, allow me to ask, why am I called upon to speak here to-day? What have I, or those

I represent, to do with your national independence? Are the great principles of political freedom and of natural justice, embodied in that Declaration of Independence extended to us? and am I, therefore, called upon to bring our humble offering to the national altar, and to confess the benefits and express devout gratitude for the blessings resulting from your independence to us?

After reciting a brief history of American independence, Douglass gets to his main point, the fact that African Americans cannot celebrate this holiday themselves.

Would to God, both for your sakes and ours, that an affirmative answer could be truthfully returned to these questions! Then would my task be light, and my burden easy and delightful. For who is there so cold, that a nation's sympathy could not warm him? Who so obdurate and dead to the claims of gratitude, that would not thankfully acknowledge such priceless benefits? Who so stolid and selfish, that would not give his voice to swell the hallelujahs of a nation's jubilee, when the chains of servitude had been torn from his limbs? I am not that man. In a case like that, the dumb might eloquently speak, and the "lame man leap as an hart."

But, such is not the state of the case. I say it with a sad sense of the disparity between us. I am not included within the pale of this glorious anniversary! Your high independence only reveals the immeasurable distance between us. The blessings in which you, this day, rejoice, are not enjoyed in common.—The rich inheritance of justice, liberty, prosperity and independence, bequeathed by your fathers, is shared by you, not by me. The sunlight that brought life and healing to you, has brought stripes and death to me. **This Fourth [of] July is *yours,* not *mine.* *You* may rejoice, *I* must mourn. To drag a man in fetters into the grand illuminated temple of liberty, and call upon him to join you in joyous anthems, were inhuman mockery and sacrilegious irony. Do you mean, citizens, to mock me, by asking me to speak**

While pronouncing himself spokesman for American slaves, Douglass addresses the fact that blacks are not included in the inheritance of liberty and freedom represented by the Fourth of July. Indeed, since the early 19th century, most blacks who did celebrate Independence Day did so on July 5 because when they tried to do so on July 4, they were often the victims of racial and mob violence.

to-day? If so, there is a parallel to your conduct. And let me warn you that it is dangerous to copy the example of a nation whose crimes, lowering up to heaven, were thrown down by the breath of the Almighty, burying that nation in irrecoverable ruin! I can to-day take up the plaintive lament of a peeled and woe-smitten people!

Douglass here likens American blacks to the Israelites of old. Just as they found themselves enslaved in a foreign land, so too did blacks. The implication of this was that just as God had freed Israelites from Egyptian bondage, so too would he free His new chosen people from American slavery.

"By the rivers of Babylon, there we sat down. Yea! we wept when we remembered Zion. We hanged our harps upon the willows in the midst thereof. For there, they that carried us away captive, required of us a song; and they who wasted us required of us mirth, saying, Sing us one of the songs of Zion. How can we sing the Lord's song in a strange land? If I forget thee, O Jerusalem, let my right hand forget her cunning. If I do not remember thee, let my tongue cleave to the roof of my mouth."

Fellow-citizens; above your national, tumultuous joy, I hear the mournful wail of millions! whose chains, heavy and grievous yesterday, are, to-day, rendered more intolerable by the jubilee shouts that reach them. If I do forget, if I do not faithfully remember those bleeding children of sorrow this day, "may my right hand forget her cunning, and may my tongue cleave to the roof of my mouth!" To forget them, to pass lightly over their wrongs, and to chime in with the popular theme, would be treason most scandalous and shocking, and would make me a reproach before God and the world. My subject, then fellow-citizens, is AMERICAN SLAVERY. I shall see, this day, and its popular characteristics, from the slave's point of view. Standing, there, identified with the American bondman, making his wrongs mine, I do not hesitate to declare, with all my soul, that the character and conduct of this nation never looked blacker to me than on this 4th of July! Whether we turn to the declarations of the past, or to the professions of the present, the conduct of the nation seems equally hideous and revolting. America is false to the past, false to the present, and solemnly binds herself to be false to the future. Standing with God and the crushed and bleeding slave on this occasion, I will, in the name of humanity which is outraged, in the name of liberty which is fettered, in the name of the constitution and the Bible, which are disregarded and trampled upon, dare to call in question and to denounce, with all the emphasis I can command, everything that serves to perpetuate slavery—the great sin and shame of America! "I will not equivocate; I will not excuse;" I will use the severest language I can command; and yet not one word shall escape me that any man, whose judgment is not blinded by prejudice, or who is not at heart a slaveholder, shall not confess to be right and just.

But I fancy I hear some one of my audience say, it is just in this circumstance that you and your brother abolitionists fail to make a favorable impression on the public mind. Would you argue more, and denounce less, would you persuade more, and rebuke less, your cause would be much more likely to succeed. But, I submit, where all is plain there is nothing to be argued. What point in the antislavery creed would you have me argue? On what branch of the subject do the people of this country need light? Must I undertake to prove that the slave is a man? That point is conceded already. Nobody doubts it. The slaveholders themselves acknowledge it in the enactment of laws for their government. They acknowledge it when they punish disobedience on the part of the slave. There are seventy-two crimes in the State of Virginia, which, if committed by a black man, (no matter how ignorant he be), subject him to the punishment of death; while only two of the same crimes will subject a white man to the like punishment. What is this but the acknowledgement that the slave is a moral, intellectual and responsible being? The manhood of the slave is conceded. It

The abolitionist movement was by no means unified. While people such as Frederick Douglass and William Lloyd Garrison thought it best to denounce slavery and slaveholders in the harshest terms and call for immediate emancipation, others favored plans for gradual emancipation and not being as confrontational.

is admitted in the fact that Southern statute books are covered with enactments forbidding, under severe fines and penalties, the teaching of the slave to read or to write. When you can point to any such laws, in reference to the beasts of the field, then I may consent to argue the manhood of the slave. When the dogs in your streets, when the fowls of the air, when the cattle on your hills, when the fish of the sea, and the reptiles that crawl, shall be unable to distinguish the slave from a brute, *then* will I argue with you that the slave is a man!

This period saw a rise in arguments against black humanity and black equality. Pseudo-scientific racism posited different origins for blacks and whites and relied on things such as phrenology to classify human beings according to characteristics such as the size of one's skull.

For the present, it is enough to affirm the equal manhood of the Negro race. Is it not astonishing that, while we are ploughing, planting and reaping, using all kinds of mechanical tools, erecting houses, constructing bridges, building ships, working in metals of brass, iron, copper, silver and gold; that, while we are reading, writing and cyphering, acting as clerks, merchants and secretaries, having among us lawyers, doctors, ministers, poets, authors, editors, orators and teachers; that, while we are engaged in all manner of enterprises common to other men, digging gold in California, capturing the whale in the Pacific, feeding sheep and cattle on the hill-side, living, moving, acting, thinking, planning, living in families as husbands, wives and children, and, above all, confessing and worshipping the Christian's God, and looking hopefully for life and immortality beyond the grave, we are called upon to prove that we are men!

Would you have me argue that man is entitled to liberty? that he is the rightful owner of his own body? You have already declared it. Must I argue the wrongfulness of slavery? Is that a question for Republicans? Is it to be settled by the rules of logic and argumentation, as a matter beset with great difficulty, involving a doubtful application of the principle of justice, hard to be understood? How should I look to-day, in the presence of Americans, dividing, and subdividing a discourse, to show that men have a natural right to freedom? speaking of it relatively, and positively, negatively, and affirmatively. To do so, would be to make myself ridiculous, and to offer an insult to your understanding.—There is not a man beneath the canopy of heaven, that does not know that slavery is wrong *for him.*

What, am I to argue that it is wrong to make men brutes, to rob them of their liberty, to work them without wages, to keep them ignorant of their relations to their fellow men, to beat them with sticks, to flay their flesh with the lash, to load their limbs with irons, to hunt them with dogs, to sell them at auction, to sunder their families, to knock out their teeth, to burn their flesh, to starve them into obedience and submission to their masters? Must I argue that a system thus marked with blood, and stained with pollution, is *wrong*? No! I will not. I have better employments for my time and strength than such arguments would imply.

Despite Douglass's easy dismissal of his need to make this argument, there were in fact many in the country who did not see slavery to be wrong at all. Thinkers such as George Fitzhugh even went so far as to argue that slavery was a better system than free labor and that poor southern whites should also be enslaved. His ideas failed to gain traction, however.

What, then, remains to be argued? Is it that slavery is not divine; that God did not establish it; that our doctors of divinity are mistaken? There is blasphemy in the thought. That which is inhuman, cannot be divine! Who can reason on such a proposition? They that can, may; I cannot. The time for such argument is passed.

At a time like this, scorching irony, not convincing argument, is needed. O! had I the ability, and could I reach the nation's ear, I would, to-day, pour out a fiery stream of biting ridicule, blasting reproach, withering sarcasm, and stern rebuke. For it is not light that is needed, but fire; it is not the gentle shower, but thunder. We need the storm, the whirlwind, and the earthquake. The feeling

Douglass feels that the time for argumentation and equivocation is over. Slavery will only be abolished through what has come to be known as the tradition of black prophetic witness.

of the nation must be quickened; the conscience of the nation must be roused; the propriety of the nation must be startled; the hypocrisy of the nation must be exposed; and its crimes against God and man must be proclaimed and denounced.

What, to the American slave, is your 4th of July? I answer: a day that reveals to him, more than all other days in the year, the gross injustice and cruelty to which he is the constant victim. To him, your celebration is a sham; your boasted liberty, an unholy license; your national greatness, swelling vanity; your sounds of rejoicing are empty and heartless; your denunciations of tyrants, brass fronted impudence; your shouts of liberty and equality, hollow mockery; your prayers and hymns, your sermons and thanksgivings, with all your religious parade, and solemnity, are, to him, mere bombast, fraud, deception, impiety, and hypocrisy—a thin veil to cover up crimes which would disgrace a nation of savages. There is not a nation on the earth guilty of practices, more shocking and bloody, than are the people of these United States, at this very hour.

In 1852, the United States was one of the last countries in the Western world to still practice slavery. Britain and France had abolished it, and Spain had taken steps to do so. Most Latin American countries had also abolished slavery, with the exception of Cuba and Brazil.

Go where you may, search where you will, roam through all the monarchies and despotisms of the old world, travel through South America, search out every abuse, and when you have found the last, lay your facts by the side of the everyday practices of this nation, and you will say with me, that, for revolting barbarity and shameless hypocrisy, America reigns without a rival.

THE INTERNAL SLAVE TRADE

Take the American slave-trade, which, we are told by the papers, is especially prosperous just now. Ex-Senator Benton tells us that the price of men was never higher than now. He mentions the fact to show that slavery is in no danger. This trade is one of the peculiarities of American institutions. It is carried on in all the large towns and cities in one-half of this confederacy; and millions are pocketed every year, by dealers in this horrid traffic. **In several states, this trade is a chief source of wealth. It is called (in contradistinction to the foreign slave-trade)** *"the internal slave trade."* **It is, probably, called so, too, in order to divert from it the horror with which the foreign slave-trade is contemplated. That trade has long since been denounced by this government, as piracy. It has been denounced with burning words, from the high places of the nation, as an execrable traffic. To arrest it, to put an end to it, this nation keeps a squadron, at immense cost, on the coast of Africa. Everywhere, in this country, it is safe to speak of this foreign slave-trade, as a most inhuman traffic, opposed alike to the laws of God and of man. The duty to extirpate and destroy it, is admitted even by our DOCTORS OF DIVINITY. In order to put an end to it, some of these last have consented that their colored brethren (nominally free) should leave this country, and establish themselves on the western coast of Africa! It is, however, a notable fact that, while so much execration is poured out by Americans upon those engaged in the foreign slave-trade, the men engaged in the slave-trade between the states pass without condemnation, and their business is deemed honorable.**

The abolition of the Atlantic slave trade in 1807 led to the rise of the domestic slave trade in the southern states. This process witnessed more than 1 million slaves being relocated from Upper South states such as Virginia and North Carolina to newer regions of the South, especially Alabama and Mississippi.

Behold the practical operation of this internal slave-trade, the American slave-trade, sustained by American politics and America religion. Here you will see men and women reared like swine for the market. You know what is a swine-drover? I will show you a man-drover. They inhabit all our Southern States. They perambulate the country, and crowd the highways of the nation, with droves of human stock. You will see one of these human flesh-jobbers, armed with pistol, whip and bowie-knife, driving a company of a hundred men, women, and children, from the Potomac to the slave market at New Orleans. These wretched people are to be sold singly, or in lots, to suit purchasers. They are food for the cotton-field, and the deadly sugar-mill. Mark the sad procession, as it moves wearily along, and the inhuman wretch who drives them. Hear his savage yells and his blood-chilling oaths, as he hurries on his affrighted captives! There, see the old man, with locks thinned and gray. **Cast one glance, if you please, upon that young mother, whose shoulders are bare to the scorching sun, her briny tears falling on the brow of the babe in her arms. See, too, that girl of thirteen, weeping, yes! weeping, as she thinks of the mother from whom she has been torn! The drove moves tardily. Heat and sorrow have nearly consumed their strength; suddenly you hear a quick snap, like the discharge of a rifle; the fetters clank, and the chain rattles simultaneously; your ears are saluted with a scream, that seems to have torn its way to the center of your soul! The crack you heard, was the sound of the slave-whip; the scream you heard, was from the woman you saw with the babe. Her speed had faltered under the weight of her child and her chains! that gash on her shoulder tells her to move on. Follow the drove to New Orleans. Attend the auction; see men examined like horses; see the forms of women rudely and brutally exposed to the shocking gaze of American slave-buyers. See this drove sold and separated forever; and never forget the deep, sad sobs that arose from that scattered multitude. Tell me citizens, WHERE, under the sun, you can witness a spectacle more fiendish and shocking. Yet this is but a glance at the American slave-trade, as it exists, at this moment, in the ruling part of the United States.**

An important component of the sentimental literature of the 18th and 19th centuries was allowing readers to place themselves in the position of downtrodden characters. Douglass employs this literary tool to great effect in vividly portraying the horrors of the internal slave trade.

I was born amid such sights and scenes. To me the American slave-trade is a terrible reality. When a child, my soul was often pierced with a sense of its horrors. I lived on Philpot Street, Fell's Point, Baltimore, and have watched from the wharves, the slave ships in the Basin, anchored from the shore, with their cargoes of human flesh, waiting for favorable winds to waft them down the Chesapeake. **There was, at that time, a grand slave mart kept at the head of Pratt Street, by Austin Woldfolk. His agents were sent into every town and county in Maryland, announcing their arrival, through the papers, and on flaming "*hand-bills*," headed CASH FOR NEGROES. These men were generally well dressed men, and very captivating in their manners. Ever ready to drink, to treat, and to gamble. The fate of many a slave has depended upon the turn of a single card; and many a child has been snatched from the arms of its mother by bargains arranged in a state of brutal drunkenness.**

This last statement would have appealed to those interested in the temperance movement, which was one of the largest and most influential social reform movements of the 19th century.

The flesh-mongers gather up their victims by dozens, and drive them, chained, to the general depot at Baltimore. When a sufficient number have been collected here, a ship is chartered, for the purpose of conveying the forlorn crew to Mobile, or to New Orleans. From the slave prison to the ship, they are usually driven in the darkness of night; for since the antislavery agitation, a certain caution is observed.

In the deep still darkness of midnight, I have been often aroused by the dead heavy footsteps, and the piteous cries of the chained gangs that passed our door. The anguish of my boyish heart was intense; and I was often consoled, when speaking to my mistress in the morning, to hear her say that the custom was very wicked; that she hated to hear the rattle of the chains, and the heart-rending cries. I was glad to find one who sympathized with me in my horror.

Fellow-citizens, this murderous traffic is, to-day, in active operation in this boasted republic. In the solitude of my spirit, I see clouds of dust raised on the highways of the South; I see the bleeding footsteps; I hear the doleful wail of fettered humanity, on the way to the slave-markets, where the victims are to be sold like *horses, sheep,* and *swine,* knocked off to the highest bidder. There I see the tenderest ties ruthlessly broken, to gratify the lust, caprice and rapacity of the buyers and sellers of men. My soul sickens at the sight.

"Is this the land your Fathers loved,

The freedom which they toiled to win?

Is this the earth whereon they moved?

Are these the graves they slumber in?"

But a still more inhuman, disgraceful, and scandalous state of things remains to be presented.

Douglass refers to a provision of the Compromise of 1850, a strengthened Fugitive Slave Act that gave broad powers to those southerners looking for runaways in the North.

By an act of the American Congress, not yet two years old, slavery has been nationalized in its most horrible and revolting form. By that act, Mason and Dixon's line has been obliterated; New York has become as Virginia; and the power to hold, hunt, and sell men, women, and children as slaves remains no longer a mere state institution, but is now an institution of the whole United States. The power is co-extensive with the Star-Spangled Banner and American Christianity. Where these go, may also go the merciless slave-hunter. Where these are, man is not sacred. He is a bird for the sportsman's gun. By that most foul and fiendish of all human decrees, the liberty and person of every man are put in peril. Your broad republican domain is hunting ground for *men.* Not for thieves and robbers, enemies of society, merely, but for men guilty of no crime. Your lawmakers have commanded all good citizens to engage in this hellish sport. Your President, your

Secretary of State, your *lords, nobles,* and ecclesiastics, enforce, as a duty you owe to your free and glorious country, and to your God, that you do this accursed thing. Not fewer than forty Americans have, within the past two years, been hunted down and, without a moment's warning, hurried away in chains, and consigned to slavery and excruciating torture. Some of these have had wives and children, dependent on them for bread; but of this, no account was made. The right of the hunter to his prey stands superior to the right of marriage, and to *all* rights in this republic, the rights of God included! For black men there are neither law, justice, humanity, not religion. The Fugitive Slave *Law* makes mercy to them a crime; and bribes the judge who tries them. An American judge gets ten dollars for every victim he consigns to slavery, and five, when he fails to do so. The oath of any two villains is sufficient, under this hell-black enactment, to send the most pious and exemplary black man into the remorseless jaws of slavery! His own testimony is nothing. He can bring no witnesses for himself. The minister of American justice is bound by the law to hear but *one* side; and *that* side, is the side of the oppressor. Let this damning fact be perpetually told. Let it be thundered around the world, that, in tyrant-killing, king-hating, people-loving, democratic, Christian America, the seats of justice are filled with judges, who hold their offices under an open and palpable *bribe,* and are bound, in deciding in the case of a man's liberty, *hear only his accusers!*

In glaring violation of justice, in shameless disregard of the forms of administering law, in cunning arrangement to entrap the defenseless, and in diabolical intent, this Fugitive Slave Law stands alone in the annals of tyrannical legislation. I doubt if there be another nation on the globe, having the brass and the baseness to put such a law on the statute-book. If any man in this assembly thinks differently from me in this matter, and feels able to disprove my statements, I will gladly confront him at any suitable time and place he may select.

RELIGIOUS LIBERTY

I take this law to be one of the grossest infringements of Christian Liberty, and, if the churches and ministers of our country were not stupidly blind, or most wickedly indifferent, they, too, would so regard it.

Most abolitionists were religious, but many were anticlerical, denouncing what they saw to be the unholy combination of civil and religious authority in bolstering support for slavery.

Douglass's mention of John Knox and the Covenanters refers to a group of Presbyterians in 17th-century Scotland who signed a covenant pledging their nation to God. Under covenant theology, which was prevalent among the Scots and among American Puritans, any nation that does not live according to God's will is going to be destroyed.

At the very moment that they are thanking God for the enjoyment of civil and religious liberty, and for the right to worship God according to the dictates of their own consciences, they are utterly silent in respect to a law which robs religion of its chief significance, and makes it utterly worthless to a world lying in wickedness. Did this law concern the "*mint, anise, and cumin*"—abridge the fight to sing psalms, to partake of the sacrament, or to engage in any of the ceremonies of religion, it would be smitten by the thunder of a thousand pulpits. A general shout would go up from the church, demanding *repeal, repeal, instant repeal!*—And it would go hard with that politician who presumed to solicit the votes of the people without inscribing this motto on his banner. Further, if this demand were not complied with, another Scotland would be added to the history of religious liberty, and the stern old Covenanters would be thrown into the shade. A John Knox would be seen at every church door, and heard from every pulpit, and Fillmore would have no more quarter than was shown by Knox, to the beautiful, but treacherous queen Mary of Scotland.—The fact that the church of our country, (with fractional exceptions), does not esteem "the Fugitive Slave Law" as a declaration of war against religious liberty, implies that that church regards religion simply as a form of worship, an empty ceremony, and *not* a vital principle, requiring active benevolence, justice, love and good will towards man. It esteems sacrifice above mercy; psalm-singing above right doing; solemn meetings above practical righteousness. A worship that can be conducted by persons who refuse to give shelter to the houseless, to give bread to the hungry, clothing to the naked, and who enjoin obedience to a law forbidding these acts of mercy, is a curse, not a blessing to mankind. The Bible addresses all such persons as "scribes, Pharisees, hypocrites, who pay tithe of *mint, anise,* and *cumin,* and have omitted the weightier matters of the law, judgment, mercy and faith."

THE CHURCH RESPONSIBLE

But the church of this country is not only indifferent to the wrongs of the slave, it actually takes sides with the oppressors. It has made itself the bulwark of American slavery, and the shield of American slave-hunters. Many of its most eloquent Divines, who stand as the very lights of the church, have shamelessly given the sanction of religion and the Bible to the whole slave system. They have taught that man may, properly, be a slave; that the relation of master and slave is ordained of God; that to send back an escaped bondman to his master is clearly the duty of all the followers of the Lord Jesus Christ; and this horrible blasphemy is palmed off upon the world for Christianity.

For my part, I would say, welcome infidelity! welcome atheism! welcome anything! in preference to the gospel, *as preached by those Divines!* They convert the very name of religion into an engine of tyranny, and barbarous cruelty, and serve to confirm more infidels, in this age, than all the infidel writings of Thomas Paine, Voltaire, and Bolingbroke, put together, have done! These ministers make religion a cold and flinty-hearted thing, having neither principles of right action, nor bowels of compassion. They strip the love of God of its beauty, and leave the throng of religion a huge, horrible, repulsive form. It is a religion for oppressors, tyrants, man-stealers, and *thugs*. It is not that *"pure and undefiled religion"* which is from above, and which is *"first pure, then peaceable, easy to be entreated,* full of mercy and good fruits, *without partiality, and without hypocrisy."* But a religion which favors the rich against the poor; which exalts the proud above the humble; which divides mankind into two classes, tyrants and slaves; which says to the man in chains, *stay there;* and to the oppressor, *oppress on;* it is a religion which may be professed and enjoyed by all the robbers and enslavers of mankind; it makes God a respecter of persons, denies his fatherhood of the race, and tramples in the dust the great truth of the brotherhood of man. All this we affirm to be true of the popular church, and the popular worship of our land and nation—a religion, a church, and a worship which, on the authority of inspired wisdom, we pronounce to be an abomination in the sight of God. In the language of Isaiah, the American church might be well addressed, "Bring no more vain ablations; incense is an abomination unto me: the new moons and Sabbaths, the calling of assemblies, I cannot away with; it is iniquity even the solemn meeting. Your new moons and your appointed feasts my soul hateth. They are a trouble to me; I am weary to bear them; and when ye spread forth your hands I will hide mine eyes from you. Yea! when ye make many prayers, I will not hear. YOUR HANDS ARE FULL OF BLOOD; cease to do evil, learn to do well; seek judgment; relieve the oppressed; judge for the fatherless; plead for the widow."

The American church is guilty, when viewed in connection with what it is doing to uphold slavery; but it is superlatively guilty when viewed in connection with its ability to abolish slavery. The sin of which it is guilty is one of omission as well as of commission. Albert Barnes but uttered what the common sense of every man at all observant of the actual state of the case will receive as truth, when he declared that "There is no power out of the church that could sustain slavery an hour, if it were not sustained in it."

Let the religious press, the pulpit, the Sunday school, the conference meeting, the great ecclesiastical, missionary, Bible and tract associations of the land array their immense powers against slavery and slave-holding; and the whole system of crime and blood would be scattered to the winds; and that they do not do this involves them in the most awful responsibility of which the mind can conceive.

Part of the so-called Benevolent Empire included organizations such as the American Tract Society, which made a plan to deliver a tract to every inhabitant of New York City, as well as the American Bible Society. Should these organizations turn their attention to slavery, the institution would be abolished in short order, according to Douglass.

In prosecuting the anti-slavery enterprise, we have been asked to spare the church, to spare the ministry; but *how*, we ask, could such a thing be done? We are met on the threshold of our efforts for the redemption of the slave, by the church and ministry of the country, in battle arrayed against us; and we are compelled to fight or flee. From *what* quarter, I beg to know, has proceeded a fire so deadly upon our ranks, during the last two years, as from the Northern pulpit? As the champions of oppressors, the chosen men of American theology have appeared—men, honored for their so-called piety, and their real learning. The Lords of Buffalo, the Springs of New York, the Lathrops of Auburn, the Coxes and Spencers of Brooklyn, the Gannets and Sharps of Boston, the Deweys of Washington, and other great religious lights of the land have, in utter denial of the authority of *Him* by whom the professed to be called to the ministry, deliberately taught us, against the example or the Hebrews and against the remonstrance of the Apostles, they teach *that we ought to obey man's law before the law of God.*

My spirit wearies of such blasphemy; and how such men can be supported, as the "standing types and representatives of

Jesus Christ," is a mystery which I leave others to penetrate. In speaking of the American church, however, let it be distinctly understood that I mean the great mass of the religious organizations of our land. There are exceptions, and I thank God that there are. Noble men may be found, scattered all over these Northern States, of whom Henry Ward Beecher of Brooklyn, Samuel J. May of Syracuse, and my esteemed friend (Rev. R. R. Raymond) on the platform, are shining examples; and let me say further, that upon these men lies the duty to inspire our ranks with high religious faith and zeal, and to cheer us on in the great mission of the slave's redemption from his chains.

RELIGION IN ENGLAND AND RELIGION IN AMERICA

One is struck with the difference between the attitude of the American church towards the anti-slavery movement, and that occupied by the churches in England towards a similar movement in that country. There, the church, true to its mission of ameliorating, elevating, and improving the condition of mankind, came forward promptly, bound up the wounds of the West Indian slave, and restored him to his liberty. There, the question of emancipation was a high religious question. It was demanded, in the name of humanity, and according to the law of the living God. The Sharps, the Clarksons, the Wilberforces, the Buxtons, and Burchells and the Knibbs, were alike famous for their piety, and for their philanthropy. The anti-slavery movement *there* was not an anti-church movement, for the reason that the church took its full share in prosecuting that movement: and the anti-slavery movement in this country will cease to be an anti-church movement, when the church of this country shall assume a favorable, instead of a hostile position towards that movement.

Americans! your republican politics, not less than your republican religion, are flagrantly inconsistent. You boast of your love of liberty, your superior civilization, and your pure Christianity, while the whole political power of the nation (as embodied in the two great political parties), is solemnly pledged to support and perpetuate the enslavement of three millions of your countrymen. You hurl your anathemas at the crowned headed tyrants of Russia and Austria, and pride yourselves on your Democratic institutions, while you yourselves consent to be the mere *tools* and *body-guards* of the tyrants of Virginia and Carolina. You invite to your shores fugitives of oppression from abroad, honor them with banquets, greet them with ovations, cheer them, toast them, salute them, protect them, and pour out your money to them like water; but the fugitives from your own land you advertise, hunt, arrest, shoot and kill.

You glory in your refinement and your universal education yet you maintain a system as barbarous and dreadful as ever stained the character of a nation—a system begun in avarice, supported in pride, and perpetuated in cruelty. You shed tears over fallen Hungary, and make the sad story of her wrongs the theme of your poets, statesmen and orators, till your gallant sons are ready to fly to arms to vindicate her cause against her oppressors; but, in regard to the ten thousand wrongs of the American slave, you would enforce the strictest silence, and would hail him as an enemy of the nation who dares to make those wrongs the subject of public discourse! You are all on fire at the mention of liberty for France or for Ireland; but are as cold as an iceberg at the thought of liberty for the enslaved of America.

The period from 1770 to 1850 is known as the Age of Revolutions because of the revolutions that occurred throughout both the Western Hemisphere and Europe. France went through successive revolutions, as did Greece, Hungary, and many Latin American nations. Americans often supported these efforts, sometimes by volunteering to fight.

You discourse eloquently on the dignity of labor; yet, you sustain a system which, in its very essence, casts a stigma upon labor. You can bare your bosom to the storm of British artillery to throw off a threepenny tax on tea; and yet wring the last hard-earned farthing from the grasp of the black laborers of your country. You profess to believe "that, of one blood, God made all nations of men to dwell on the face of all the earth," and hath commanded all men, everywhere to love one another; yet you notoriously hate, (and glory in your hatred), all men whose skins are not colored like your own. You declare, before the world, and are understood by the world to declare, that you *"hold these truths to be self evident, that all men are created equal; and are endowed by their Creator with certain inalienable rights; and that, among these are, life, liberty, and the pursuit of happiness;"* and yet, you hold securely, in a bondage which, according to your own Thomas Jefferson, *"is worse than ages of that which your fathers rose in rebellion to oppose,"* a *seventh part* of the inhabitants of your country.

Fellow-citizens! I will not enlarge further on your national inconsistencies. The existence of slavery in this country brands your republicanism as a sham, your humanity as a base pretence, and your Christianity as a lie. It destroys your moral power abroad; it corrupts your politicians at home. It saps the foundation of religion; it makes your name a hissing, and a bye-word to a mocking earth. It is the antagonistic force in your government, the only thing that seriously disturbs and endangers your *Union.* It fetters your progress; it is the enemy of improvement, the deadly foe of education; it fosters pride; it breeds insolence; it promotes vice; it shelters crime; it is a curse to the earth that supports it; and yet, you cling to it, as if it were the sheet anchor of all your hopes. Oh! be warned! be warned! a horrible reptile is coiled up in your nation's bosom; the venomous creature is nursing at the tender breast of your youthful republic; *for the love of God, tear away,* and fling from you the hideous monster, and *let the weight of twenty millions crush and destroy it forever!*

THE CONSTITUTION

But it is answered in reply to all this, that precisely what I have now denounced is, in fact, guaranteed and sanctioned by the Constitution of the United States; that the right to hold and to hunt slaves is a part of that Constitution framed by the illustrious Fathers of this Republic.

Then, I dare to affirm, notwithstanding all I have said before, your fathers stooped, basely stooped.

"To palter with us in a double sense:
And keep the word of promise to the ear,
But break it to the heart."

And instead of being the honest men I have before declared them to be, they were the veriest imposters that ever practiced on mankind. This is the inevitable conclusion, and from it there is no escape. But I differ from those who charge this baseness on the framers of the Constitution of the United States. It is a slander upon their memory, at least, so I believe. There is not time now to argue the constitutional question at length—nor have I the ability to discuss it as it ought to be discussed. The subject has been handled with masterly power by Lysander Spooner, Esq., by William Goodell, by Samuel E. Sewall, Esq., and last, though not least, by Gerritt Smith, Esq. These gentlemen have, as I think, fully and clearly vindicated the Constitution from any design to support slavery for an hour.

Fellow-citizens! there is no matter in respect to which, the people of the North have allowed themselves to be so ruinously imposed upon, as that of the pro-slavery character of the Constitution. In that instrument I hold there

Another division in the abolitionist movement concerned the relationship between the U.S. Constitution and slavery as well as whether abolitionists should participate in politics. William Lloyd Garrison argued that the Constitution supported slavery and thus that the American political system was too corrupt to be reformed from within. Douglass initially agreed but had changed his mind by the 1850s.

is neither warrant, license, nor sanction of the hateful thing; but, interpreted as it ought to be interpreted, the Constitution is a GLORIOUS LIBERTY DOCUMENT. Read its preamble, consider its purposes. Is slavery among them? Is it at the gateway? or is it in the temple? It is neither. While I do not intend to argue this question on the present occasion, let me ask, if it be not somewhat singular that, if the Constitution were intended to be, by its framers and adopters, a slave-holding instrument, why neither slavery, slave-holding, nor slave can anywhere be found in it. What would be thought of an instrument, drawn up, legally drawn up, for the purpose of entitling the city of Rochester to a track of land, in which no mention of land was made? Now, there are certain rules of interpretation, for the proper understanding of all legal instruments. These rules are well established. They are plain, common-sense rules, such as you and I, and all of us, can understand and apply, without having passed years in the study of law. I scout the idea that the question of the constitutionality or unconstitutionality of slavery is not a question for the people. I hold that every American citizen has a right to form an opinion of the constitution, and to propagate that opinion, and to use all honorable means to make his opinion the prevailing one. Without this right, the liberty of an American citizen would be as insecure as that of a Frenchman. Ex–Vice-President Dallas tells us that the Constitution is an object to which no American mind can be too attentive, and no American heart too devoted. He further says, the Constitution, in its words, is plain and intelligible, and is meant for the home-bred, unsophisticated understandings of our fellow-citizens. Senator Berrien tells us that the Constitution is the fundamental law, that which controls all others. The charter of our liberties, which every citizen has a personal interest in understanding thoroughly. The testimony of Senator Breese, Lewis Cass, and many others that might be named, who are everywhere esteemed as sound lawyers, so regard the constitution. I take it, therefore, that it is not presumption in a private citizen to form an opinion of that instrument.

Now, take the Constitution according to its plain reading, and I defy the presentation of a single pro-slavery clause in it. On the other hand it will be found to contain principles and purposes, entirely hostile to the existence of slavery.

I have detained my audience entirely too long already. At some future period I will gladly avail myself of an opportunity to give this subject a full and fair discussion.

Allow me to say, in conclusion, notwithstanding the dark picture I have this day presented of the state of the nation, I do not despair of this country. There are forces in operation, which must inevitably work the downfall of slavery. "The arm of the Lord is not shortened," and the doom of slavery is certain. I, therefore, leave off where I began, with hope. While drawing encouragement from the Declaration of Independence, the great principles it contains, and the genius of American Institutions, my spirit is also cheered by the obvious tendencies of the age. Nations do not now stand in the same relation to each other that they did ages ago. No nation can now shut itself up from the surrounding world, and trot round in the same old path of its fathers without interference. The time was when such could be done. Long established customs of hurtful character could formerly fence themselves in, and do their evil work with social impunity. Knowledge was then confined and enjoyed by the privileged few, and the multitude walked on in mental darkness. But a change has now come over the affairs of mankind. Walled cities and empires have become unfashionable. The arm of commerce has borne away the gates of the strong city. Intelligence is penetrating the darkest corners of the globe. It makes its pathway over and under the sea, as well as on the earth. Wind, steam, and lightning are its chartered agents. Oceans no longer divide, but link nations together. From Boston to London is now a holiday excursion. Space is comparatively annihilated. Thoughts expressed on one side of the Atlantic are, distinctly heard on the other.

The far off and almost fabulous Pacific rolls in grandeur at our feet. The Celestial Empire, the mystery of ages, is being solved. The fiat of the Almighty, "Let there be Light," has not yet spent its force. No abuse, no outrage whether in taste, sport or avarice, can now hide itself from the all-pervading light. The iron shoe, and crippled foot of China must be seen, in contrast with nature. Africa must rise and put on her yet unwoven garment. "Ethiopia shall stretch out her hand unto God." In the fervent aspirations of William Lloyd Garrison, I say, and let every heart join in saying it:

God speed the year of jubile
The wide world o'er
When from their galling chains set free,
Th' oppress'd shall vilely bend the knee,
And wear the yoke of tyranny
Like brutes no more.
That year will come, and freedom's reign,
To man his plundered fights again
Restore.

God speed the day when human blood
Shall cease to flow!
In every clime be understood,
The claims of human brotherhood,
And each return for evil, good,
Not blow for blow;

That day will come all feuds to end.
And change into a faithful friend
Each foe.

God speed the hour, the glorious hour,
When none on earth
Shall exercise a lordly power,
Nor in a tyrant's presence cower;
But all to manhood's stature tower,
By equal birth!
That hour will come, to each, to all,
And from his prison-house, the thrall
Go forth.

Until that year, day, hour, arrive,
With head, and heart, and hand I'll strive,
To break the rod, and rend the gyve,
The spoiler of his prey deprive—
So witness Heaven!
And never from my chosen post,
Whate'er the peril or the cost,
Be driven.

Source: Frederick Douglass, "What to the Slave Is the Fourth of July?" Oration Delivered in Corinthian Hall, Rochester, New York, July 5, 1852 (Rochester: Lee, Mann, American Building, 1852).

Foundation of the Confederacy

Alexander Stephens, "Cornerstone Speech"

1861

INTRODUCTION

Alexander Stephens was a slaveholder and politician from Georgia. He served the state in the U.S. House of Representatives from 1843 to 1859 and again after the Civil War. During the conflict Stephens served as the vice president of the Confederate States of America, and in the early 1880s he would be elected governor of Georgia and served until his death just four months after taking office. Stephens gave the "Cornerstone Speech" in Savannah, Georgia, on March 21, 1861. By this point a number of Lower South states had already seceded from the Union and formed the Confederate States of America. The question of slavery would of course be a prominent one in the Confederate constitutional convention and similar conventions in Southern states. Stephens asserted in this speech that slavery provided the economic, political, and moral foundation of Southern society and was the basis for the conflict with the North.

Stephens gave this speech in March 1861. Thus, the last 90 days to which he refers had been marked by the secession of seven Southern states and the formation of the Confederate States of America.

We are in the midst of one of the greatest epochs in our history. The last ninety days will mark one of the most memorable eras in the history of modern civilization.

. . . [W]e are passing through one of the greatest revolutions in the annals of the world—seven States have, within the last three months, thrown off an old Government and formed a new. This revolution has been signally marked, up to this time, by the fact of its having been accomplished without the loss of a single drop of blood. [Applause.] This new Constitution, or form of government, constitutes the subject to which your attention will be partly invited.

In many respects the Confederate States of America Constitution was the same as that of the U.S. Constitution, the main exception being amendments and provisions regarding the institution of slavery.

In reference to it, I make this first general remark: It amply secures all our ancient rights, franchises, and privileges. All the great principles of Magna Charta are

retained in it. No citizen is deprived of life, liberty, or property, but by the judgment of his peers, under the laws of the land. The great principle of religious liberty, which was the honor and pride of the old Constitution, is still maintained and secured. All the essentials of the old Constitution, which have endeared it to the hearts of the American people, have been preserved and perpetuated. . . . So, taking the whole new Constitution, I have no hesitancy in giving it as my judgment, that it is decidedly better than the old. [Applause.]

Allow me briefly to allude to some of these improvements. The question of building up class interests, or fostering one branch of industry to the prejudice of another, under the exercise of the revenue power, which gave us so much trouble under the old Constitution, is put at rest forever under the new. We allow the imposition of no duty with a view of giving advantage to one class of persons, in any trade or business, over those of another. All, under our system, stand upon the same broad principles of perfect equality. Honest labor and enterprise are left free and unrestricted in whatever pursuit they may be engaged in. . . .

Stevens refers primarily to the different ways that tariffs affected the Northern and Southern economies. Tariffs are taxes on imported goods from another country and were imposed by Congress to both raise revenue and promote American manufacturing, which was located primarily in the North. Tariffs on imported goods would generally cause other countries to raise their own tariffs on American exports. Since most of those exports came from the products of slave labor—cotton, tobacco, indigo, and rice—Southerners generally felt that tariffs were an unequal tax that raised the interests of Northerners above Southerners.

But not to be tedious in enumerating the numerous changes for the better, allow me to allude to one other—though last, not least: the new Constitution has put at rest forever all the agitating questions relating to our peculiar institutions—African slavery as it exists among us—the proper status of the negro in our form of civilization. This was the immediate cause of the late rupture and present revolution.

While many historians have debated the true cause(s) of the Civil War, attributing it to slavery, state's rights, different cultures, and economic issues, Stephens clearly states that agitation over slavery was the "immediate cause" of the problems between the two sections.

Jefferson, in his forecast, had anticipated this, as the "rock upon which the old Union would split." He was right. What was conjecture with him, is now a realized fact. But whether

Stephens refers to the "necessary evil" period of proslavery thought, when individuals such as Thomas Jefferson decried the existence of slavery in a republican society and hoped that it would soon vanish. Some of these people freed their slaves (George Washington being a prime example), others advocated African colonization, and still others pushed for gradual emancipation plans.

he fully comprehended the great truth upon which that rock stood and stands, may be doubted. **The prevailing ideas entertained by him and most of the leading statesmen at the time of the formation of the old Constitution were, that the enslavement of the African was in violation of the laws of nature; that it was wrong in principle, socially, morally and politically. It was an evil they knew not well how to deal with; but the general opinion of the men of that day was, that, somehow or other, in the order of Providence, the institution would be evanescent and pass away. This idea, though not incorporated in the Constitution, was the prevailing idea at the time. The Constitution, it is true, secured every essential guarantee to the institution while it should last, and hence no argument can be justly used against the constitutional guarantees thus secured, because of the common sentiment of the day. Those ideas, however, were fundamentally wrong. They rested upon the assumption of the equality of races. This was an error. It was a sandy foundation, and the idea of a Government built upon it—when the "storm came and the wind blew, it fell."**

This paragraph is indicative of the degree to which Southern views on slavery evolved from the American Revolutionary era to the Civil War. By 1860, many slaveholders rejected the "necessary evil" view and instead saw slavery as a "positive good." In their minds, slavery was not contrary to the laws of nature because the laws of nature declared that blacks were inferior to whites and that all men were not created equal. While these thinkers accepted Thomas Jefferson's racial views toward blacks, they rejected his universal statements in the Declaration of Independence regarding natural rights.

Our new Government is founded upon exactly the opposite ideas; its foundations are laid, its cornerstone rests, upon the great truth that the negro is not equal to the white man; that slavery, subordination to the superior race, is his natural and moral condition. [Applause.] This, our new Government, is the first, in the history of the world, based upon this great physical, philosophical, and moral truth. This truth has been slow in the process of its development, like all other truths in the various departments of science. It is so even amongst us. Many who hear me, perhaps, can recollect well that this truth was not generally admitted, even within their day. The errors of the past generation still clung to many as late

as twenty years ago. Those at the North who still cling to these errors with a zeal above knowledge, we justly denominate fanatics. All fanaticism springs from an aberration of the mind; from a defect in reasoning. It is a species of insanity. One of the most striking characteristics of insanity, in many instances, is, forming correct conclusions from fancied or erroneous premises; so with the anti-slavery fanatics: their conclusions are right if their premises are. They assume that the negro is equal, and hence conclude that he is entitled to equal privileges and rights, with the white man. . . . I recollect once of having heard a gentleman from one of the Northern States, of great power and ability, announce in the House of Representatives, with imposing effect, that we of the South would be compelled, ultimately, to yield upon this subject of slavery; that it was as impossible to war successfully against a principle in politics, as it was in physics or mechanics. That the principle would ultimately prevail. That we, in maintaining slavery as it exists with us, were warring against a principle—a principle founded in nature, the principle of the equality of man. The reply I made to him was, that upon his own grounds we should succeed, and that he and his associates in their crusade against our institutions would ultimately fail. The truth announced, that it was as impossible to war successfully against a principle in politics as well as in physics and mechanics, I admitted, but told him it was he and those acting with him who were warring against a principle. They were attempting to make things equal which the Creator had made unequal.

In the conflict thus far, success has been on our side, complete throughout the length and breadth of the Confederate States. It is upon this, as I have stated, our social fabric is firmly planted; and I cannot permit myself to doubt the ultimate success of a full recognition of this principle throughout the civilized and enlightened world.

As I have stated, the truth of this principle may be slow in development, as all truths are, and ever have been, in the various branches of science. It was so with the principles announced by Galileo—it was so with Adam Smith and his principles of political economy. It was so with Harvey, and his theory of the circulation of the blood. It is stated that not a single one of the medical profession, living at the time of the announcement of the truths made by him, admitted them. Now, they are universally acknowledged. May we not therefore look with confidence to the ultimate universal acknowledgment of the truths upon which our system rests? It is the first Government ever instituted upon principles in strict conformity to nature, and the ordination of Providence, in furnishing the materials of human society. **Many Governments have been founded upon the principles of certain classes; but the classes thus enslaved, were of the same race, and in violation of the laws of nature. Our system commits no such violation of nature's laws. The negro by nature, or by the curse against Canaan, is fitted for that condition which he occupies in our system. The architect, in the construction of buildings, lays the foundation with the proper material—the granite—then comes the brick or the marble. The substratum of our society is made of the material fitted by nature for it, and by experience we know that it is the best, not only for the superior but for the inferior race, that it should be so. It is, indeed, in conformity with the Creator. It is not for us to inquire into the wisdom of His ordinances or to question them. For His own purposes He has made one race to differ from another, as He has made "one star to differ from another in glory."**

Leaders of the Confederacy such as Stephens thought their society was superior to the North, because while Northerners exploited white workers and fostered class divisions, Southerners treated all white men with respect (in theory) and discriminated and exploited only those deemed inferior—blacks.

The great objects of humanity are best attained, when conformed to his laws and degrees [*sic*], in the formation of Governments as well as in all things else. Our Confederacy is founded upon principles in strict conformity with these laws. This stone which was rejected by the first builders "is become the chief stone of the corner" in our new edifice.

Source: Alexander H. Stephens, "Cornerstone Address, March 21, 1861," in *The Rebellion Record: A Diary of American Events with Documents, Narratives, Illustrative Incidents, Poetry, Etc.,* Vol. 1, edited by Frank Moore (New York: Putnam, 1862), 44–46.

Finally Free

Emancipation Proclamation
1863

INTRODUCTION

Abraham Lincoln and military commanders for the Union ran into an unexpected problem early in the Civil War. This problem involved what to do with slaves who ran to Union lines when the army was nearby. Some generals in the field returned slaves to their owners, but others believed that this was foolish, as slaves were a valuable wartime ally. This view led to slaves being dubbed "contraband-of-war," a designation that affirmed their status as property but also allowed them to be seized to undermine the Confederate war effort. The Emancipation Proclamation was thus a formal recognition of what had largely been the practice on the ground. Now slaves in areas occupied by the Confederacy were deemed to be free, an announcement that changed the nature of the Civil War from one being fought to preserve the Union to a war about slavery. Blacks were also allowed to join the army as a result of the proclamation, leading to hundreds of thousands of enlistments and a recognition of an important right of citizenship.

By the President of the United States of America:

A Proclamation.

Abraham Lincoln had been considering the Emancipation Proclamation for a couple of months at this point but decided to issue it on the heels of the Battle of Antietam, which was essentially a stalemate but allowed Lincoln to claim a victory. He wanted to issue the proclamation from a position of military strength and not out of weakness or necessity.

The Emancipation Proclamation is sometimes attributed to having freed the slaves. It did free some slaves but not all of them. The pronouncement only applied to those areas in rebellion. Therefore, slaves in states such as Missouri that were not part of the Confederacy remained in bondage, although the Lincoln administration did push these regions to adopt emancipation plans.

Whereas, on the twenty-second day of September, in the year of our Lord one thousand eight hundred and sixty-two, a proclamation was issued by the President of the United States, containing, among other things, the following, to wit:

"That on the first day of January, in the year of our Lord one thousand eight hundred and sixty-three, all persons held as slaves within any State or designated part of a State, the people whereof shall then be in rebellion against the United States, shall be then, thenceforward, and forever

free; and the Executive Government of the United States, including the military and naval authority thereof, will recognize and maintain the freedom of such persons, and will do no act or acts to repress such persons, or any of them, in any efforts they may make for their actual freedom.

"That the Executive will, on the first day of January aforesaid, by proclamation, designate the States and parts of States, if any, in which the people thereof, respectively, shall then be in rebellion against the United States; and the fact that any State, or the people thereof, shall on that day be, in good faith, represented in the Congress of the United States by members chosen thereto at elections wherein a majority of the qualified voters of such State shall have participated, shall, in the absence of strong countervailing testimony, be deemed conclusive evidence that such State, and the people thereof, are not then in rebellion against the United States."

Now, therefore I, Abraham Lincoln, President of the United States, by virtue of the power in me vested as Commander-in-Chief, of the Army and Navy of the United States in time of actual armed rebellion against the authority and government of the United States, and as a fit and necessary war measure for suppressing said rebellion, do, on this first day of January, in the year of our Lord one thousand eight hundred and sixty-three, and in accordance with my purpose so to do publicly proclaimed for the full period of one hundred days, from the day first above mentioned, order and designate as the States and parts of States wherein the people thereof respectively, are this day in rebellion against the United States, the following, to wit:

Arkansas, Texas, Louisiana, (except the Parishes of St. Bernard, Plaquemines, Jefferson, St. John, St. Charles, St. James

Lincoln puts forth this policy as a measure of war, drawing on his advanced powers as commander in chief during war. While he was certainly ideologically opposed to slavery, his executive power would only allow him to confiscate enemy property if necessary as a war measure.

Ascension, Assumption, Terrebonne, Lafourche, St. Mary, St. Martin, and Orleans, including the City of New Orleans) Mississippi, Alabama, Florida, Georgia, South Carolina, North Carolina, and Virginia, (except the forty-eight counties designated as West Virginia, and also the counties of Berkley, Accomac, Northampton, Elizabeth City, York, Princess Ann, and Norfolk, including the cities of Norfolk and Portsmouth[)], and which excepted parts, are for the present, left precisely as if this proclamation were not issued.

And by virtue of the power, and for the purpose aforesaid, I do order and declare that all persons held as slaves within said designated States, and parts of States, are, and henceforward shall be free; and that the Executive government of the United States, including the military and naval authorities thereof, will recognize and maintain the freedom of said persons.

And I hereby enjoin upon the people so declared to be free to abstain from all violence, unless in necessary self-defence; and I recommend to them that, in all cases when allowed, they labor faithfully for reasonable wages.

This is one of the most significant parts of the Emancipation Proclamation and one that is often overlooked, namely the fact that blacks were to be admitted into the Union armies. Military service is an essential badge of citizenship that African Americans had been traditionally denied. By allowing them to serve in the military, Lincoln in essence pronounced them citizens.

And I further declare and make known, that such persons of suitable condition, will be received into the armed service of the United States to garrison forts, positions, stations, and other places, and to man vessels of all sorts in said service.

And upon this act, sincerely believed to be an act of justice, warranted by the Constitution, upon military necessity, I invoke the considerate judgment of mankind, and the gracious favor of Almighty God.

In witness whereof, I have hereunto set my hand and caused the seal of the United States to be affixed.

Done at the City of Washington, this first day of January, in the year of our Lord one thousand eight hundred and sixty three, and of the Independence of the United States of America the eighty-seventh.

By the President: ABRAHAM LINCOLN

WILLIAM H. SEWARD, Secretary of State.

Source: Emancipation Proclamation, January 1, 1863, in Presidential Proclamations, 1791–1991, Record Group 11, General Records of the United States Government, National Archives.

The Meaning of the War

Abraham Lincoln, Second Inaugural Address
1865

INTRODUCTION

Abraham Lincoln gave his second inaugural address just weeks before the formal end of the Civil War. Having just been reelected president over Democrat George McClellan, one of his former generals, Lincoln was now looking forward to the task of reconstructing the nation. In order to look forward, however, he believed that the nation must take careful account of its past and recognize that this war was likely a punishment by God for America's sin of slaveholding. Out of the massive bloodshed of the conflict would arise a new dedication to the principles of freedom, he claimed, marking the rebirth of the American nation.

Lincoln gave this address in March 1865 when Confederate armies were reeling from assaults by Generals William Sherman and Ulysses Grant. Within a month the Civil War would be over.

At this second appearing to take the oath of the presidential office, there is less occasion for an extended address than there was at the first. Then a statement, somewhat in detail, of a course to be pursued, seemed fitting and proper. Now, at the expiration of four years, during which public declarations have been constantly called forth on every point and phase of the great contest which still absorbs the attention, and engrosses the energies of the nation, little that is new could be presented. The progress of our arms, upon which all else chiefly depends, is as well known to the public as to myself; and it is, I trust, reasonably satisfactory and encouraging to all. With high hope for the future, no prediction in regard to it is ventured.

On the occasion corresponding to this four years ago, all thoughts were anxiously directed to an impending civil-war. All dreaded it—all sought to avert it. While the inaugural address was being delivered from this place, devoted altogether to *saving* the Union without war, insurgent agents were in the city seeking to *destroy* it without war—seeking to dissolve the Union, and divide effects, by negotiation. Both parties deprecated war; but one of them would *make* war rather than let the nation survive; and the other would *accept* war rather than let it perish. And the war came.

One eighth of the whole population were colored slaves, not distributed generally over the Union, but localized in the Southern part of it. These slaves constituted a peculiar and powerful interest. All knew that this interest was, somehow, the cause of the war. To strengthen, perpetuate, and extend this interest was the object for which the insurgents would rend the Union, even by war; while the government claimed no right to do more than to restrict the territorial enlargement of it.

Speaking to the cause of the Civil War, Lincoln clearly sees it to be slavery. While Southerners would brook no interference with the institution, Northerners said that they did not want it to expand. Their free-soil ideology was not abolitionist per se but was viewed as such by Southerners, who believed that if slavery could not expand it would die out.

Neither party expected for the war, the magnitude, or the duration, which it has already attained. Neither anticipated that the *cause* of the conflict might cease with, or even before, the conflict itself should cease.

Both sides expected a quick war from the outset but ended up witnessing the bloodiest conflict in American history. Slavery, the cause of the war, was severely undermined with the Emancipation Proclamation and would be dealt a death blow by the Thirteenth Amendment.

Each looked for an easier triumph, and a result less fundamental and astounding. Both read the same Bible, and pray to the same God; and each invokes His aid against the other. It may seem strange that any men should dare to ask a just God's assistance in wringing their bread from the sweat of other men's faces; but let us judge not that we be not judged. The prayers of both could not be answered; that of neither has been answered fully. The Almighty has His own purposes. "Woe unto the world because of offences! for it must needs be that offences come; but woe to that man by whom the offence cometh!" If we shall suppose that American Slavery is one of those offences which, in the providence of God, must needs come, but which, having continued through His appointed time, He now wills to remove, and that He gives to both North and South, this terrible war, as the woe due to those by whom the offence came, shall we discern therein any departure from those divine attributes which the believers in a Living God always ascribe to Him? Fondly do we hope—fervently do we pray—that this mighty scourge of war may speedily pass away. **Yet, if God wills that it continue, until all the wealth piled by the bond-man's two hundred and fifty years of unrequited toil shall be sunk, and until every drop of blood drawn with the lash, shall be paid by another drawn with the sword, as was said three thousand years ago, so still it must be said "the judgments of the Lord, are true and righteous altogether."**

Dating back to Phillis Wheatley and Thomas Jefferson, writing on slavery had posited that a just God would have his revenge on a nation that practiced it. Lincoln, it seems, agrees with this sentiment, referring to the Civil War as a righteous judgment of God.

With malice toward none, with charity for all, with firmness in the right as God gives us to see the right, let us strive on to finish the work we are in, to bind up the nation's wounds, to care for him who shall have borne the battle and for his widow and his orphan, to do all which may achieve and cherish a just and lasting peace among ourselves and with all nations.

Source: Abraham Lincoln, "Second Inaugural Address," 1865, in *Inaugural Addresses of the Presidents of the United States* (Washington, DC: U.S. Government Printing Office, 1989), http://www.bartleby.com/124/pres32.html.

Timeline

1619

Approximately 20 Africans are sold into slavery or indentured servitude in Virginia.

1641

Massachusetts becomes the first British North American colony to legalize slavery.

1662

Virginia declares that the children of slaves will follow the status of the mother, making slavery hereditary.

1667

Virginia passes a law decreeing that baptism does not grant freedom to slaves.

1688

Pennsylvania Quakers approve the first antislavery petition in what would become the United States.

1700

Samuel Sewall pens *The Selling of Joseph: A Memorial.* Pennsylvania legalizes slavery.

1705

Virginia passes a law decreeing that masters who kill slaves will not be punished. Massachusetts makes marriages between whites and blacks illegal.

1739

Slaves near Charleston, South Carolina, rebel against their masters and attempt to flee to Spanish Florida. The rebellion is put down, and many slaves are executed.

1764

Parliament passes the Sugar Act, spurring a crisis with the colonies. James Otis pens *The Rights of the British Colonies Asserted and Proved,* the first pamphlet written by a white man that argues for racial equality.

1773

Phillis Wheatley publishes her book *Poems on Various Subjects, Religious and Moral.* Slaves in Boston submit two petitions to the Massachusetts legislature calling for freedom. They also form a committee to advocate for slaves, the first anti-slavery committee in the colonies.

1775

The Pennsylvania Abolition Society is formed. The royal governor of Virginia, Lord Dunmore, offers freedom to slaves who will fight for the British. Prince Hall forms the African Masonic Lodge in Boston.

1776

The Society of Friends (Quakers) in Pennsylvania prohibit their members from holding slaves, becoming the first religious body to take such action.

1777

Prince Hall and other blacks in Massachusetts submit another petition to the legislature calling for their freedom. Vermont becomes the first state to abolish slavery.

1780

Paul Cuffe submits his petition to the Massachusetts legislature calling for no taxation without representation. Pennsylvania passes a gradual abolition law.

1781

Thomas Jefferson pens the first edition of *Notes on the State of Virginia.*

1783

A court case ends in Massachusetts that is widely interpreted as abolishing slavery in the state.

1784
Connecticut and Rhode Island pass gradual abolition laws.

1787
Gouverneur Morris gives his speech at the Constitutional Convention urging the abolition of slavery. The delegates take no action on slavery, enact the Three-Fifths Clause, and provide for the continuation of the slave trade until 1807. The Northwest Ordinance prohibits slavery in the Northwest Territory.

1792
Congress excludes blacks from military service.

1793
Eli Whitney invents the cotton gin. The first Fugitive Slave Law is passed by Congress.

1803
The Louisiana Purchase is passed, doubling the territory of the United States, including future slave states such as Mississippi and Alabama.

1807
Congress prohibits the international slave trade.

1819
The Missouri Crisis erupts over the question of whether or not slavery should expand into the new state.

1822
Denmark Vesey's planned uprising is foiled, and nearly 40 slaves are executed.

1827
Freedom's Journal, America's first black newspaper, begins publication in New York.

1829
The case of *North Carolina vs. Mann* is adjudicated in the North Carolina Supreme Court. David Walker publishes his *Appeal to the Coloured Citizens of the World.*

1831
William Lloyd Garrison begins publishing *The Liberator.* Virginia debates abolition but ultimately decides against it in the last serious movement by southerners to

abolish slavery. Nat Turner leads an uprising in Southampton, Virginia, that results in the death of 57 whites.

1832
The New England Anti-Slavery Society is formed in Boston.

1833
Maria Stewart delivers her address in the African Masonic Hall. Britain abolishes colonial slavery, which would take effect in 1834.

1835
Antiabolition riots break out in cities across the North, including Boston and Philadelphia.

1836
Angelina Grimké publishes *An Appeal to the Christian Women of the South.* Congress adopts the Gag Rule, which immediately tables all antislavery petitions.

1837
Charles Ball publishes his narrative *Slavery in the United States.* Frederick Douglass escapes from slavery in Maryland.

1840
The issue of women's rights divides the American Anti-Slavery Society. The Liberty Party runs its first candidate for president.

1846–1848
The United States fights a war with Mexico that many northerners condemn as an attempt to acquire more slave territory.

1848
The Free Soil Party is formed to advocate for restrictions on the spread of slavery to new territories in the West.

1850
The Compromise of 1850 is passed, admitting California as a free state, passing a stronger fugitive slave law, and abolishing the slave trade in Washington, D.C.

1852
Harriet Beecher Stowe publishes *Uncle Tom's Cabin,* a work that galvanizes the antislavery movement. Frederick Douglass gives his speech "What to the Slave Is the Fourth of July?"

1854
The Kansas-Nebraska Act is passed, creating two separate territories and allowing for popular sovereignty on the issue of slavery. This latter component repeals the Missouri Compromise.

1856
The Republican Party is formed out of a coalition of Free Soilers, northern Democrats, and former Whigs. Fighting between proslavery and antislavery forces breaks out in Bleeding Kansas in what becomes a rehearsal for the Civil War.

1857
The *Dred Scott* decision is handed down by the U.S. Supreme Court denying citizenship to slaves and free blacks in the country while also allowing slavery in the territories.

1859
John Brown leads an unsuccessful raid on Harpers Ferry that is meant to incite a slave rebellion. The raid galvanizes the North and South over the issue of slavery.

1860
Abraham Lincoln is elected president, and South Carolina secedes from the Union one month later.

1861
The Civil War begins in April. Ten more states follow South Carolina's lead, and together they establish the Confederate States of America.

1862
Slavery is abolished in the territories and in Washington, D.C.

1863
The Emancipation Proclamation frees all slaves in areas under rebellion.

1865
The Civil War ends. Slavery is abolished by the Thirteenth Amendment.

Further Reading

Adams, Catherine, and Elizabeth H. Pleck. *Love of Freedom: Black Women in Colonial and Revolutionary New England.* Oxford: Oxford University Press, 2010.

Aptheker, Herbert. *Abolitionism: A Revolutionary Movement.* Boston: Twayne, 1989.

Aptheker, Herbert, ed. *A Documentary History of the Negro People in the United States,* Vol. 1, *From the Colonial Times through the Civil War.* New York: Carol Publishing Group, 1990.

Bacon, Jacqueline. *Freedom's Journal: The First African-American Newspaper.* Lanham, UK: Lexington Books, 2007.

Bailey, Richard. *Race and Redemption in Puritan New England.* Oxford: Oxford University Press, 2011.

Bay, Mia. *The White Image in the Black Mind: African-American Ideas about White People, 1830–1925.* Oxford: Oxford University Press, 2000.

Berlin, Ira. *Many Thousands Gone: The First Two Centuries of Slavery in North America.* Cambridge, MA: Harvard University Press, 1998.

Brooks, Joanna, and John Saillant, eds.. *"Face Zion Forward": First Writers of the Black Atlantic, 1785–1798.* Boston: Northeastern University Press, 2002.

Brown, Christopher Leslie. *Moral Capital: Foundations of British Abolitionism.* Chapel Hill: University of North Carolina Press, 2006.

Bruns, Roger, ed. *Am I Not a Man and a Brother: The Antislavery Crusade of Revolutionary America, 1688–1788.* New York: Chelsea House Publishers, 1977.

Cameron, Christopher. *To Plead Our Own Cause: African Americans in Massachusetts and the Making of the Antislavery Movement.* Kent, OH: Kent State University Press, 2014.

Carey, Brycchan. *From Peace to Freedom: Quaker Rhetoric and the Birth of American Antislavery, 1657–1761.* New Haven, CT: Yale University Press, 2012.

Carretta, Vincent. *Phillis Wheatley: Biography of a Genius in Bondage.* Athens: University of Georgia Press, 2011.

Carretta, Vincent, ed. *Unchained Voices: An Anthology of Black Authors in the English-Speaking World of the 18th Century.* Lexington: University Press of Kentucky, 1996.

Clavin, Matthew J. *Toussaint Louverture and the American Civil War: The Promise and Peril of a Second Haitian Revolution.* Philadelphia: University of Pennsylvania Press, 2010.

Davis, David Brion. *Inhuman Bondage: The Rise and Fall of Slavery in the New World.* Oxford: Oxford University Press, 2006.

Davis, David Brion. *The Problem of Slavery in the Age of Revolution, 1770–1823.* Ithaca, NY: Cornell University Press, 1975.

Davis, David Brion. *The Problem of Slavery in Western Culture.* Oxford: Oxford University Press, 1967.

Douglass, Frederick. "What to the Slave Is the Fourth of July?" In *Narrative of the Life of Frederick Douglass, an American Slave: Written by Himself, with Related Documents,* edited by David W. Blight, 146–171. Boston and New York: Bedford/St. Martin's, 2003.

Drescher, Seymour. *Abolition: A History of Slavery and Antislavery.* Cambridge: Cambridge University Press, 2009.

Dubois, Laurent. *Avengers of the New World: The Story of the Haitian Revolution.* Cambridge, MA: Harvard University Press, 2004.

Egerton, Douglas R. *Death or Liberty: African Americans and Revolutionary America.* Oxford: Oxford University Press, 2009.

Finkelman, Paul. *Defending Slavery: Proslavery Thought in the Old South; A Brief History with Documents.* Boston and New York: Bedford/St. Martin's, 2003.

Forbes, Robert Pierce. *The Missouri Compromise and Its Aftermath: Slavery and the Meaning of America.* Chapel Hill: University of North Carolina Press, 2007.

Frey, Sylvia. *Water from the Rock: Black Resistance in a Revolutionary Age.* Princeton, NJ: Princeton University Press, 1991.

Garrison, William Lloyd. *Thoughts on African Colonization.* 1832; reprint, New York: Arno, 1969.

Gates, Henry Louis, Jr.. *The Trials of Phillis Wheatley: America's First Black Poet and Her Encounters with the Founding Fathers.* New York: Basic Civitas Books, 2003.

Goodman, Paul. *Of One Blood: Abolitionism and the Origins of Racial Equality.* Berkeley: University of California Press, 1998.

Greene, Lorenzo Johnston. *The Negro in Colonial New England.* 1942; reprint, New York: Atheneum, 1971.

Hinks, Peter P. *To Awaken My Afflicted Brethren: David Walker and the Problem of Antebellum Slave Resistance.* University Park: Pennsylvania State University Press, 1997.

Howard-Pitney, David. *The Afro-American Jeremiad: Appeals for Justice in America.* Philadelphia: Temple University Press, 1990.

Howe, Daniel Walker. *What Hath God Wrought: The Transformation of America, 1815–1848.* Oxford: Oxford University Press, 2007.

Hume, David. *Essays, Moral and Political.* Edited by Eugene F. Miller. Indianapolis: Liberty Fund, 1987.

Jacobs, Donald M., ed. *Courage and Conscience: Black and White Abolitionists in Boston.* Bloomington: Indiana University Press, 1993.

Jefferson, Thomas. *Notes on the State of Virginia.* Philadelphia: Prichard and Hall, 1788.

Jordan, Winthrop. *White over Black: American Attitudes toward the Negro, 1550–1812.* Chapel Hill: University of North Carolina Press, 1966.

Levesque, George A. *Black Boston: African American Life and Culture in Urban America, 1750–1860.* New York: Garland, 1994.

Mason, Matthew. *Slavery and Politics in the Early American Republic.* Chapel Hill: University of North Carolina Press, 2006.

Mayer, Henry. *All on Fire: William Lloyd Garrison and the Abolition of Slavery.* New York: Norton, 2008.

Melish, Joanne Pope. *Disowning Slavery: Gradual Emancipation and "Race" in New England, 1780–1860.* Ithaca, NY: Cornell University Press, 1998.

Miller, Floyd J. *The Search for a Black Nationality: Black Colonization and Emigration, 1787–1863.* Urbana: University of Illinois Press, 1975.

Minardi, Margot. *Making Slavery History: Abolitionism and the Politics of Memory in Massachusetts.* Oxford: Oxford University Press, 2010.

Nash, Gary B. *Forging Freedom: The Formation of Philadelphia's Black Community, 1720–1840.* Cambridge, MA: Harvard University Press, 1988.

Newman, Richard S. *Freedom's Prophet: Bishop Richard Allen, the AME Church, and the Black Founding Fathers.* New York: New York University Press, 2008.

Newman, Richard S. *The Transformation of American Abolitionism: Fighting Slavery in the Early Republic.* Chapel Hill: University of North Carolina Press, 2002.

Porter, Dorothy, ed. *Early Negro Writing, 1760–1837.* Boston: Beacon, 1971.

Quarles, Benjamin. *Black Abolitionists.* New York: Oxford University Press, 1969.

Rael, Patrick. *Black Identity and Black Protest in the Antebellum North.* Chapel Hill: University of North Carolina Press, 2002.

Richardson, Marilyn, ed. *Maria Stewart: America's First Black Woman Political Writer.* Bloomington: Indiana University Press, 1987.

Rosenthal, Bernard. "Puritan Conscience and New England Slavery." *New England Quarterly* 46 (1973): 62–81.

Saillant, John. *Black Puritan, Black Republican: The Life and Thought of Lemuel Haynes, 1753–1833.* Oxford: Oxford University Press, 2003.

Sassi, Jonathan D. "'This Whole Country Have Their Hands Full of Blood This Day': Transcription and Introduction of an Antislavery Sermon Manuscript Attributed to the Reverend Samuel Hopkins." *Proceedings of the American Antiquarian Society* 112, Part 1 (2004): 29–92.

Shields, John C. "Phillis Wheatley's Use of Classicism." *American Literature* 52 (1990): 97–111.

Sinha, Manisha. "To 'Cast Just Obliquy' on Oppressors: Black Radicalism in the Age of Revolution." *William and Mary Quarterly,* 3rd Series, 64 (2007): 149–160.

Smith, Samuel Stanhope. *An Essay on the Causes of the Variety of Complexion and Figure in the Human Species: To Which Are Added Strictures on Lord Kaims's Discourse, on the Original Diversity of Mankind.* Philadelphia: Robert Aiyken, 1787.

Staudenraus, P. J. *The African Colonization Movement, 1816–1865.* New York: Columbia University Press, 1961.

Sweet, John Wood. *Bodies Politic: Negotiating Race in the American North, 1730–1830.* Baltimore: Johns Hopkins University Press, 2003.

Van Cleve, George William. *A Slaveholder's Union: Slavery, Politics, and the Constitution in the Early American Republic.* Chicago: University of Chicago Press, 2010.

Walker, David. *David Walker's Appeal, in Four Articles: Together with a Preamble, to the World.* Edited by Sean Wilentz. New York: Hill and Wang, 1995.

Wheatley, Phillis. *Complete Writings.* Edited by Vincent Carretta. New York: Penguin, 2001.

Winch, Julie. *A Gentleman of Color: The Life of James Forten.* Oxford: Oxford University Press, 2002.

Wood, Peter. *Black Majority: Negroes in Colonial South Carolina from 1670 through the Stono Rebellion.* New York: Knopf, 1974.

Yee, Shirley J. *Black Women Abolitionists: A Study in Activism, 1828–1860.* Knoxville: University of Tennessee Press, 1992.

Zilversmit, Arthur. *The First Emancipation: The Abolition of Slavery in the North.* Chicago: University of Chicago Press, 1967.

Index

About the Author

Christopher Cameron is an assistant professor of history at the University of North Carolina at Charlotte. He received his MA and PhD in American history from the University of North Carolina at Chapel Hill. His research and teaching interests include early American history, the history of slavery and abolition, and American religious and intellectual history. Cameron's book *To Plead Our Own Cause: African Americans in Massachusetts and the Making of the Antislavery Movement* was published by Kent State University Press in 2014.